1993

Although a "longing for Zion" has always existed in Judaism, Zionism's call for the Jews' return to Palestine is a distinctly modern phenomenon. This book investigates Zionism's reception by bourgeois West European Jews from 1897 to 1914, with regard to the movement's approach toward those who were not seen as the potential immigrants to Palestine. The episodes considered here – the institution of the Zionist Congress, debates about a secular-national culture, idealization of Zionist heroes and a "New Jewish Man," Zionist art, presentations of Palestine, and the Jewish National Fund – helped foster European Jewry's identification with Zionism. These partially succeeded in establishing a 'supplemental nationality,' shaping Western Jewry's perceptions of the movement and profoundly influencing modern notions of Jewish identity. The Zionists were able to 'nationalize' part of Western Jewry because they drew on the liberal view of nationalism which had spawned Jewish emancipation, combined with vague and unobjectionable elements of Jewish culture which did not always imply a deep commitment – especially *zedakah*, the tradition of giving to charity. Even though the "problem of culture" is typically portrayed as a divisive force in the movement, this study contends that a shared ideal of culture helps account for the attraction of middle-class, assimilated Jewry to Zionism.

ZIONIST CULTURE AND WEST EUROPEAN JEWRY BEFORE THE FIRST WORLD WAR

ZIONIST CULTURE AND WEST EUROPEAN JEWRY BEFORE THE FIRST WORLD WAR

MICHAEL BERKOWITZ
Assistant Professor of History, The Ohio State University

Published by the Press Syndicate of the University of Cambridge
The Pitt Building, Trumpington Street, Cambridge CB2 1RP
40 West 20th Street, New York, NY 10011-4211, USA
10 Stamford Road, Oakleigh, Victoria 3166, Australia

First published 1993

Printed in Great Britain at the University Press, Cambridge

A catalogue record for this book is available from the British Library

Library of Congress cataloguing in publication data

Berkowitz, Michael.
Zionist culture and West European Jewry, 1897–1914/Michael Berkowitz.
p. cm.
Includes bibliographical references and index.
ISBN -521-42072-5
1. Zionism–Europe–History. 2. Jews–Europe–History–20th century.
3. Jews–Europe–Civilization. 4. Europe–Ethnic relations.
5. Europe–History–1871-1918. I. Title.
DS 149.B395 1993
320.5'4'09569404–dc20 92-8986 CIP

ISBN 0 521 42072 5 hardback

I dreamed I had a lovely fatherland.
The sturdy oak
Grew tall there, and the violets gently swayed.
Then I awoke.

I dreamed a German kiss was on my brow,
and someone spoke
The German words: "I love you!" (How they rang!)
Then I awoke.

Heinrich Heine, translated by Aaron Kramer

Not all are free who mock their chains.

G. E. Lessing, "Nathan der Weise," IV, 4

All men dream, but not equally. Those who dream by night in the dusty recesses of their minds wake in the day to find that it was vanity: but the dreamers of the day are dangerous men, for they may act their dream with open eyes, to make it possible . . .

T. E. Lawrence, *The Seven Pillars of Wisdom*

Don't you realize that we don't even have a people yet?

Nahum Sokolow, 1903

After all, we did not intend to be schnorrers.

Theodor Herzl, 1897

We were victorious too early . . .

Gershom Scholem, in a letter to Walter Benjamin, 1931

CONTENTS

ILLUSTRATIONS

PREFACE AND ACKNOWLEDGEMENTS

This book, on the invention of a Zionist culture among assimilated Western Jews in the early twentieth century, concerns the question: what does it mean to be a Jew in the modern world? In light of the prewar Zionist agenda, one of the great successes of the movement was that the myths and symbols it put forward were largely accepted as part of an authentic, generic Jewish identity. Articulating a view that was initially and overwhelmingly rejected by assimilated Jewry, the Zionists asserted that a Jewish national regeneration had begun, that a unified Jewry already existed, and that Palestine was a Jewish homeland with a uniquely Jewish national landscape – which would become the basis of a flourishing, mass Jewish settlement. In order to activate a sense of belonging to a Jewish nation among the Jews of Europe, Zionism's leadership was compelled to devise tools to fashion a unified people and an earthly nation where none existed.

The processes and products of this effort, what the Zionists themselves referred to as the creation of a national culture, is the subject of this book. I have explored the political style, myths, and symbols that helped engender the unity and growth of Zionism, and fostered Jewish identification with the Zionist program in Central and Western Europe from 1897 to 1914.

Without questioning the legitimacy of Zionism as a national liberation movement, for all that that entails, I have examined it as a European–Jewish national movement, from the perspective of its reception among primarily middle-class Western Jewish men – who were assumed to be a main group from which Zionism's leadership would emerge. I believe that the movement established enduring paradigms of perception within this constituency, which would remain consistent for those who rarely, if ever, were seen as the likely immigrants to Jewish Palestine. These perceptions have had a fateful impact on the ways Western Jews see themselves and their relationship to the Zionist project.

What I have found striking and chosen to investigate about Zionism is not that the poor, persecuted, or religiously motivated turned to Zionism – which is not to say that poverty, anti-Semitism, and messianism are factors to be taken lightly. Instead, I have been interested in the attraction and sustained commitment of relatively comfortable Jews to the movement. So that is the first problem: why and how did Zionism work among assimilated European Jewry, west of the Pale of Settlement? The answer, in brief, is that the movement created a form of nationalist thought and participation that drew on aspects of the European nationalisms acceptable to Jews; it was a product of a specific subculture of assimilated Jewry; and it incorporated aspects and symbols of traditional Judaism providing a common core of mythology for the movement.

The second problem with which I deal is: what kept these people who called themselves Zionists together? I was intrigued by the degree to which the historiography of the Zionist Movement underscores bitter factional divisions and widely divergent, idiosyncratic ideologies. I have sought to answer the questions: if their quarrels were as important as the historiography implies, why didn't the movement become more diffuse?, or, if they are so busy arguing with each other, what is it that holds them together? In short, Zionism was able to survive and grow because its members and increasing numbers of Jews could wholeheartedly agree about a vague set of myths and symbols, which might mean different things to different people. Even after their most acrimonious debates, Zionists could lock arms, sing "Hatikvah" under the blue and white flag, and tears would well in their eyes.

What I have done, therefore, is to examine the most important factors of cohesion, self-consciously controlled or fabricated by the movement, that nurtured Western Jewish commitment to Zionism. I look at the institution of the Zionist Congress, the theories and debates about language and culture, the image of a new man and heroism put forward by the movement, the artistic expressions of the movement to concretize its national ideals, the representations of Palestine to provide a sense of the old/new Jewish homeland, and the chief fundraising mechanism of the movement, the Jewish National Fund.

My main conclusion is that the Zionist Movement achieved the partial nationalization of Western Jewry by inventing a supplementary nationality – one that could coexist with other national identifications. Zionism succeeded in the West because the Zionists invented a way for Jews to be good Zionists while remaining in the nations where they lived, apparently without conflict with their being good Germans, Austrians, or Englishmen. With this approach, I will not consider the aforementioned elements of anti-Semitism and religious messianism, or Jewish literature and the non-Zionist press, beyond their application to official Zionist efforts to nationalize the Jews – because these were not explicitly invented or regulated by the Zionist Organization.

Not surprisingly, much of the phenomena I deal with has only occasionally been the concern of historians of Zionism. Zionism was, in fact, born into an age when what one saw was at least as important as what one read. Nevertheless, there has been little investigation of the visual imagery that summarized, transmitted, and symbolized the Zionist project. The images appropriated or created by the early Zionists are simply taken as assumptions that need not be qualified or studied. This attests to the ultimate success of these myths and symbols, but it leaves an important gap in the historical comprehension of Zionism.

Along with papers, memoirs, newspapers, and journals I have analyzed pictures, postcards, promotional booklets, fundraising materials, and artifacts. I found that such "agitation and propaganda" (terms which were not then connoted negatively) was taken very seriously as part of the attempt to impart a Zionist national culture. Another main subject of this study is the debate on the creation of a secular, national culture, or Hebrew culture – the so-called *Kulturdebatte*. Hebrew was not simply or immediately acclaimed as the new national language of the Jews by a plurality of Zionists. There was deep-rooted resistance to Hebrew, which foreshadowed important divisions within the movement. Overall, however, the thought and debates on culture, along with the actual attempt to revitalize Hebrew as a living language of the Jews, and the material culture of Zionism complemented each other in producing the basis of a new, supplemental nationality. All of these aspects showed Zionism as embodying a complete Jewish civilization. I have therefore sought to reconfigure and analyze how the early Zionists thought, talked about, saw, and experienced their nascent national culture.

*

The conception of the thesis upon which this book is drawn would have been impossible without George L. Mosse. I consider it my great fortune to have worked with him at the University of Wisconsin and the Hebrew University of Jerusalem. This work owes its largest intellectual debt to his books and his teaching. Professor Mosse's concern, humor, warmth, and friendship are a magnificent complement to his academic counsel. He is an ideal mentor, and an outstanding exemplar of a Judaic tradition which holds that "the honor of your student should be as dear to you as yourself" (*Pirkei Avot* 4: 15).

A sensitivity to the importance of pictures as an agent of memory, history, and culture was instilled in me by my father, William Berkowitz, who does not know that he is a cultural historian. As an employee of Eastman Kodak in Rochester, New York, it was a matter of course that he became an amateur photographer; he is quite good. My father's awareness of aesthetics was also passed on to my sister and me through the stream of pictorial histories and popular science books that entered our home. Perhaps my mother's funny and perceptive comments as we looked at these images was my first training in historical analysis.

In the course of my graduate studies at Madison, Sterling Fishman's graciousness, encouragement and advice were a consistent and invaluable part of my experience; I also benefited from working with Robert L. Koehl. Steven Kale helped me refine this project in its formative stage; he is a superb colleague and friend. From my student years and beyond, from Madison, Jerusalem, Vienna, Boston, Canton (New York), Los Angeles, New York, Columbus, and Tel Aviv, I also would like to acknowledge the assistance of Kitty Kameon, Bud Burkhard, Maureen Flynn, Jeffrey Watt, Monys Hagen, William Schara, Greg Moule, Dennis Koepke, Amira Proweller, Ulrich Lehmann, Derek Penslar, Marsha Rozenblit, Miriam Dean-Otting, Alexander Orbach, Jacob Heilbrunn, Susan Shapiro, David Harari, Carol Selkin, Miriyam Glazer, Elliot Dorff, Sue Lemkuil, Kevin McAleer, Richard Freund, Ernest Oliveri, and Andrew N. Bachman. Andy tirelessly tracked down a number of Hebrew references, helped with translations, and was an essential source of goodwill and spirit in Jerusalem and Madison. Joel Truman lent his expertise in cultural history and thoughtful editing skills to drafts of the dissertation; I warmly thank him for his generosity and friendship.

In Israel I was assisted by the (now emeritus) Director of the Central Zionist Archives, Dr. Michael Heymann, and his staff. Dr. Heymann gave of his vast knowledge of Zionism, and he patiently answered long lists of questions during several meetings; his suggestion of looking into the promotions of the Jewish National Fund proved especially fruitful in my investigation. Dr. Heymann's breadth of knowledge is clearly the greatest resource for a scholar of Zionism. At the Zionist Archives I also was assisted by Moshe Schaerf, Chaya Harel, and Adina Eshel; Shalom Ben-Reuven, Jacob Harlap, and the photographic unit of the Jewish National Library painstakingly photographed the various materials included in this book.

Reuven Koffler, Photoarchivist and Curator of Special Collections of the Central Zionist Archives, gave my project a great amount of time and consideration, and I appreciate his kindness and friendship. His dedication to locating sources and helping me understand them was superlative. Pinchas Selinger, Curator of the Herzl Papers and the unofficial social director of the Archives, was tremendously helpful in a number of capacities. His paleographic skills and historical insights are truly remarkable, and are only surpassed by his warm-heartedness, intellect, and sense of humor. Research in archives is often said to be a dreary business; Reuven and Pinchas made me look forward to working in the basement of the Sochnut, a feat which should not be underestimated. They were always generous in sharing their knowledge and friendship.

I also want to thank my friends and colleagues who were fellow Sochnut basement-dwellers: Esther Redmount, Ernst Pawel, Roza El-Eini, Sharman Kadish, Gordon Horwitz, Mascha Hoff, Dan Bitan, Moshe Halavy, Angelika Kipp, Michael Brenner, and Michael Konrad. Steven Aschheim, Ezra Mendelsohn, Shmuel Almog, Gabriel Motzkin, and Joseph Wenkert offered sound advice and support during my stays in Jerusalem.

Chapter 5 of this book originally appeared as an article in *Studies in Contemporary Jewry: An Annual, Vol. VI: [Art and Its Uses:] The Visual Image and Modern Jewish Society*, edited by Ezra Mendelsohn, Copyright (c) 1990 by Oxford University Press, Inc. It has been reprinted with their permission. Richard Cohen, as guest symposium editor for *Art and Its Uses*, was very helpful in reading and commenting on early drafts of the chapter.

As a Monkarsh Fellow at the University of Judaism in Los Angeles, I especially enjoyed the friendship, generosity, and important advice of Steven Lowenstein and Steven Zipperstein. They helped with everything from technical points to a reconceptualization of my original thesis. Steve Zipperstein's forthcoming biography of Ahad Ha-Am is certain to be one of the most important works in the field in several years.

Financial assistance for the many stages of this book was provided by the Melton Center for Jewish Studies and History Department of the Ohio State University, the Institute for German History and Wiener Library of Tel Aviv University, the Lucius N. Littauer Foundation, the Monkarsh Fellowship of the University of Judaism, the Graduate School and History Department of the University of Wisconsin-Madison, the Wisconsin Society for Jewish Learning, the Bureau of Jewish Education of Rochester, New York, the Lady Davis Fellowship Trust of the Hebrew University, and the Memorial Foundation for Jewish Culture.

My friends, many of whom have already been listed, deserve great praise; Michael A. McHale and Eli Shibi-Shai merit special mention. They help me keep things in perspective. My parents, William and Gloria, my sister, Edie, and my wife, Deborah, are the most important; they have my deepest gratitude for their love and support in every way, and it is to them that this is dedicated.

Tel Aviv and Columbus

INTRODUCTION

The early Zionist Movement sought to define and create a Jewish national culture in order to activate a sense of belonging to a Jewish nation among the Jews of Europe.[1] The elements of a Zionist culture to be considered here are the parts of a movement, in Central and Western Europe from 1897 to 1914, that were employed to foster Jews' identification with the Zionist program through changing their national self-consciousness.[2]

The processes and products of Zionism's attempt to create a Jewish national culture help explain why the movement persisted and developed within a milieu that overwhelmingly rejected Jewish-national political assumptions, a milieu in which official membership in Zionist organizations never numbered more than a fraction of assimilated Jews before the First World War.[3] Yet, despite an originally hostile or at best indifferent audience, Zionism accomplished more than simply "keeping and nourishing ideas – and an organization to embody them."[4] It exemplified a view of the world which afforded even peripheral participants in Zionism a glimpse of the movement's whole effort. The Zionist *Weltanschauung* held that Jews under Zionism were creating a culture which affirmed Jewish distinctiveness, while incorporating the most admirable aspects of the civilizations with which the Jews had had contact.[5] It worked its way into the ideology of the Jewish middle-class by drawing heavily on that group's ideal of nationalism, which emanated from the Jews' greatest hopes for a fruitful emancipation in the early nineteenth century.[6] Zionist culture, consciously and unconsciously, also amplified the criticism of Judaism and Jewry articulated in the Haskala beginning in the eighteenth century; it comprised an impulse to regenerate patterns of Jewish life and thought that were seen as corrupt or decayed.[7]

To be sure, Zionism owed a great deal to the Judaic liturgy and motifs claiming that national redemption would come from a collective return to Zion. Equally important in the movement's genesis was the notion of defending the interests and rights of severely persecuted Jews.[8] Yet the Western Jews' secular liberal faith was also significant, allied with the notion of the decadence and regenerative potential of Jewry. A main tenet of this creed was the primacy of *Bildung*, which "combines the meaning carried by the English word 'education' with notions of character formation and moral education."[9] This was rooted in the classical humanist tradition from the time of the War of Liberation, emanating from the thought of Lessing, Schiller, Goethe, and Fichte – complemented by the Haskala – and was framed by the *fin-de-siècle* nationalist forms familiar to Jews.[10] Accompanying the establishment of a modern Jewish nation, Zionist culture envisioned a continuous process of educational and moral regeneration, progressing toward greater freedom of the nation and humankind. A large part of Zionism's attraction for Western Jews can be traced to this merger between culture and politics that the movement embraced and expressed in the images of a viable cultural order: Zionism was to be the consummation of Jewish Emancipation.[11]

Zionist politics began with cultural presuppositions, and Zionism sought to endow Jews with a complete way of life, or at least to influence the tenor of their lives. "Culture" in early Zionism was not a precise formulation based on the Hebrew language or certain texts, but rather a mood, and a kind of comportment. It comprised respectability (as defined by middle-class European society), Jewish cohesion, and an enthusiastic (but not chauvinistic) Jewish patriotism. West European Zionist culture also incorporated an abiding respect for education, literature, and the arts, with a special reverence for what formerly had been regarded as "Jewish culture," laying stress on its "national" (as opposed to theological) content through the revival of Hebrew. Zionists disagreed, however, over the extent to which the Hebrew revival should occupy the movement. Culture in Zionism exalted a belief in the interconnectedness of the fate of all Jews.[12] It annexed itself to the prophetic tradition "concerned less with the salvation of the individual soul than with the holiness of the nation" and maintained that the revitalized nation of the Jews would spark the advancement of humankind.[13] A radical anti-assimilationism, which was a confession of the serious failure of emancipation in Europe, was inherent in Zionist culture; however, the work toward the establishment of a Jewish people and state, and the idealization of the incipient Jewish society in Palestine was consistently wrapped in the mantle of Enlightenment ideals and aspects of nationalism that Jews had known in Central and Western Europe.[14] Zionist culture also included a potential to criticize its own national myths, in the tradition of Heinrich Heine; consequently, it not only tolerated dissent, but at times deemed it vital to its culture.

Most Zionists would have largely agreed with Moses Mendelssohn's understanding of culture as esteem of secular education, and "an improvement in manners, morals, and taste," along with the retention of "tradition." This would allow for "the achievement of the dignity requisite to operate within the educated gentile society;"[15] Zionism's additional condition was that Jews should be regarded as equals, as a nation. Theodor Herzl summarized a similar view of Jewish culture in a speech by the President of the Jewish Academy in his utopian novel, *Altneuland* (1902): "We are in duty bound to increase beauty and wisdom upon the earth, unto our last breath."[16] In short, Zionism encompassed a form of *Bildung* with a Jewish national consciousness, striving toward the end-goal of building a Jewish national home in Palestine. In his address to the First Zionist Congress (1897), Herzl attempted to clarify the misperception that Zionism was a fundamentalist Jewish movement which sought to combine religious orthodoxy with nationalism: "We have no intention of yielding one bit of the [secular] culture we have acquired. On the contrary, we are aiming for a broadening of culture, such as any increase in knowledge brings." Herzl maintained that the material and spiritual products of the Jews – regardless of their Jewish self-consciousness – comprised Jewish culture, and that the Jews' creations as the members of a Jewish nation would be their national culture.[17]

Herzl's formulation was consistent with the perceptions of Zionist culture held until 1914 by most Western and Central European Zionists.[18] Hugo Bergman, a leader of the "Prague Circle" of Zionists, "one of the germinal groups in the intellectual history of modern Jewry," offered a cogent synopsis of this view in 1913: "Jewish culture cannot be identified simply as Hebrew culture. As Hegel said, the culture of a people is their total possessions in an 'objective spirit.' Everything that is an expression of its spirit comprises the culture of a people. Language and literature are a part of this objective spirit, but are not its totality. National laws, as well as national dance, proverbs, dress, folk songs, jokes, fairy tales, children's games, and in their broadest parameters, the ways of conceiving schooling and sports – however disparate – belong to a people's culture."[19] David Yellin, a noted Hebrew educator in Palestine, concurred that national culture consists of "everything which strengthens the national sentiment in a people – a feeling which produces in its component parts the consciousness that together they form one whole, with a natural striving to cherish and develop the possessions that belong to it."[20]

This book reconstructs and analyzes segments of the Zionists' initial instruments of nationalization as they were received by Western Jews.[21] Chapter 1 details Western perceptions of the Zionist Congresses, which were held annually from 1897 to 1901, and biennially from 1903 to 1913. These were the chief mediators of Zionism that exhibited the movement's political style; to a large extent the Congresses embodied the prewar Zionist Organization, and showed how Zionism was related to European nationalist models.

The following two chapters of this book detail the debate on "the problem of culture" (*Kulturfrage*) in the context of the Congresses, and how it was influenced by, and in turn affected the political liturgy and festivities of the Congresses. Delegates at the Zionist Congresses did not speak in a vacuum, or simply echo ongoing polemics from the Jewish press; their words were part of a Zionist event in Europe, accompanied by great fanfare and publicity. They talked about and demonstrated the advancement of a national culture which not only grew and developed, but incited counter-trends, and acted as a lightning rod for dissenting views about the essence and direction of the movement. It will furthermore be argued, against the grain of most historiography of the movement, that the cohesion of Western Zionism was partly based on common attitudes toward *Kultur*. Chapter 4 discusses the lionization of Zionist heroes through the Congresses, and the conceptualization of the Zionists' "New Man." Beginning in Chapter 5, the more material expressions of Zionist culture, which were not exclusively tied to the Congress days, will be explored. These are analyzed as the artistic and photographic dimensions of the movement, which enabled Jews literally to see a Zionist national culture. While Zionist art was more suggestive and subject to interpretation, the movement's photography was often augmented by travelogue-type or scientific reports and purported to carry great authority and veracity. Specifically, the visualization of Zionist culture in Palestine will be investigated in Chapter 6. Finally, the Jewish National Fund (JNF), the main fundraising unit of Zionism, which was the principal instrument connecting Western Jewry to the Zionist project, will be analyzed as the most effective transmitter of the myths and symbols inciting Western Jewish participation in Zionism. It was the means by which most Jews experienced the movement by 1914 and integrated it into their lives. The JNF, together with the Congress as an institution, the so-called *Kulturdebatte*, and the visual depictions of the movement continually referred to each other and helped concretize a discourse on Zionism that represented the entirety of the movement to prewar Western Jewry.

Interestingly, major trends in Zionist historiography have impeded the investigation of how Zionism was conveyed and understood in the form of myths and symbols through these aspects of Zionist national culture. In particular, the history of Zionism has tended to examine "the problem of culture," or *Kulturfrage* in early Zionism within the contexts of the Hebrew revival, political feuds, or biography. Furthermore, historians of Zionism have been mainly concerned with what Zionists said and wrote about culture in the movement. They tend to neglect what Zionists at that time saw as culture and grasped as culture.[22] In large part, this is due to their categorical avoidance of sources which were used as "propaganda" and "agitation."[23] As an end result, historians have ignored or obscured the implications of the popular means by which the movement was received in Europe for the first generation of Zionism's existence. Yet these very means of popular dissemination represented vital aspects of *Kultur* to the early Zionists.

The novelty of the attempt to bring forth a Zionist national culture in Western Jewish history also has been deemphasized due to the assumption of many writers that the longing for a Jewish home in Palestine was always deeply ingrained in the Jewish consciousness, and that the advent of modern Zionism was a more or less predetermined event.[24] The history of Zionism has often been depicted from the perspective of Jewish statehood, and the processes that contributed to this are seen as part of a messianic or secular-national teleology.[25] From this point of view, the notion that there might not have been a Jewish State, a substantial Jewish presence in Palestine, or a viable Zionist Movement is virtually unthinkable. Moreover, a teleological standpoint takes for granted the existence of a Jewish people with a common culture. This assumption is questionable. When the Zionist leader Nahum Sokolow observed in 1903 that "we don't even have a people yet," he underscored a diametrically opposed idea.[26] The early Zionists' first major task was the creation of the Jewish people as a national-cultural entity.[27]

Early Zionism confronted the reality of a Jewry deeply splintered along religious, geographical, linguistic, social, economic, and political lines, coupled with a Jewish community in Palestine that was a small, precarious, and heterogeneous minority.[28] This compelled the movement to invent ways to overcome these awesome obstacles. One of the most important developments in the service of this goal was the fabrication of a national culture with which European Jews could identify without setting foot in Palestine. The national culture fashioned by the early Zionists, therefore, played a vital role in establishing the movement as a possible though supplemental nationality for the Jews of Central and Western Europe. It was a prodigious force in the Jews' conception of a Jewish State, comprising an established Jewish settlement in Palestine and a Jewish people defined on the basis of an autonomous nationality. And one could be part of this nationality without living in the territory that served as its focus.

The analysis which follows probes the reception of Zionist culture primarily by Western and Central European Jews who identified with the movement. Such Jews were "characterized by a high degree of assimilation in the majority cultures of which they were a part, a detachment from both Yiddish and orthodoxy, a completed secondary school degree, and a strong likelihood of university or professional education. Socioeconomically, they were usually middle class, highly urbanized, and had fewer children than the surrounding population."[29] There were numerous university students in the Zionists' ranks, many of whom had recently emigrated from Eastern Europe, whose incomes were chronically lower than their middle-class tastes and outlook.[30] Ideas and images of Zionist culture were available to this group in cafes, university and Jewish community reading rooms, Zionist society reading rooms and social groups, and through literary or journalistic subscriptions.[31] They were conveyed in many forms: through participation in the Zionist Congresses and local meetings; through verbatim reports of such events in the Zionist press and in bound volumes; and through periodicals, newspapers, books, pictures, postcards, and materials produced or expressly endorsed by the Zionist Organization.

The apprehension of Zionism by bourgeois European Jewry around the turn of the century was significant because it established enduring paradigms for Western Jewish perceptions of the Zionist project. Such perceptions were in fact adopted by some Jews who went on to forge new lives for themselves in Palestine, usually after 1918, but most Western Zionists remained in Europe and were not called on by the movement to accept this ultimate challenge. Zionist culture did not immediately foresee the European Jewish bourgeoisie as the settlers of Zion, nor did it consistently appeal to them to immigrate in order to solve their own "Jewish Problem." Nevertheless, Zionism regarded all of its followers as full members of the Jewish nation. The "vicarious nationalism" that it engendered is quite possibly a unique feature of Zionism. Although the reception of Zionism occurred as part of the dialectic between Zionist culture as imagined by the movement's founders, and the realities of the Jewish and non-Jewish world, its paradigms have become an important part of the self-identity of Western Jews. This was in force long before the actual birth of the Jewish State.

The officially sanctioned, extra-territorial dimension of Zionism in one sense assisted in reducing the movement to an interest or cause in which one could be involved when time and energy permitted. It also abetted Zionism's perception by Western Jews as something ultimately meant for Jews other than themselves, or a charity, whereby participation meant giving money. At the outset, Zionism purported to replace the Jews' diverse national sentiments with loyalty to a Jewish nation. For Western Jews it emerged as a contingent national identity; one could be a Zionist, and remain a good German or Englishman, as the vast majority did. Yet from a different perspective, Zionism even in its prewar phase was able to relate a matrix of myths and symbols intimating the possibility that "Israel might live again as a nation" in the modern world for the assimilated Jews of Europe – that could be transformed into real intellectual, social, and political alternatives. At the conclusion of the last Zionist Congress before the First World War, an editorial in London's *Jewish Chronicle* summed up the Zionist world which appeared to be unfolding through Zionist culture: "When we think about the gymnastic displays on the one hand, and the determination to found a university on the other, and remember all else that is going forward – the serious development of colonisation work in Palestine, for instance – it seems that the 'three Ms' demanded at one time – Mind, Muscle, and Men – are now forthcoming by the Jews in their effort to become a nation."[32]

CHAPTER ONE

CONGRESS-ZIONISM IN MOTION

The preeminent institution of the prewar Zionist Movement was its Congress, which convened on eleven occasions: seven times in Basel and once each in London, the Hague, Hamburg, and Vienna. The Zionist Congress was a novel innovation in Jewish political life, since it represented the first attempt to create a forum for Jewish national self-definition and policy that would include the whole of Jewry. The First Congress, which met during August 29–31, 1897 in Basel, Switzerland, fostered a political liturgy, national ceremonies, and a variety of myths which to a large extent determined the content of Zionist culture for the Jews of Central and Western Europe. Thereafter, succeeding Congresses provided the single most powerful force in transmitting Zionist goals and ideals to the party faithful and the broader Jewish audience. Their inspirational impact was visible not only to direct participants; it also enabled delegates and spectators to represent the movement enthusiastically in their communities as living extensions of Zionist culture.[1]

Shmarya Levin, an East European Jew who became a leading Zionist emissary to the West, conveyed a vivid sense of the Congresses that was widely shared when he recalled that

> the impression of the Congress was ineffaceable. The praesidium on the tribune, with the majestic figure of Herzl at its head, called up in my mind the descriptions of the ancient Sanhedrin. I forgot for the moment our condition, helpless and unprotected. I only saw before me the representatives of an ancient, cultural people, and I believed that with the power behind them they would move mountains and build up worlds.[2]

Indeed, the Congress became the framework and symbol that helped assure the coherence, viability, and respectability accorded Jewish nationalism though Zionism. With the parliament of the incipient Jewish State in its center, the Congress developed a pattern of visual imagery, interactive deliberations, and ancillary activities which became a microcosm of the new Jewish civilization that Zionism hoped to engender. It concretized the idea that a Zionist national culture had been called into existence while simultaneously providing a means for the dissemination of much of the movement's culture. The Congresses cultivated, as well, a carefully groomed image of statesmanlike respectability in European gentile culture at large, establishing the central myth that the Zionists represented the whole of Jewry, on a nearly equal footing with the existing governments of the world.

In many respects, the Zionist Congresses enjoyed rapid success in developing effective secularized liturgy and ceremonial forms. Already at the First Congress, for example, one of the most significant parts of this liturgy found its expression in its opening session, featuring the entrance of the praesidium to tremendous ovations. Herzl's presidential address to the assembly followed, and was complemented by an assessment of the Jewish condition delivered by Max Nordau, the second great embodiment of early Zionism. Characteristically, the opening and close of the principals' speeches were greeted by choruses of cheers, applause, and hat, handkerchief, and flag waving. The rhythms of nationalism thus initiated at the First Congress sustained the perception of the institution as the nucleus of a nascent Jewish State and were powerfully reinforced by subsequent national homage. Indeed, it might be said that this is the way that all European political movements proceeded; the very normalcy of Jewish nationalism, in this regard, was crucial for its acceptance.[3]

Interestingly, though the evolving spectacle of the Zionist Congresses came to satisfy Herzl's penchant for imagery and detail, the institution of the Congress itself was far from his original design. In fact, Zionism's primary institution materialized in large part through improvisation. Herzl himself had initially favored a popular newspaper as the chief instrument for drawing attention to Zionism, but was forced to drop this project because of insufficient finances.[4] Later, in *Der Judenstaat* (1896) he called for "the center of the incipient Jewish movement" to be an elitist body he termed "the Society of Jews." At this stage in his thinking, Herzl hoped to gather a number of well-known Jews from business, politics, the arts, and the rabbinate and had made a point of visiting well-placed Jews in London and the continent by November 1895. From Herzl's perspective it was most important to win the backing of Jewish industrialists, dignitaries, and financiers; they would comprise the movement's central policy-making body, and it would be their duty to perform the "political and scientific" tasks necessary for the foundation of the Jewish State.[5] His "Society" was to be, in effect, a committee of notables which Herzl also envisioned would provide the movement with much of its necessary capital.

The influence of Nordau, Herzl's trusted colleague, helped transform the idea of a "Society of Jews" into that of a "Zionist Congress." There is no suggestion in Herzl's voluminous writings that portended a deliberate imitation of an existing legislative body, such as the French Chamber of Deputies or Austrian Parliament for the First Congress – although his familiarity with these assemblies undoubtedly played some part. Herzl drew his famous sketch of the "Jewish Parliament" between the First and Second Congresses.[6] Nordau was chiefly concerned that Zionism should be perceived by Jews and non-Jews as a democratic movement, and should therefore assume the form of a representative assembly. He believed that in order for Zionism to succeed, the Jewish masses, the Eastern Jews themselves would have to participate in the governance of the movement. It is doubtful that Nordau sincerely believed that Zionism ought to be rigorously democratic; but, because he felt that the most prominent European Jews would remain aloof from the plan, Nordau pressed Herzl to alter his proposal.[7] Nordau's advice was corroborated by Herzl's father, Jakob, in whom the leader also placed a good deal of confidence.[8]

Herzl reiterated this idea at a crucial planning session in Vienna, attended mostly by members of small Jewish nationalist societies from Berlin and Vienna, which decided to call "a general Zionist Congress" to be held in Munich. By demanding an all-encompassing forum on the *Judenfrage* rather than a convention which included Jewish charitable societies, Herzl managed to cast the nascent movement as a grand exercise in state-building – while also incorporating the movement's directive of saving the most wretched Jews.[9] Predictably, the notion of the Zionist Congress as a representative body was ridiculed. Nonetheless, had it not assumed a parliamentary appearance in 1897, the movement probably would have incurred many more accusations that "the Zionists represented no one but themselves" – as an editorial in the *Jewish Chronicle* charged shortly before the Congress.[10]

As is now well known, the initial choice of Munich as the Congress site turned out to be problematic for the Zionists, due to the objections it elicited from that city's *Israelitische Kultusgemeinde* (Jewish religious community). In order to expose the Munich *Kultusgemeinde* as mean-spirited, Herzl published the correspondence between the Zionist office and its potential host community in *Die Welt*. At this time, the Zionists emphasized that the movement was by no means antithetical to German nationalism, and that the Congress would be completely compatible with the desire of most German Jews to be dutiful citizens. The insistence on harmony between an individual's loyalty to Zionism and loyalty to his or her European state thus appeared quite early in the movement's formative phase. The notion that one could be a confirmed Zionist while fulfilling all obligations of citizenship in another European country was soon taken for granted as a crucial tenet in the Zionist culture of Western Jewry.

Meanwhile, Herzl had to find a replacement site for Munich; this part of the story is less well known. He turned to one of his Zionist colleagues in Zurich, David Farbstein, for help in finding and preparing an alternate location.[11] To both Herzl and Farbstein, the chief conditions which the site had to meet were accessibility for the Eastern Jews, and respect for the requirement of many delegates for kosher food. That limited the choice immediately to cities in German Switzerland, which helped assure the Germanic tenor of the Congress. Herzl had never seriously contemplated holding the meeting in a language other than German, but he began to see advantages to a site in German Switzerland.[12] Here the Zionists could conduct their business in the lingua franca and apparently be as open as possible about their affairs. This, Herzl thought, would help to demonstrate the antithesis of the anti-Semitic vision of mysterious Jewish conspiratorial gatherings.

The opportunity to observe kosher dietary laws during a Congress in Switzerland was a consideration of no small significance. Indeed, had this been overlooked, numerous delegates might not have attended, given the already prohibitive cost of travel and lodging for many prospective participants.[13] Moreover, the insistence on keeping kosher helped legitimate Herzl's promise that Zionism would respect orthodox Judaism. It was also consistent with Herzl's shrewd sense of the need to adapt Zionist culture to everyday Jewish habits; if the

Viennese would have *Salzstangel* in the Promised Land, the orthodox should have *Kashrut* on the way, in Switzerland.[14] The Congress' planners were aware that it was not beyond Jewish critics of Zionism, or even orthodox Zionists, to use the issue of observing the dietary laws as a litmus test for respect of orthodoxy.[15] In the Congress itself, they likewise encouraged the presence of rabbis on the podium as a symbol of the movement's claim to have united the secular and religious.

The Zionists finally selected the Swiss German city of Basel. As opposed to the situation in Munich, Farbstein reported that the Congress organizers could expect no resistance from Basel's Jewish community, though he added that local Jewish support was unlikely. "They can neither help nor damage us," Farbstein wrote Herzl about the Basel Jews. "They will not be useful to us, because they are so cowardly, and it would only hurt them in the eyes of the local population if they were to bar us. The Jews here are not respected; they play no role in public life; they are either small-time clothing sellers or peddlers."[16]

This Jewish-communal vacuum in Basel proved curiously attractive to Farbstein and Herzl. It is clear that they perceived with disdain a Jewish population that conformed to the stereotype of materialistic, largely superfluous retail-trade Jews. Yet the apathy of such a community seemed less detrimental than the possible opposition of a more prosperous, established Jewish population. Furthermore, since there was no community where they could anticipate an unqualified welcome by the Jewish leadership, and they were least likely to be feted by one that was wealthy and cultured, the lackluster community in Basel was probably the best they could imagine. The appearance of harmony with the Jewish population was all important in order not to shatter the myth of the Zionists' confluence with general Jewish interests.

Of other possible Congress sites, Farbstein had noted that Zurich, his own home, possessed a "cultured population," which could prove a valuable backdrop for the Congress. In ultimately choosing Basel, however, Congress organizers believed that it had many of the same qualities as Zurich, including a "nice Jewish restaurant." The rabbi, a "respectable, orthodox community-leader type, would not denounce the movement as long as he was certain that the Zionists were not atheists." Thus, it did not appear that the Jewish community of Basel, "the oldest in Switzerland," would place any major obstacles in the

Zionists' way. Equally important, as far as the political climate was concerned, Basel was "not as infamous from a political-revolutionary point of view" as Zurich. It would cause far less consternation for Russian Jews to ask permission to travel to Basel, than to the "old Nihilists' City," Zurich. This was perhaps the decisive factor in the selection of Basel over Zurich. Herzl did not wish for Zionism to appear sympathetic with revolutionary socialism, an impression he feared would automatically arise given the expected presence of a large group of Russian Jews. Zurich might send the wrong message.[17]

This raises the question of representation at the Congress, to which Zionist planners devoted a good deal of attention. Echoing Nordau's advice, Farbstein wrote Herzl that "it was of paramount importance that Jews from all countries and social classes be represented. The Congress should include not only Germans and Austrians, but Galicians and Russians – especially some orthodox rabbis. It would be very good if they could use their influence to bring along 'a Galician rabbi in his long coat.'"[18] The latter comment implies that the Zionists' inclusion of the orthodox at the First Congress was in part a cosmetic touch – there is little hint that they desired a thoughtful dialogue with the religious. Nevertheless, it illustrates a sensitivity for one type of symbolism which Herzl perceived as essential.[19] From the start, most Western Zionists realized that the consent, or at least acquiescence of the rabbis – especially in the East – was the key for building a mass movement. In the service of that goal, what better sign could there be of Zionism's continuity with traditional Judaism than a Galician rabbi in a long coat? As part of its appeal to the orthodox Jewish masses, as well as to reassure Western Jews that Zionism comprised all of Jewry, Zionist culture would continually use images of orthodox, Eastern rabbis to suggest the movement's solidarity with traditional Judaism.

Just as Zionist Congress organizers carefully sought not to alienate prospective delegates from Eastern Europe, they attentively cultivated the goodwill of their Swiss hosts. In this regard, after Basel was selected, Farbstein advised Herzl to tailor the publicity of the movement to complement the national sentiments of the Basel Swiss. "The Swiss are nationalistic," he reported, "but they are intolerant of chauvinism. Above all, emphasize that we carry our colors openly, as opposed to those who are ashamed of their Jewish nationality." Here Farbstein hit on a delicate task. In the face of the Swiss Jews' disinterest in Jewish nationalism, the priority was to project the strongest possible positive image, without provoking the enmity of the gentile Swiss.

"The general public is sympathetic towards us, because they already hate the cowardice of our opponents. We can use the shallowness of Swiss nationalism to our benefit, by claiming that we chose Switzerland because we were impressed by its 'spirit of freedom.'"[20] The Jewish community of Basel was inviting because it seemed so weak that it could allow for the acceptance and exhibition of Zionism. Likewise, the relatively anachronistic, patriotic version of Swiss nationalism appeared as perhaps the most fertile – or the least hostile – ground for the Zionists' seed to be sown.

"You must not allow our movement to appear as a fruit of anti-Semitism," Farbstein warned Herzl, fearing that it might be seen as a movement that primarily wished to redress grievances, ferment political change, or otherwise threaten the status quo of the tranquil city. "Preferably, stress the suffering of innocent, poor Jews – as a result of anti-Semitism – as the most essential point." Obviously, Farbstein was referring to the Pale of Settlement. "The democratic Swiss are anti-Semitic, in that they are against the rich Jews, but they can empathize with a movement of the poor. Making the social-political side preeminent will be very useful to us, and so will underscoring the moral dimension. As far as possible, let them know that the rich Jews and the hypocritical reform rabbis are our enemies. The Swiss hate Plutocrats and snobs."[21] It is not clear if this part of Farbstein's advice had much of an influence on Herzl himself. Yet the recommendation to cast the Zionist mission as the rescue of the most desperate Eastern Jews was indeed prescient. It would soon become an article of faith in Zionist cultural pronouncements.

In short, the architects of the Zionist Congress consciously adopted a tone that was calculated to appeal to their Swiss hosts' love of domestic tranquility and humanitarian impulses. This not only served to sharpen Zionists' focus on saving their downtrodden brethren in the East, but also helped to solidify the middle-class character of the Congress – a trait which extended to matters of dress and personal comportment, giving the movement entry into wider bourgeois Jewish circles throughout Europe. Ironically, Herzl himself was not completely in tune with this style. Despite his quintessentially bourgeois tastes, the Zionist founder had envisioned a very regimented division of labor within the movement, with secular Jewish elites at the apex.[22] In contrast, the Congress' deliberate avoidance of aristocratic flamboyance and stress on middle-class respectability took into account both the Swiss aversion to ostentation and bourgeois Jewish attitudes throughout Central and Western Europe. Zionism was presented in a style both the Swiss and Jews could understand. Judging from the reception of the Swiss public and press, the Zionism that emerged from the Congress was well within the boundaries of prescribed behavior for German Switzerland. In many respects the political and social proclivities of Basel left an indelible imprint on the Zionism of the Western Jews, as Zionism had self-consciously and fatefully molded itself to its "temporary" capital city.

The cordial relationship that quickly developed between the Congress and Basel's Jewish community also lent credence to the idea that Zionism existed in harmony with contemporary Jewish religious life. Already at the inaugural Congress of 1897, references to Jewish prayer and the Shabbat services during the proceedings helped integrate the Zionists' political liturgy with traditional Jewish liturgy. At the close of the Friday afternoon preliminary session, the delegates were informed of the services to be held at the Basel synagogue. "As the meeting at which Dr. Herzl presided broke up," the *Jewish Chronicle* reported, "Herzl laughingly remarked that the cantor had promised to sing *Lecha Dodi* in especially fine style and that it was long since he had heard the hymn."[23] Shortly thereafter, the Basel synagogue hosted the first "Kongress-Sabbath," at which Herzl was called to the Torah after the rabbi warmly greeted the visiting delegates. On this occasion, and at successive Congresses, the Basel congregation prided itself as the place of worship for Jews "from the four corners of the earth – standing together – calling for redemption through returning to Zion." After the First Congress, Basel's rabbi wrote an article praising Max Nordau, whom he had found extraordinarily inspiring.[24]

The planning that went into the prewar Zionist Congresses gave great weight to the symbolic importance of the Congress' delegate composition. In this regard, Zionist organizers took pains to strike a balance between youth and old age, with the former given a vital role. Farbstein believed that large-scale participation by students would create a vivid lasting impression of the inaugural congress as a festival of youth. He also sought to enlist a smaller group of Jewish university students as a sort of honor guard to assure the orderliness of the event. Herzl too had envisioned middle-class Jewish youth as the vanguard of Zionism. He wrote that young educated Jews possessed a vast untapped reservoir of energy which could be harnessed to invigorate the Jewish State.[25] As suggested in his utopian novel *Altneuland*, at present they formed "a proletariat of intellectuals" [*Bildungsproletariat*] comprised of

> budding physicians, newly-baked jurists, freshly graduated engineers. They had just completed their professional studies, and now they had nothing to do . . . They were really a kind of superior proletariat, victims of a viewpoint that had dominated middle-class Jewry twenty or thirty years before: the sons must not be what the fathers had been. They were to be freed from the hardships of trade and commerce. And so the younger generation entered the liberal professions en masse. The result was an unfortunate surplus of trained men who could find no work, but were at the same time spoiled for a modest way of life. They could not, like their Christian colleagues, slip into public posts . . . Nevertheless, they had the obligations of their "station in life," an arrogant sense of class distinction, and degrees that they could not back up with a shilling.[26]

The reality for prewar Zionism in Europe was not that far from this assessment. Many activists who found their way into the movement in fact belonged to a new "reserve army" of Jewish university students.[27] Their ranks would include some of the more significant crafters of a Zionist national culture, such as Heinrich Loewe, Berthold Feiwel, Davis Trietsch, and Theodor Zlocisti.

To complement Zionism's link with the future through the students, Farbstein also sought to establish a sense of continuity with proto-nationalist and *Hibbat-Zion* leaders by displaying their pictures in the hallway. These included Hirsch Kalischer (1795–1874), Moses Montefiore (1784–1885), Moses Hess (1812–75), Peretz Smolenskin (1840–85), Eliahu Gutmacher (1795–1874), David Gordon (1831–86), Alexander Zederbaum (1816–93), and Leon Pinsker (1821–91).[28] Congress organizers likewise made a point of giving occasional ceremonial functions at the proceedings to elderly delegates. This was a sign of Zionist respect for age and experience in what was largely a youthful event. The balance between symbols of youth and age helped to cast the movement as part of an unfolding historical epoch with ties to the past and future. In so doing, it set a precedent for Zionist culture's later emphasis on the exaltation of its own history. Such emphasis was in fact already manifest during the inaugural Congress when several motions were made to immediately print and disseminate the major speeches of the event separately from the Congress protocol. This went along with the decided effort to faithfully record the protocol verbatim; in so doing, the Zionists recalled the functioning of European national assemblies, such as the Reichstag.

For many delegates, the entry into history by way of Zionism began on the train to Basel. "We travelled to Basel with our hearts full of joyous anticipation," wrote Berthold Feiwel in *Die Welt*. "The trip is a charming introduction to the Congress. It is a Congress in a train car, totally improvised, a Congress in miniature. Upon arrival we were a proper, stately assembly. What excitement incurred when another 'Baseler' was discovered and introduced to the rest! A heart-felt, brotherly handshake, and a joyful getting-to-know each other. Most of us were familiar through common friends or newspaper work. Our Zionism provides us with a friendship in a few minutes, as if we had known each other for years."[29]

The sense of solidarity so expressed was a central feature of the Zionist experience and was strongly enhanced at the Zionist Congresses in many ways. In the context of this institution, Jews from Central and Western Europe for the first time were able to feel as if they had come together as friends and brothers on the same plane as non-Jewish citizens of a European state. The camaraderie which they enjoyed was similar to the cult of male friendship popular in early German nationalism.[30] Perhaps the greatest symbol of national solidarity through friendship was the relationship between Herzl and Nordau. Although each was a preeminent symbol of early Zionism in his own right, these men together, as friends, colleagues, and compatriots of a nation-building process demonstrated the mutual respect and duty they hoped would unite all Jewry in the Zionist cause. Though apocryphal, an often repeated anecdote from the early Zionist period conveys the strong image of loyalty and fellowship which the two leaders cultivated in the service of the movement. According to the tale, Herzl was prompted to consult Nordau – a doctor who specialized in nervous diseases – by a mutual friend, who feared that Herzl's ramblings about a Judenstaat were symptomatic of a nervous disorder. After a few days of intense conversation, Nordau embraced Herzl and exclaimed "If you are crazy then so am I!"

In fact, the relationship between Herzl and Nordau was not immune to the petty rivalries that occur between ambitious visionaries, or, for that matter, in almost any collegial relationship.[31] Publicly, though, the two men always made a point of addressing each other warmly and in glowing terms. They further allowed their friendship to be

1. Herzl and Max Nordau New Year's postcard.

2. Opening scene of the Second Zionist Congress (1898) by Menahem Okin.

memorialized and idealized in a number of pictures and postcards, and in a widely reproduced painting of the opening of the Second Congress [Figures 1 and 2].[32] In the context of the Congress the Zionists thus celebrated male friendship as evidence of their nation-building capacity. A pronounced manliness was part of the culture needed to build the Jewish State.[33]

Indeed, Herzl had always envisioned Zionism as a means by which Jews could "become real men."[34] His attitude, shared by most early Zionists, was an internal and external disavowal of the anti-Semitic stereotype of Jewish men as un-manly, and it affirmed the European-wide equation of manliness and rightful membership in the nation. The way to a "new Jewish existence" could only be reached though participation in a "society of friends," or "a special type of comradeship" that was possible for Jewish men only through Zionism.[35] This myth reflected the reality of a movement, which like the larger society, was male-dominated. The inaugural assembly of 250 Zionists included only around twelve female delegates, and women were not accorded voting rights until the Second Congress. To be a Zionist was to "take a manly stand" and be a manly man, asserting the Jews' rightful place among the peoples of the world.[36]

In addition, the notion that all Zionists were friends, heightened in the Congress days, helped instill a sociability that muted the sometimes bitter and divisive controversies that were played out in the press. "We embraced and kissed each other," reported one of the accounts of *Die Welt*. "We didn't know who. But then again, we already knew that we were brothers. And after we embraced and kissed each other again, we introduced ourselves. Upon saying our names, we kissed another time, as we were friends. Friends and comrades, who had before then never seen each other got to know each other personally and established friendships. It was as if an electrical spark flew from heart to heart, igniting them . . . All at once we understood every language. Amid the multi-toned confusion of modern languages, only one call rose up from us: *Ivri onochi*! [I am a Hebrew!]"[37]

The experience of Zionist solidarity was reinforced by organized forms of sociability in the Congress setting. For many during the Congress, the most memorable episode not emanating from the praesidium was the *Commers* evening – a fraternal Zionist gathering, replete with poetry recitations, songs, hale and hearty toast, and well-wishing. The *Commers* was no small affair. Attended by around 200 persons in 1897, and much larger crowds in later Congresses, it reminded students and recent graduates of the fraternal bonds of their Jewish university organizations; even during the acrimonious Sixth

Congress (1903) when the Uganda plan was hotly debated, the *Commers* was an occasion for joyful solidarity. Beyond this it provided a poignant display of the symbiosis of early German and Jewish nationalism which Zionism engendered.[38]

Commersfeste had been an integral part of the German fraternity tradition. As they evolved in the Zionist setting, they featured Hebrew songs, including "Hatikvah" along with the Latin standard "Gaudeamus" and musical adaptations from the works of German classical literature.[39] Lyrics from Goethe, Lessing, and Schiller and other works in this tradition were also the stock of non-Jewish organizations. Typically, the lyrics of some of these were changed to replace references to Germany with allusions to the Jewish Fatherland of *eretz Israel*. From the original Zionist *Commers* programs, it was not always clear what was sung by student choruses as opposed to the whole assembly, or what offerings were sung (as opposed to being recited), and who deserved credit for some of the Zionist lyrical twists.[40] But Zionist adaptations were prominently featured, as in the altered version of one patriotic German song (*Der Wacht am Rhine*), which the student chorus sang at the end of the *Commers* evening

> There where the cedar kisses the sky,
> And where the Jordan quickly flows by,
> There where the ashes of my father lie,
> In that exalted Reich, on sea and sand,
> Is my beloved, true Fatherland.[41]

The Jews' "true Fatherland" was no longer that of the Rhine and the oak, but the Jordan and the cedar.

Besides the *Commers*, during the evening hours after Congress sessions – and at later Congresses during afternoon breaks – other opportunities for sociability and discussion presented themselves to the delegates. Before the question of Hebrew language and literature became central to the official Congress agenda, it was primarily handled in informal after-hours meetings. Concerts, which later included symphonic versions of the Hebrew songs from the *Commers* and works by Jewish composers, and sports shows of Jewish athletes, quickly found their way into Congress programs; by the Eleventh Congress (1913), delegates could anticipate seeing a Zionist play, lantern slideshows, and even a movie.[42] In line with the general trend in European society, the Congress' diversions became increasingly visually oriented.

Nevertheless, the role of song as an emotionally unifying factor at the prewar Congresses remained of vital importance. During *Commersfest* music-making, for example, images of the ruins of Zion and new life in Jewish Palestine wafted almost surrealistically with the verses of Germanic drinking songs and ballads.[43] Although beer was served, there was no hint that drunkenness influenced the participants' enthusiasm. Heinrich Loewe, Berthold Feiwel, and Theodor Zlocisti, who were active in many aspects of Zionist culture, wrote and adapted lyrics especially for such occasions. Loewe even wrote ballads that were sung by non-Jewish German student groups.

In addition, although it could easily be claimed that Zionist social gatherings simply mimicked their counterparts in countless gentile voluntary associations, the inclusion of songs such as *Nes Ziona* glorifying the pioneers of a Jewish colony in Palestine and especially *Hatikvah*, which concluded most evenings and was sometimes sung over and over again, marked these occasions as distinctively Jewish events. Above all, the uniquely Zionist songs augmented the participants' awareness that they belonged together because of discrimination or their exclusion from the mainstream – an attitude which Herzl perceived as one of the foundations of nationality. *Die Welt* wrote shortly after the First Congress that the delegates' voices in unison seemed a public, enthusiastic denunciation of "the shame of their centuries of exile."[44] While all German students were familiar with some of the musical repertoire, only Jews intoned the verses of *Hatikvah* which afforded a traditional Jewish visage of exile and redemption. For Zionists who knew some Hebrew, the words of *Hatikvah* took on added meaning in the context of the Congress:

> Within their hearts,
> Jews' souls yearn
> Looking eastward
> An eye beholds Zion
>
> Our hope is not yet lost
> The ancient hope to return to our Fatherland
> The city where David dwelt
>
> Tears fall from our eyes
> Pouring like rain
> As thousands have tread
> Across our fathers' graves
>
> As long as our finest yearnings
> Arise to our eyes
> On the ruins of our Temple
> One eye still cries

As long as the Jordan majestically rolls
The water will flow to its banks
And the Sea of Galilee, in loud voice
Thunderously does quake

There are yet roads
To the Temple's desolate gate
Among Jerusalem's ruins
Where the daughter of Zion weeps

As long as pure tears
Fall from thee my people's eyes
And throughout the night for Zion they cry
In the midst of the night it will rise

As long as blood courses through our veins
And as long as our blood flows,
While upon the graves of our fathers
dew still falls,

As long as the love for the nation
Exists in the heart of the Jew
We can still hope even now
That God will have mercy on us anew

Listen, my brother, in all the lands
Listen to the voice of our prophets who spoke
Only the death of the one last Jew
Will mark the end of our hope.[45]

Of all the songs which could be heard at the Zionist Congresses *Hatikvah* was the favorite. Sung to the tune of a Romanian folk song (or, as some believe, a German or Polish patriotic tune), the lyrics of *Hatikvah* were written around 1878 by Naftali Herz Imber, a Hebrew poet who lived briefly in Palestine. The song was already popular with Jewish organizations such as *Jung-Israel* and the *Vereine juedischer Studenten* for several years prior to the inaugural Congress.[46] Despite this, between the First and Second Congresses, Herzl and Nordau decided to hold a contest to pick an official anthem for the movement. They did so primarily because the creator of *Hatikvah*, Imber, was a shady character hardly suited for the honor of national poet. With a reputation for drunkenness, philandering, *schnorring*, and swindling, Imber actually delighted at times in jeering the Zionist Movement.[47] The results of the Zionist anthem contest were disappointing, however, in part because Herzl and Nordau apparently could not read the Hebrew submissions. It is an indication of how seriously they perceived the role of song in the movement that they obviously spent hours poring over those offerings they could read in German, French, English, and Italian. Thus, ironically, while Imber's personality continued to be a nightmare for the Zionists' carefully cultivated image of respectability, his song remained the people's choice.[48]

Indeed, *Hatikvah* became one of the most moving parts of the succeeding Zionist Congresses. The Eleventh Congress (1913), for example, was widely considered to have opened uninspiringly. With Herzl long dead and Nordau absent, and delegate enthusiasm at an unprecedented low, its official proceedings "disillusioned new-comers and disappointed the old 'Congress hands,'" according to the *Jewish Chronicle*. "Compared with the opening of previous Congresses, it was like a *minyan* in relation to a big synagogue." Nonetheless, "*Hatikvah* saved the situation; the audience sang the Anthem; the tune was the same – they were glad. At least that had not changed."[49]

While songs such as *Hatikvah* obviously played a major role in fostering unity at Zionist functions, the Congresses set forth important visual symbols as well. The First Congress officially commenced on Sunday morning, August 29, 1897 in the large Concert Room of the Basel *Stadtcasino*, a public auditorium near the center of the city. As the delegates entered, they passed beneath a flag with a Star of David and a banner proclaiming "Zionisten-Kongress." The flag outside the building had a white background, blue stripes on the top and bottom, and a simple blue heptagon in the center [Figure 3]. This design was advocated by David Wolffsohn, Herzl's successor as President of the Zionist Organization, to recall the blue stripes of the *talit*, the Jewish prayer shawl.[50] The Star of David was applied to nearly every visual representation of Zionism, from this time forward. Gershom Scholem noted that for the early Zionists, the Star "possessed two qualities which recommended it as a new symbol. It was well known because of its general dissemination through the centuries, with its appearance on every new synagogue, as well as on the seals of Jewish communities, the philanthropic societies and the like." Yet until the nineteenth century it had no national connotation. According to Scholem, "in the contemporary consciousness the Star of David lacked any clear connection with religious conceptions and associations. This fault became a virtue . . . it addressed hopes for the future, for redemption" and for the reconstitution of the Jewish nation.[51]

Like so many issues in Zionist culture, the design of the movement's flag had been the subject of much discussion. Before the First Congress, Max Bodenheimer, the founder of a Jewish national society in

3. Postcard of the Basel Stadtcasino from the First Zionist Congress (1897).

Cologne and an early devotee of Herzl, had proposed to symbolize both the Zionist movement and the Congress with "a vignette in red, gold, and blue, in the middle of which appeared the Star of David with the Lion of Judah, surrounded by twelve small stars symbolizing the twelve tribes of Israel." Herzl did not completely approve of this image; he objected to the twelve small stars – perhaps because they appeared cluttered – so he submitted a sketch of his own. The more simple and traditional the symbol, reasoned Herzl, the more effective it would probably be. "Assume," he wrote to Bodenheimer, in presenting a modification, "that the scrawl in the middle [of a Star of David] is the lion, that in each of the small triangles [inside the Star, surrounding the lion] there is a [smaller] star, and that there is a star above."[52] Herzl's version, which became the flag at the head of the Congress hall until the leader's death in 1904, was a synthesis of his proposed flag in *Der Judenstaat* and the plans of Wolffsohn and Bodenheimer. Its likeness was transmitted to European Jews through the numerous photographic postcards depicting the Congress in action [Figure 4].[53]

The close attention to detail which Herzl dedicated to the Zionist flag is not surprising in an aspiring nation-builder whose formative years were spent amid the competing nationalisms of the Habsburg Dual Monarchy. For Herzl the national banner served as a leadership

4. Original Zionist flag, in a postcard from the Third Zionist Congress (1899).

tool ensuring the loyalty of the masses and rallying them to action. Its design was therefore a matter of deadly seriousness. "By no means," Herzl assured Bodenheimer, "is the flag a plaything for me. If you intend to lead, you need flags and trumpets, otherwise you cannot convey your words of command."[54]

Earlier in *Der Judentstaat* he asserted in a similar vein that "anyone who wants to lead many men must raise a symbol over their heads." To a lesser degree, Herzl believed that the flag could convey something of its movement's programmatic content. In *Der Judenstaat* he proposed to circle the Star of David with seven pentagonal stars, representing the seven-hour work day that Zionism would introduce as part of a progressive social engineering scheme.[55] This design, however, never left the pages of Herzl's pamphlet. In the end, the more conservative design – the Star of David and the *talit* stripes – proved to be a most enduring symbol of the Zionist Movement. At the Seventh Zionist Congress of 1905, an announcement that the Zionist flag had flown among the flags of the nations of the world at the St. Louis World's Fair of 1904 set off perhaps the greatest display of jubilation at that Congress; later, the same flag was adopted by the modern State of Israel some fifty years after the First Congress.[56]

Two additional features of the Zionist Congress which heightened the impression that the proceedings within had world-historical importance were the assembly hall's spatial and seating arrangements. The concert-hall floor, where the delegates to the First Congress were seated, did not have room to hold many more than the two hundred-plus Zionists in attendance. On the other hand, the visitors' gallery in the balcony was ample, seating another few hundred at capacity and housing large numbers of those who were underrepresented in the Congress proper. At least one observer noted that the "old and young women and the elderly" in the gallery appeared to be even more emotional than the delegates, "following the goings-on with rapt attention," and punctuating the deliberations and speeches with "loud, enthusiastic clapping and handkerchief waving." The audience also conveyed the impression that Zionism did speak for a broader audience, and the presence of a large gallery likewise served as evidence to dispel the myth of secret Jewish gatherings. It offered, as *Die Welt* wrote, a "symbol of candor, of sincerity, and loyalty to the complete openness of Zionism." At least some observers claimed that the preponderance of women as spectators, especially young women, invigorated the delegates' sense of manly self-assertion in calling for the founding of the Jewish State.[57]

The assembly hall itself was no different from many European concert rooms. Outfitted with marble columns, oak furnishings, and scattered banners displaying the Lion of Judah or Star of David, its overall appearance, as seen in photographs, was reminiscent of a legislative chamber. To further enhance the aura of dignity at the Congress, Herzl provided a dress code. The vast majority of delegates followed his instructions on their *Mitglieds-Karten*: "For the festive opening session, black formal wear and white tie is required."[58]

One of the anecdotes often repeated in Zionist lore calls attention to the significance of the delegates' attire. Max Nordau, who had a reputation for exposing "conventional lies" and hypocrisy in his works of cultural criticism, arrived at the opening session in a simple suit coat. Herzl implored him to change into more appropriate clothes, remarking: "The people must accustom themselves to associating the Congress with everything that is festive and dignified." Nordau complied, returning in his "official uniform." Alex Bein, Herzl's biographer, has noted that Herzl's dress code and other expressions of his "theatrical impulses" were mocked by anti-Zionists and a few of the movement's adherents as well. For skeptics and people unsympathetic to the cause, the *schwarze Festkleidung und weisse Halsbinde* seemed wholly ridiculous. They were taken as glaring examples of the political Zionists' pretentiousness and morally bankrupt attempt to mimic the gentile European bourgeoisie. Nevertheless, the use of formal attire may well have contributed to most delegates' sense of partaking in a profound ceremony. For the average participant, Bein also notes that "something was needed to symbolize the break with the ordinary, the proclamation of something great and beautiful in the dream which had brought them together."[59] The sense of participation in a new epoch and the solidarity this promoted were forcefully underscored by the liturgical techniques and ceremonial speechmaking which characterized the Congress proceedings themselves.

The ceremonial parts of the inaugural Congress illustrate this clearly. The first person chosen to ascend the podium was Dr. Karl Lippe of Jassy, Rumania. Because he was thought to be the oldest delegate and represented a bridge to the pre-Herzlian nationalist movement, Lippe was given the honor of introducing the entire assembly.[60] His address as well as his person reinforced the Zionists' urge to establish continuity with the earlier efforts at Jewish nationalization, while also showing how political Zionism had transcended its predecessors. Lippe portrayed the Kattowitz Conference of 1883, the "Lovers of Zion" attempt at consolidation that might have been considered a forerunner to the Zionist Congress, as representative of a mere fraction of Eastern Jews. The current Congress, however, stood for the totality of Jewry. The glowing praise for the new organization and its leaders, and generally upbeat tone assumed by Lippe (despite the fact that he spoke much longer than Herzl had directed) demonstrated the considerable skill with which the Congress orchestrators managed to put forward the best face of inner Zionist harmony at the early Zionist assemblies. Lippe's strong opinion that the colonization of Palestine should be enacted immediately was actually in sharp conflict with Herzl's approach.[61]

The opening ceremony also demonstrated the Zionists' ability to integrate their political liturgy with the religious liturgy of traditional Judaism. An image that most likely stayed in the minds of the delegates was that "Old Doctor Lippe of Jassy mounted the rostrum, covered his white head with his hat, and made a blessing." Lippe intoned the Sheheheyanu, a Hebrew prayer to mark the commencement of a special occasion: "*Baruch atah adanoi, eloheynu melech haolam, shehehayanu, vekiyemanu, vehegianu, lazman hazeh.*" (Blessed art Thou,

O Lord Our God, King of the Universe, who has kept us alive, sustained us, and brought us to this time.)[62]

This had the effect of framing the official proceedings with a liturgical rite that was common to all delegates and even the most assimilated Western Jews. Its impact was reinforced by the presence of the rabbis – the most familiar symbol of orthodox Judaism – seated at the back of the stage facing the delegates, and by scattered references to Jewish prayer throughout the remainder of the Congress. All of this served to underscore the idea that Zionism was in harmony with traditional Jewish religious life and proved important in laying the foundations of the movement's later mass appeal.

Completing the opening ceremonies at the inaugural assembly, the two chief Zionist leaders, Herzl and Nordau, delivered their initial addresses. The main speeches which took place at this and remaining Congresses in Herzl's lifetime stand out because of the thunderous ovations which proceeded and followed them. In contemporary press reports, as well as in a great many Zionist memoirs, they are in fact recalled as uniquely transfiguring emotional experiences. The extent to which Congress organizers consciously encouraged or sought to elicit such intense leadership adulation is difficult to gauge in retrospect. But, intended or not, the acclamational style intensified delegate solidarity at the Congresses and bolstered the young movement's recruitment and myth-making capacities.

The *Jewish Chronicle*'s report on the First Congress conveys a sense of this adulatory style in its account of the reception Herzl received when he first ascended the tribune. "To say that he received an ovation is to use too mild an expression. Such cheering, such excitement" took the British observer by surprise, for it was of an intensity "rarely experienced in England, and it was some minutes before the meeting resumed the calm that had hitherto characterized it. A less strong man than Dr. Herzl would have been unnerved by his reception."[63] It is most difficult to find a personal account of the First Zionist Congress that does not emphasize the exhilaration generated by the physical presence of Herzl. At the podium of the incipient state, he appeared to embody simultaneously a cultured Viennese, a dignified European statesman, a messianic incarnation, and the ideal new man that Zionism aspired to create [Figure 5]. The impact of the perception of Herzl, in the context of the meticulously staged assembly – as opposed to the Herzl one saw in the hall or small meeting, was detailed time and again. "It was extraordinary! What had happened? This was

5. Most reproduced portrait of Herzl.

not the Dr. Herzl I had seen hitherto, with whom I was in discussion as recently as last night," recorded one of the delegates.

Before us rose a marvelous and exalted figure, kingly in bearing and stature, with deep eyes in which could be read quiet majesty and unuttered sorrow. It

> is no longer the elegant Dr. Herzl of Vienna; it is a royal scion of the House of David, risen from among the dead, clothed in legend and fantasy and beauty. Everyone sat breathless, as if in the presence of a miracle . . . The dream of two thousand years was on the point of realization; it was as if the Messiah, son of David, confronted us; and I was seized by an overpowering desire, in the midst of this storm of joy, to cry out, loudly, for all to hear: "*Yehi hamelech*!" Hail to the King![64]

Another delegate, also struck by the "metamorphosis" of Herzl, recalled that "we all felt that we were a part of a new epoch" in Jewish history – which began with the ascent of Herzl to the podium.[65]

The fantasies of the delegates were not lost on the leader. Bein has commented on Herzl's understanding that "every response, every gesture had symbolic significance."[66] This was not, to say the least, a new awareness for Herzl. From the outset of the movement, he often wrote of the necessity of the leader to be encased in myths of power and grandeur. Further, in that his Zionism was nurtured in the same environment as Freudian psychoanalysis, it is not surprising that Herzl sought to utilize the interplay of levels of consciousness in his public appearances.[67] Like his colleague, the playwright Arthur Schnitzler, he was able to draw on current assumptions about the unconscious mind without directly referring to the new science of psychoanalysis.

Interestingly, in his later years, Herzl seems to have developed an acute intuitive sense of how to manipulate large group dynamics to his movement's advantage. He wrote occasionally of this comprehension in language reminiscent of the "philosopher of the crowd," Gustav LeBon, and claimed to have refined his understanding of crowd behavior by watching large-scale street demonstrations while a political correspondent in Paris, the same milieu which LeBon had studied. It was shortly after his entrance into Jewish politics, at a mass meeting in London, that Herzl described himself as becoming the focus of the kind of events at which he had formerly been an observer. "As I sat on the platform of the workingmen's stage . . . I experienced strange sensations. I saw and heard my legend being born. The people are sentimental; the masses do not see clearly. A light fog is beginning to rise around me and it may perhaps become the cloud in which I shall walk."[68] From this time on, Herzl did not hesitate to put his growing insight to use in the creation of positive myths about the national reconstitution of the Jews.

Herzl's Congress address, too, became inextricably linked with the messianic allusions and perceptions of the audience, which would be recalled by numerous portraits and postcards of the Zionist leader circulated after the Congress. "We want to lay the foundations of the edifice which will someday house the Jewish nation. The cause is so great that we should speak of it only in the simplest terms." His speech reiterated the assembly's concern with overturning anti-Semitic stereotypes and in reeducating Jews and non-Jews alike about the authentic and potential Jewish character. "Since time immemorial the world has been misinformed about us." Yet, taking Farbstein's advice, Herzl muted the significance of anti-Semitism as the impetus of the movement, stressing instead Zionism's strong humanitarian impulses and sincere respect for Jewish tradition.

> The feeling of solidarity with which we have been so frequently and violently reproached was in the process of disintegration when we were attacked by anti-Semitism. Anti-Semitism gave it new strength. We have returned home, as it were. Zionism is a return to Jewishness even before there is a return to the Jewish land. We, the sons who have returned, find in our father's house many things in urgent need of improvement; above all, we have brothers who have sunk deep into misery. However, we have been made welcome in the old home, because it is well known that we do not harbor the presumptuous notion of undermining what is time-honored.

In his address, Herzl accentuated the myth that the unity of Jewry could be achieved only through the movement. To make his point, Herzl used the rhetorical technique of wildly exaggerating the extent of Zionism's accomplishments and following:

> Zionism has already brought about something remarkable and heretofore regarded as impossible: a close alliance between the ultra-modern and ultra-conservative elements of Jewry. The fact that this has come to pass without undignified concessions on the part of either side and without intellectual sacrifices is additional proof, if such proof be needed, for the peoplehood of the Jews. A union of this kind is possible only on a national basis.[69]

Henceforth nearly all Zionist cultural pronouncements would clothe themselves in the rhetoric of unity and consensus in an effort to rally mass support on the basis of a self-fulfilling prophecy.

In another statement which was to be reformulated countless times, Herzl implored his audience to "let our profession of faith be solemnly repeated." The obvious vagueness of the reference to faith was intentional. In obscuring the boundary between Jewish nationalism as a secular ideology and Judaism's traditional religious faith, Herzl created a pledge of commitment which could mean all things to all people. Because of its very nebulousness the Zionist "profession of faith" became a powerful liturgical device, akin in some ways to the Yom Kippur service, in which the collective admission of sins, vows, and mutual responsibility is stressed. "The formal avowal," which implied public participation in Zionist rites, represented "the will to change or rededicate one's life." Robert Weltsch, a second-generation Zionist, recalled that "to the young Jew of this period, an acquaintance with Theodor Herzl's Zionism and the message of his life became the converting experience. He experiences the joy in confessing his faith, the joy that gives strength. This confession of regained solidarity is a return to Jewishness . . . It has been Herzl's achievement to create an outward expression for this confession."[70] Indeed, there is evidence that the quasi-religious loyalties aroused by Herzl's rhetoric extended beyond the circle of those who experienced the Congress first-hand. As early as 1911, one sympathetic observer would argue that the conversion experience had been widely transmitted through pictures, newspaper reports, and reprints of the *Stenographisches Protokoll*.[71]

Finally, Herzl set a recurrent theme in Zionist culture when he proclaimed that "enlightenment and reassurance shall go forth" as the beacon from the Congress. "Let people everywhere find out what Zionism really is; not a kind of chiliastic horror," but "a moral, lawful, humanitarian movement directed toward the age-old goal of our people's longing." Herzl insisted that precisely the Congress' enlightened humanitarian strivings would make it a permanent fixture in Jewish life; it would "govern as a wise ruler," and "provide for its own perpetuation, so that we will never again disperse" and become "ephemeral and ineffectual . . . And our Congress shall live forever . . . let [it] be earnest and high-minded, a source of welfare to the unhappy, of defiance to none, of honor to all Jewry, and worthy of a past whose renown, though already far distant in time, is eternal."[72]

Herzl's concluding words, though detached from the Congress sound like platitudes, solemnly reaffirmed the collective task which lay ahead of the Zionist Movement and triggered another round of wild acclamation. The *Jewish Chronicle* reported that tremendous cheering greeted Herzl as he finished his address, "and from all parts of the room men flocked to shake his hand."[73] Max Bodenheimer later suggested that the tumultuous ovation he received owed much to the fact that Herzl was widely perceived as the living personification of the Zionist cause.[74] Herzl's own pithy summary of his role – "At Basel I founded the Jewish State" – did much to propagate a "founder myth" within the movement, after it was published posthumously from his diaries.[75] All of this became part of the canon of Zionism and helped endow the fledgling movement with it first unifying hero and most significant prewar symbol.

If Herzl's inaugural Congress speech paved the way for his lionization as Zionism's ideal man, the assembly's official keynote speaker, Max Nordau, became the paragon of the Zionist critical intellect. Nordau's lasting contribution to all of the prewar Zionist Congresses, save the last, was a report on the general situation of world Jewry, which became an integral part of the institution's political liturgy. Nordau provided in some respects the perfect complement to Herzl. Like Herzl, he was a journalist and *litterateur*, writing primarily in German. His authority as a physician and scientist, though, enhanced his position as a best-selling author; and Nordau's reputation in the secular world was far greater than the movement's founder. Even allowing for a small number of books published per edition, the fact that Nordau's *Conventional Lies of Our Civilization* (1883) merited at least seventy-three printings, and was translated into more than fifteen languages testifies to an extraordinary readership. As a featured journalist for such newspapers as the Budapest *Pester Lloyd*, Berlin's *Vossische Zeitung*, the *Frankfurter Zeitung*, and the *Neue Freie Presse* of Vienna, he enjoyed an even larger audience.[76]

Although Nordau did not deal with specifically Jewish topics in his books and articles before 1897, his traditional Jewish background as the son of a modest rabbi constituted part of the mythology which formed his public image.[77] Even before he appeared at the First Congress, many Jews identified Nordau as a representative of Jewish concerns, and as an exemplar of distinctively Jewish characteristics.[78] Esteemed for his mastery of many different fields, and thought to be a sincere, honest, and bold critic of his environment, Nordau seemed to embody such core Zionist virtues as hard work, discipline, and responsibility. This image made him a highly effective symbol of Zionism from the moment he sided with Herzl. Herzl maintained that the Jewish State must be founded in a serious and reasonable manner, in order to impress both the Jewish and non-Jewish world; who better, then, to help establish it than the man who concluded in his anti-modernist tract *Degeneration* (1892–3):

> Whoever preaches the absence of discipline is an enemy of progress; and whoever worships his 'I' is an enemy to society. Society has for its first premise neighborly love and the capacity for self-sacrifice; and progress is the effect of

ever more rigorous subjugation of the beast in man, of an ever tenser self-restraint, and ever keener sense of duty and responsibility.[79]

Nordau's stature as a moralist was enhanced by his appearance. Possessed of a full white beard and robust countenance, his looks inevitably gave rise to comparisons with the ancient sages or prophets [Figure 6]. His iconoclasm led several devotees to see him as a modern-day Jeremiah.[80] Nordau's summary of the state of world Jewry, for many Zionists, was tantamount to a brilliant and moving High Holiday sermon. Though relatively unsophisticated, it was more analytic than the speech of Herzl. Yet it also contained a number of slogans that were easily adopted as received canon, the most famous being Nordau's opening remark, "Jewish misery has two forms, the material and the moral." While the bulk of Nordau's talk addressed the latter – the Western Jews' spiritual dilemma and its causes – it also contained the implicit message that Zionism's principal aim was to save the Jews of Eastern Europe from further degradation and persecution by securing a Jewish homeland.[81]

All in all, Nordau's keynote address produced an impact close to that of Herzl. The *Jewish Chronicle* reported that it was repeatedly interrupted by wild bouts of cheering and applause and that at the close, "roused to a fever heat of excitement, the Congress rose to a man and cheered Dr. Nordau again and again." Other delegates testified to a truly historic phenomenon. To the young Chaim Weizmann, for example, Nordau's speech seemed the most eloquent and forceful presentation of the *Judenfrage* from a Jewish perspective that the world had been compelled to consider.[82]

How infectious the atmosphere of leadership acclamation must have been during the Congress proceedings can be seen in the reaction of Ahad Ha-Am to Nordau's presentation. As a correspondent for the Hebrew daily *Ha-Shiloach*, Ahad Ha-Am came and left the Basel Congress incredulous at the movement. Nonetheless, he admitted to being fully caught up in the nationalistic jubilation aroused by Nordau's speech:

If I could enter into a pact with the angel of oblivion I would make him vow to obliterate from the hearts of the delegates all traces of what they saw and heard at Basel, leaving them only one memory. [I am referring to] the memory of that great and sacred hour when they all stood together as brothers. These forlorn men of Israel had come from all corners of the earth with their hearts full of feelings of holiness, their eyes were lovingly and proudly directed to their noble brother [Max Nordau] standing on the

6. Most reproduced portrait of Nordau.

platform, preaching wonders to his people, like of the prophets of days of yore. The memory of this hour, had it not been followed by many other hours which deprived the first impression of its purity, could have turned the assembly into one of the most distinguished events in the history of our people.[83]

As these comments indicate, by the time he left Basel, Ahad Ha-Am – with his aversion to mass politics – had largely regained his critical distance. But the "nationalization" of many others continued apace.[84] A floodgate of postcards and pictures followed Nordau's triumphant Congress appearance. By all accounts, the "state of world Jewry" address that Nordau went on to deliver at the next nine Congresses through 1911 came to be received as Zionist gospel by the vast majority of Zionists.[85] In the end, Nordau's appeal as a Zionist leader contributed significantly to the movement's cohesion during its prewar phase. The fact that Nordau was able to sustain great popularity among Zionists – while his reputation as an intellectual plummeted among the general European public – is telling. It suggests the extent to which all shades of Zionism remained colored by the older virtues of the liberal Enlightenment, such as respect for law, faith in gradual progress, and esteem for the voice of ethical conscience – within a broader cultural milieu that was growing increasingly fascinated by anti-rationalistic forms of discourse.

While no other Zionist approached the visibility or repute of a Herzl or Nordau, other individuals made substantial contributions to the establishment of common goals and unifying myths within the Congress setting as well. At the first assembly, for example, Hermann Schapira, a Heidelberg mathematics professor, introduced the concept of what became known as the Jewish National Fund (JNF). He was remembered for a moving address which proposed to set up a general subscription fund for the purchase of land for Jewish settlement in Palestine and the establishment of a secular Jewish university. Schapira, who was actually the oldest delegate at the Congress (rather than Karl Lippe) and extremely popular with the well-represented German and Austrian university students, also formed the subject of a well-known anecdote in Zionist lore. This purported to show the movement's role as a surrogate family to its supporters. Told in several versions, perhaps the most trustworthy account, related by Max Bodenheimer with a touch of Yiddishkeit, has a dozen Heidelberg students dancing around the popular Schapira at the end of the

Commers evening. "What do I want with children?," the childless Schapira called out. "These are all my sons!"[86]

Besides the key Congress personalities, other features of the proceedings had a strong integrative effect on the movement. Ironically, that segment of the inaugural Congress which generated the most discordant and heated discussion was the platform debate which gave rise to Zionism's central sacred text. Known as the "Basel Program," this was a very general statement of the movement's objectives. It represented a compromise between those who wanted to assert the movement's state-building emphasis, and those who wished to assure Jewry and the world that Zionism would encroach on other nation's political affairs as gingerly as possible. The Basel Program remained unamended for almost a half-century. Its strength lay in its very vagueness, which enabled all factions within Zionism to see their purposes mirrored in its text. In effect, the Basel Program became a nurturing catechism. It was repeatedly and successfully invoked during the movement's crucial formative stages to assure that Zionism proceeded along a moderate, public, and legal course.

However generalized it may have been on many questions, the consensus which appeared with the promulgation of the Basel Program contributed to a great show of solidarity and new wave of acclamation during the Congress' closing ceremony. In his remarks on this occasion, Herzl praised the moderation of the Congress' politics. His concluding thoughts reinforced another primary Zionist myth, that of purification through manual labor, especially labor close to the soil. Herzl called up the image of the Jewish farmer that had been consecrated in the Basel Program and would be popularized in numerous Congress postcards. "If we call on the downtrodden to set their hands to the plow, do we even have to ask if they prefer work to defenselessness and misery? Just ask them! On the day when the plow again rests in the toughened hands of the Jewish farmer, the Jewish Problem will be solved." According to several eyewitness depictions, Herzl's closing speech and a final rendition of "Hatikvah" again triggered an acclamatory display fully equal to the earlier pandemonium.[87] Even allowing for hyperbole in most sympathetic accounts, it seems clear that the inaugural Congress – and most of its successors before the First World War – provided a powerful emotional experience for participants which, through effective follow-up agitation, created a steadily expanding circle of Zionist "converts."

In retrospect, then, the Zionism which emerged from the Congress days was a surprisingly complete microcosm of the cultural apparatus and political style which the prewar movement required to make its way both in Western Jewish circles and bourgeois Europe at large. Already before the turn of the century, it was equipped with national heroes, an anthem and flag, a humanitarian rationale, and diverse myths, symbols, and liturgical activities with a proven capacity to inspire demonstrations of solidarity and "missionary work." There is little doubt that Zionism would not have caught the eye of middle-class Jews as rapidly as it did – even though it remained a minority movement – had it been perceived as the pet project of a political journal or the cause of a snobbish coterie, as Herzl first envisioned. The strength of Congress Zionism was its participatory emphasis. In this regard, the ebb and flow of acclamatory display, encouraged by the structure of the Congresses, was particularly important as a liturgical technique. It effectively elicited groundswells of emotional solidarity at many times when the extent of Zionist unity and the movement's actual following was questionable.

Congress Zionism, to be sure, was not without its contradictory aspects. The movement adopted the prescription of Jewish religious law that Jews should settle in the Promised Land, and departing Congress delegates took leave of one another saying "Next year in Jerusalem" – the familiar closing benediction of the Passover Seder. But the Congresses came to flourish so comfortably in Switzerland that they often gave the impression that "the land of milk and honey" was Basel. More than once this prompted scorn for the thought of middle-class Zionists, who seemed wedded to the creature comforts of their European milieu, actually settling Palestine.[88] More serious perhaps was the fact that many early Zionists had not totally renounced certain forms of anti-Semitic prejudice and stereotyping which they claimed to be combatting. They proclaimed their respect for Jewish traditions, but some were scornful of Yiddish culture and implicitly used the dirty, chaotic *Shtetl* as a foil to idealized depictions of Basel. They spoke of solidarity with the downtrodden Eastern Jewish masses, but took pains to dissociate themselves from what they saw as the moral debasement of the objects of their charity. This was reflected in the *Jewish Chronicle*'s closing comments on the First Congress which mentioned that over one-third of the delegates had come from the East, not including Galicia:

Nearly all of them appeared to be men of high intellectual power, and not a few of them are of commanding presence. Among these cultured representative men was a *Chazan* [cantor], who is conversant with a number of Western languages, including English, in which he expresses himself with clearness. The splendid types of Russian and Polish Jews who attended the Congress in such large numbers would have been a revelation to many Londoners, apt to judge the standard of their brethren in those countries by the specimens they habitually see in the East End.[89]

In many ways, these contradictions were to be expected in an essentially middle-class movement nurtured in a Central European setting. Yet along with such parochial prejudices, the cultural and organizational ferment produced by the movement was a remarkably creative process. During its Congress phase, Zionism for a few days provided its faithful with total immersion in a national Jewish world. The delegates stayed in hotels housing other Zionists, took their meals together, wore Stars of David and Zionist ribbons on their lapels, talked of Jewish matters, sang Jewish songs, exalted Jewish heroes, gathered under Jewish flags, and drank wine from grapes grown in Palestine – all of this in Basel, a model of bourgeois European normalcy. The Congress experience exemplified the degree to which prewar Zionism already styled itself as a government in exile, awaiting transplantation; while simultaneously, through the display of an extra-territorial Zionist culture, it affirmed that Zion could exist anywhere that Jews gathered in peace. These conflicting moments would frame much of the cultural debate within Zionism, which increasingly occupied the movement's discourse in the last prewar decade.

CHAPTER TWO

THE EMERGENCE OF HEBREW AND DISSENT

A vital part of the historiography and popular recollection of early Zionism concerns the great debate on culture within the movement. This controversy, by and large, has been interpreted as indicating that Zionism was more divided than united on the issue of "culture." In fact, a shared concept of culture among Zionists was one of the more important sources of cohesion of the movement for Western Jews. Studies of this debate have tended to focus on the growth and adoption of the Hebrew language, and specific events in which different concepts of Zionist culture seemed to have been the basis of bitter conflict – namely, the furor about Herzl's utopian novel, *Altneuland*, the conflict about the so-called Uganda plan advanced by the British government, and the resolution in favor of *Gegenwartsarbeit* [present-day work] of the 1906 Helsingfors Conference.

Because modern Hebrew prevailed as the dominant language in the *Yishuv* and was later enshrined as an official language of the State of Israel, many discussions of the *Kulturfrage* ["the problem of culture"] give prominence to the proponents of the Hebrew revival.[1] The thought of Asher Ginsberg, the self-styled Ahad Ha-Am, has been generally accepted as the standard by which to judge and explicate the *Kulturfrage*.[2] Ahad Ha-Am was a leader of the modern Hebrew revival whose ideas and followers attained positions of great influence in Zionism. Much of Zionist historiography assumes that the so-called "cultural Zionism" of Ahad Ha-Am, stressing the primacy of modern Hebrew in reviving the Jewish nation and the gradual development of a "cultural center" in the *Yishuv*, was widely divergent from Herzl's "political" Zionism – with the ideology of Ahad Ha-Am proving "far superior" to that of Herzl.[3] Such evaluations suggest that early Zionist ideas about "culture" represented an extremely divisive force in the movement's formative years.

A major problem with this assessment is that it is hard pressed to explain the uninterrupted growth of organized Zionism among Western Jews after the inaugural Zionist Congress of 1897, while the notion of culture was becoming ever more important in the movement. The belief that there existed an unbridgeable gap between the "political" and "cultural" wings of Zionism overlooks the relatively harmonious relations between the movement's "factions": they jointly popularized and disseminated many of the vital unifying myths, symbols, and ideological postulates of Zionism throughout the prewar period. Indeed, the argument can be made that the intensive and successful *Propagandaarbeit* of these years was possible because there was a fundamental accord in the Zionists' cultural outlook, not a fundamental divergence.

What were the chief cultural ideals that the Zionists held in common? Above all, most leaders and activists – except for Ahad Ha-Am himself, who chose a path of lonely, principled dissent – shared an appreciation of the prerequisites needed to establish a Jewish nation. They were parties to a tradition going back to Herder and the early German nationalists, such as Fichte and Jahn, who saw language and folkways as the primary manifestations of a people's distinctive national essence, and emphasized the role of education, physical culture, and purifying labor in the creation of a nation. They also were witness to the actual nation-building process that occurred throughout the nineteenth century in the ethnic-national awakenings of the peoples of Central and Eastern Europe. Most early Zionists therefore grasped that a sense of nationhood could only be cemented through shared national heroes, symbols, songs, and myths – that is, a national culture. They understood, as well, that the ultimate guarantor of unity was statehood in a common territory that the nation could call its own, although this particular insight was emphasized most by the "political" Zionists who stood closest to Herzl.

Although the Zionists emulated European models, what made their plan recognizably Jewish and attractive to Jewish nationalists was that Jewish myths, symbols, legends, images, and the ancestral homeland of *eretz Israel* served as the wellspring of Zionism. Furthermore, they embraced many of the attitudes that had animated the *Haskala*. German, Italian, Austrian, Swiss, and English features served as the vehicles, but not the substance of Zionist culture.[4] The immutable core of the mythology represented by Herzl and his followers held that in order to flourish individually and collectively, Jews must reconstitute themselves as a nation with its center in Palestine, and that the essence of Judaism would be manifested as "justice, truth, liberty, progress, humanity, and beauty."[5] Despite the pain and passions invoked by the Uganda plan, the focus of the Zionists' territorial effort was always understood to be Palestine.[6] Judaism was to have a vague but certainly visible role; although Zionists disagreed over what variety of Judaism should prevail in the movement, there was no question of its prominence: "We recognize our historic destiny," Herzl wrote and often repeated, "only by the faith of our fathers."[7] Those who joined Herzl also sensed that he was "occupied with a work of infinite grandeur . . . a mighty dream" which harmonized with the greatest hopes of the modern Hebraists – to restore Jewish dignity and honor through the creation of a Jewish nationality, expressing a self-conscious solidarity with the Jewish past and future.[8]

All of these presuppositions entered into the meaning of a word often used in early Zionism: *Kultur*. Insofar as the term related to the goal of reconstituting a Jewish nation, the overarching consensus about *Kultur* suggests that the cultural debates within the prewar movement rested on a shared intellectual terrain. However acrimonious the debates appeared to be at times, the points of disagreement were largely tactical in nature and rarely seriously impeded the movement's progress. The fact that many Zionist leaders from the different factions had close personal ties based on mutual friendship and respect further reinforced the movement's underlying unity.

Nevertheless, during the last prewar Zionist Congress in Vienna (1913), a critic writing in the *Jewish Chronicle* remarked that "the all dominating thought of the Congress is *Kulturarbeit*, i.e., schools, books, literary work, and academic studies . . . The first word of every speaker was *Kultur*. Sometimes one was under the impression that Zionism has been reduced to a kind of Hebrew literary society."[9] Though somewhat overstated, this observation is significant. It suggests the extent to which cultural ideals in prewar Zionism came to encompass less and less of the Jewish people as they were – living in the diaspora and speaking languages other than Hebrew. From the outset of the movement, and then more intensely after Herzl's death, cultural issues as defined by Ahad Ha-Am moved toward the center of discussion in Zionism. Increasingly, these issues became involved in the quest to define a modern Jewish nation. The debates on culture further inspired a panoply of effective "propaganda and agitation" techniques along with rhetorical strategies that helped bestow the perception that the Zionist Congresses were legitimately formulating a cultural policy for the Jewish masses.

The *Kulturdebatte* at the Zionist Congresses would yield valuable insights into the differing socio-cultural ideals of major groups within European Jewry. Slowly they came to provide a sounding board for diverse Jewish constituencies. Around 1900, an important phalanx in the Zionists' ranks was established, known as the "Democratic Faction." This was the first self-proclaimed party within the Zionist Movement, consisting mostly of young men, led by Martin Buber, Berthold Feiwel, E. M. Lilien, Leo Motzkin, and Chaim Weizmann. They advocated a more deliberate concentration on culture, in the sense of aesthetic and scientific education along with the Hebrew revival, as a central and obligatory component of Zionism. They have been noted for their role in organizing "cultural Zionist" dissent from the mainstream, setting a precedent for the formation of parties within Zionism.[10]

Yet a closer examination of the group reveals a great degree of loyalty to Herzl and political Zionism.[11] The historian David Vital has written that one of the most famous images of early Zionism, a photograph taken of Herzl in the center of the Faction at the Fifth Congress reveals "the ambivalence of its members' attitude to him" [Figure 7].[12] This is by no means clear. Instead, one might infer that the Faction's insistence on being photographed with the leader was more significant than Herzl's solemn expression, which did not in any case differ markedly from his austere gaze in other portraits. More important, the case can be made that the Faction's members, particularly through their publishing house, *Juedischer Verlag*, performed yeoman service in disseminating the concepts and symbols of political and cultural Zionism alike. Furthermore, it is unlikely that the Faction would have dissolved as it did after a few years had it perceived the necessity of a continuing crusade against the political Zionists. A more accurate interpretation of this development is that the group's policies became so much a part of the Zionist Organization that its existence was superfluous. The activities and fate of the Faction therefore indicate the overlap between political and cultural Zionism and the extent of their mutual interpenetration.

In general, before 1902, the *Kulturdebatte* in Zionism had been

7. Theodor Herzl and the "Democratic Faction" at the Fifth Zionist Congress (1901).

primarily a dispute between groups of East European Zionists, whom Herzl deftly managed to sidestep by keeping the movement's official position on culture as vague as possible.[13] In Zionism's early years, Herzl hoped to keep the issue of overtly propagating a Jewish national culture at bay, so as to alienate orthodox Jewry as little as possible. He wished not to offend the small percent of the orthodox who had declared themselves in favor of the movement, and to forestall the erection of barricades that might prevent the masses of East European orthodox – who generally opposed Zionism – from joining the movement in the future. As yet, most orthodox feared that the promoters of Jewish culture wanted to replace their traditional religion with a modern, secularized Jewish ideology and way of life, where they would have little say.[14]

For the most part, such views were not groundless. Many cultural Zionists did articulate a forceful anti-clerical stance. They aspired, at the very least, to "trim the excesses" of rabbinic Judaism and threatened to alter existing Jewish communal structures upon which the traditional religious elites relied for their existence.[15] The spiritual objections of orthodoxy, that Zionism represented a false, or premature messianism, are well known. The material grounds for rejecting Zionism – that the movement was a threat to orthodox livelihoods, with its potential of establishing a network of Zionist *chadarim, yeshivot* and communal organizations – are less apparent or admitted.[16] Yet as a recent study of Russian Zionism details, "there was fear among orthodox circles that the changes sought by the Zionists would result in radical changes in the realm of education. The establishment of only a few educational institutions by Zionists led anti-Zionist orthodox Jews to view Zionism as a qualitatively new danger. It was seen as a threat which was likely to oust them from their main source of livelihood – teaching." Quite possibly Herzl's "pragmatic view of Judaism" allowed him to see that "material as well as religious motivations were intertwined," in the ever-present threat that the orthodox would counterattack "and virtually declare war on the Zionist Movement."[17]

The problem of culture for those who officially joined the Zionist Organization was somewhat different. It might be summarized as the extent to which Zionism should strive to build a new, secular Jewish culture, versus the extent that orthodox Judaism should determine the culture of Zionism. Some perceived this issue as the perpetually "mishandled stepchild" of inner-Zionist relations.[18] For those who considered themselves cultural Zionists, as well as those who carried the banner of orthodoxy in the movement and opposed the development of a secular Hebrew culture, it purported to answer the question: "what does it mean to be a Zionist?" If any two concepts of *Kultur* in Zionism were truly antithetical, it was these in their extreme forms. Such *Weltanschauungen* were in contentious opposition during the prewar years, and similar tensions are still being exercised in the modern State of Israel.

Following the example of the Democratic Faction, in Vilna in 1902 orthodox Zionists organized as the *Mizrahi* party, taking their name from the Hebrew *merkaz ruhani* meaning "spiritual center;" they primarily sought to carve out a secure place for the orthodox in Zionism. Pushing democratic and socialist ideals beyond those advocated by the Democratic Faction, a group of socialists, known as Labor or *Poale-Zion* later established themselves under the rubric of the Basel Program and Marxism in 1906.[19] The attitudes of spokesmen from these groups toward the initiatives of the *Kulturisten*, who desired and worked for a greater emphasis on Hebrew culture emanating from the center of the movement, shed a great deal of light on the obstacles that early Zionism faced in its efforts to woo large sections of orthodox Jewry and the East European Jewish working classes.[20] On the other hand, the cultural debates within Zionism clearly indicate the bases of cohesion among those who called themselves Zionists, most particularly among Western Jews.

The idea that Hebrew should and could provide a vital rallying point for a distinctive Jewish national spirit and polity was never an unchallenged goal in Zionism. It was not realized without cogent criticism both from the ranks of orthodox Jewry as well as from the Jewish left and articulate defenders of Yiddish culture. The propagation of the Hebrew idea was further complicated by the decentralized and unstructured nature of the so-called "Culture Committees" charged with its dissemination. In view of the scattered personal initiatives upon which Zionist *Kulturarbeit* so frequently relied, it is all the more remarkable how quickly the language, which Herzl doubted could ever be learned by Western Jews, gained sway in the movement. Yet by 1913, portions of the Zionist Congresses were conducted mainly in Hebrew, and Hebrew was acknowledged in principle as the official language of the movement. One of the central unifying themes of Zionism attained widespread acceptance in less than two decades.

In the process by which the approbation of Hebrew and other Zionist myths and symbols took root, it is important to remember that ideological content, cultural forms, and modes of transmission were closely intertwined. Strictly speaking, their interconnection was the essence of the dissemination process. For analytical purposes, however, there is value in treating these components separately. Therefore, while the current chapter focuses largely on the rhetorical exchanges and intellectual debates which accompanied the spread of the Hebrew idea, subsequent chapters will concentrate on other specific myths and constructs, as well as chief art forms and vehicles of communication which entered into the totality of Zionist *Kulturarbeit*, to demonstrate the unifying features of Zionist culture.

The first major "cultural" speech at the Zionist Congresses was delivered in 1897 by Marcus Ehrenpreis, a "modern" rabbi and Hebraist from Djakovar, Croatia. Born in Lemberg and educated at the *Hochschule der Wissenschaft des Judentums* in Berlin and several German universities, he would be one of the major figures representing cultural Zionism at this and subsequent forums. During the First Congress, Ehrenpreis addressed the assembly on the subject of "the New Hebrew Literature." Though his speech cannot be considered one of the assembly's highlights – he began resentfully by noting that the agenda left his talk to "the twelfth hour," with very little time allotted for discussion, it nonetheless broached most of the fundamental concerns of the *Kulturisten*.[21]

Ehrenpreis emphasized the development and widespread dissemination of the Hebrew language and literature among Jews as a primary means of imbuing them with the requisite national spirit in order to prepare them for life in a reconstituted Jewish nation. Hebrew culture as such would invigorate and enrich the old/new homeland of the Jews, Palestine, as well as providing a link with the Jewish past and future. Its cultivation would serve as a common basis for the new Jewish civilization.[22]

Even if the Jews of Central and Western Europe had been totally unaware of the Hebrew movement, Ehrenpreis' ideas were certainly familiar. Numerous national groups repeated the motto of Herder that "men hold nothing more dear than the speech of their fathers," and Schlegel, who declared in that "every important and independent nation has the right of possessing a literature unique to itself; the meanest barbarism is that which would oppress the speech of a people and a country, or exclude it from all higher learning . . . it is mere prejudice which leads us to consider languages that have been neglected, or that are unbeknown to ourselves, as incapable of being brought to a higher perfection."[23] Even assimilated Jews were not as far removed from support or sympathy for the Hebrew movement as might be assumed.[24] For Ehrenpreis' perspective to become operative, though, it remained for Jews to accept the idea that the Jewish people were a distinct nationality, and not just a religious collectivity.

Ehrenpreis knew that most secular Jews tended to identify Hebrew with Judaism's liturgical rites which they neither understood nor considered very important. He was adamant in pointing out that Hebraism "was not a variety of orthodoxy or reaction, and it was well within the realm of progress and modernity."[25] This qualification is noteworthy in illustrating the *Kulturisten*'s basically secular orientation. With it, Ehrenpreis suggested a continuity with the proto-Zionist *Hibbat Zion* societies of Jewish national writers, whom religious Jews had regarded as radical secularizers.[26] This would arouse special animosity among the orthodox clergy not only on theological grounds, but because of its threat to rabbinical livelihoods, as we have seen. When Ehrenpreis went on to demand that all Jews have access to free Hebrew courses, this helped set the program of cultural Zionism on a potential collision course with the orthodox establishment. Interestingly, though, the typical assimilated Western Jew reading the protocols of the First Zionist Congress would probably not have imagined the rabbis as Ehrenpreis' opponents; they had not been afforded an opportunity to respond. On the contrary, Ehrenpreis' fusion of imagery and content, with rabbis in the backdrop and high praise for Hebrew created a strong impression of harmony on the issue of a national language.

Ehrenpreis further proclaimed that a "new Hebrew literature" was already being produced by poets, researchers, publicists, and publishing concerns. Still, the revival of Hebrew was sporadic, unorganized, and unnoticed by the general European public. The activities comprising it needed to be coordinated and fitted into a pragmatic program within the Zionist Movement.[27] At the close of this speech, Ehrenpreis proposed two resolutions to promote such coordination: (1) that the Congress found a general Hebrew-speaking society to establish free courses for Hebrew instruction, and (2) that the Congress elect a commission for Hebrew literature as a section of the executive committee. He hoped the latter committee would establish and support Hebrew periodicals and works, encourage young Hebrew writers and scholars by funding their travel (to enhance their education), and otherwise generally advance the role of Hebrew. Following his address, a "permanent" Hebrew literature commission, made up of Ehrenpreis, Ahad Ha-Am, Armand Kaminka, Nahum Sokolow, and Eliezer Ben-Yehuda was established by acclamation.[28]

The Ehrenpreis speech was punctuated with insistence that Zionist political leaders devote more resources and attention to the needs of the Hebrew movement. This, too, set the tone for a posture which many *Kulturisten* would assume at future Congresses.[29] Yet it is significant that Ehrenpreis placed no conditions on Herzl's movement in order for it to be allied with the Hebraists. Like most cultural Zionists, he treated the Hebrew movement and political Zionism as a unified cause because this was "natural."[30] Characteristically, Ehrenpreis portrayed the new Hebrew literary culture as a major province, if not the very heart, of Zionism. Nevertheless, in publicly acknowledging the close affinity between the aims of Zionism and Hebraism, he presented his differences with Herzl as a fraternal dispute rather than an irreconcilable doctrinal schism. Most *Kulturisten* were likewise careful not to overstep certain rhetorical boundaries in their subsequent calls for greater Zionist commitment to Hebrew.[31]

It is significant that after the First Congress, Ehrenpreis became a principal defender of "Congress-Zionism" against its well-publicized denunciation by Ahad Ha-Am. Ahad Ha-Am especially loathed "child-like spectacles" and an emphasis on youth culture, which he saw as prevalent in modern mass politics – including Herzl's political Zionism. Ahad Ha-Am's organic version of Zionism called for "no haste" and "no beating of drums."[32] After the First Congress, he wrote that only those believing in "a fantasy bordering on madness" can think "that as soon as the Jewish State is established millions of Jews will flock to it," "and the land will afford them sustenance. Think of the labor and the money that had to be sunk in Palestine over a long period of years before one new branch of production – vine growing – could be established there!"[33]

Although Ahad Ha-Am himself championed the idea – which could be seen as a founding national myth – that the innermost truth for Jewry was to be gleaned through their engagement with Hebrew culture, his Zionst career was more marked by a conscious stance as a vigilant critic and "razor-sharp analyst."[34] In time, he seemed to go further than anyone associated with Zionism in criticizing the use of myth in the movement for immediate political gains, emphasizing the need for gradual development over the course of generations.[35] Ahad Ha-Am strongly disparaged Zionism's deployment of slogans and political symbolism, apparently the greatest success of the First Congress: "Truth is bitter, but with all its bitterness it is better than illusion."[36] Indeed, all of this did much to establish an important and valuable tradition of dissent within Zionist culture, but made Ahad Ha-Am too controversial a figure to serve as an ultimate unifying symbol.

The main failing of Ahad Ha-Am's criticism to Ehrenpreis, who had tremendous regard for Ahad Ha-Am as a Hebraist, was his lack of latitude in allowing for the propagation of myth. To Ehrenpreis, Ahad Ha-Am's criticisms of the fledgling Zionist Organization revealed his insensitivity to the need for "imponderable elements" that Ehrenpreis saw as essential for the realization of any aspect of political or cultural Zionism.[37] Even some of the most devoted followers of Ahad Ha-Am tended to view his concept of Jewish culture as too narrow to be strictly obeyed in a living, popular political movement.[38] In contrast, regard for the "imponderable" is precisely where Herzl and most *Kulturisten* shared vital common ground.

Interestingly, the retrospective opinion of Ehrenpreis has frequently been used to substantiate the misleading notion that Herzl did not "understand" cultural Zionism.[39] Indeed, Herzl's relationship to the prescriptions of the cultural Zionists is more subtle and complex than frequently assumed. It is clear that after the First Zionist Congress of 1897, his greatest goal was securing a charter for Palestine from the Ottoman Sultan because he believed that public recognition of the Jews' national rights would provide the most effective impetus for Zionism. While Ahad Ha-Am believed that the inner world of the Jew had to be changed before a change in the Jewish condition was possible, Herzl maintained that a radical, external shift in the circumstances of Jewish life – symbolized by the charter – would in turn revolutionize Jewish consciousness. By definition, however, Herzl had to accept the Hebrew movement, because he professed that Zionism included all elements of Jewry.

Yet because he ardently wished to have all Jews under his banner, Herzl thought it best not to accentuate the proposals of cultural Zionism. He recognized that the Hebraists in Eastern Europe comprised an elitist and marginal movement. Still, to the personal dismay of Ahad Ha-Am, most members of the diffuse Hebraist movement greeted Herzl and political Zionism with great exhilaration, and its members were thrilled with the notion of becoming the avant-garde of the Jewish masses.[40]

Herzl's familiarity with Ehrenpreis, and Michael Berkowicz, who would record a very different view of Herzl's relationship to cultural Zionism than that of Ehrenpreis, assured that he was exposed to the rationale and basic facts of the Hebrew revival. Berkowicz wrote that "my visits to [Herzl's] house were frequent" after he translated *Der Judenstaat* (1896) into Hebrew, "and almost all of them were devoted to increasing his intimacy with the Hebrew world. I brought with me whatever Hebrew periodicals I received, and read to him those articles which might be of interest to him."[41] It is unreasonable to assume that Herzl's lack of Hebrew knowledge kept him from comprehending or appreciating this aspect of the Jewish risorgimento. Certainly he was able to understand the rationale for the Hebrew revival, which had originated in the *Haskala* nearly a century earlier.

Ehrenpreis records that "Herzl never really grasped the meaning of the Jewish cultural renaissance," although his refusals to strongly endorse Ehrenpreis' cultural efforts were always covered with "extraordinary politeness."[42] Perhaps Herzl's gentlemanly attitude toward his colleague led to the perception that he did not understand. Herzl, in reality, did not agree with Ehrenpreis about the urgency of the cultural Zionists' endeavors. The fact that he respected the Hebrew revival as well as orthodoxy is significant.

However, while many *Kulturisten* thought that more should have been done for their cause, Herzl's attitude allowed Hebraism to be seen as an officially sanctioned part of the cultural regeneration envisioned by Zionism.[43] In effect, it accorded the Hebraists a far greater audience for their efforts than would have been available had they struck out on their own. It also set them in a unified, national mold.

In fact, Herzl's attitude toward Hebrew became increasingly positive in the course of his Zionist career. Despite his acute sensitivity to symbols, his early Zionist writings showed little sympathy for the cultural Zionists' tendency to attribute great symbolic significance to the Hebrew language. In *Der Judenstaat*, Herzl dismissed the issue of language and national culture without much consideration: "Switzerland is a model of a federal state of various languages. The nation will be recognized by its faith, not its language." "German, of necessity, would likely be the official language," he propounded, even though Herzl held "nothing against French or English." Obviously, the majority of Jews were Yiddish speakers; this made the adoption of German logical, as the most easily assimilated language of culture for the Jewish masses. Herzl ruled out Hebrew on the grounds of practicality: "we can no longer speak to each other in Hebrew," an indisputable fact around the turn of the century.[44] Most Jews might have been able to sound out Hebrew characters, yet they had little mastery of Hebrew as an everyday spoken language.

Very soon after the publication of *Judenstaat*, however, Herzl's attitude toward the Hebrew movement underwent a marked change. He became convinced that Hebrew could serve as "a real and vital force, the instrument of self-expression of thousands of ardent Jews."[45] The symbolic disavowal of Yiddish, which to the *Kulturisten* represented the stunted cultural development of Jewry in exile, was a point with which Herzl agreed, albeit less dogmatically. Many cultural Zionists, of course, ultimately hoped to replace Yiddish and the other languages that Jewry had been compelled to acquire in the diaspora by the mass Hebraization of the Jews. Characteristically, Herzl was never vocal on the issue for tactical reasons. The impracticability of using and disseminating Hebrew, especially west of the Pale of Settlement, along with the objections of the orthodox, prevented him from promoting the Hebraization of the Jews as a major priority of the movement.

Quite possibly, Herzl also feared that the efforts of the Hebraists might embarrass the Zionist movement by failing to produce valuable cultural products. This apprehension may have stemmed from his view of the nineteenth-century Greek Revolution, which was accompanied by a cultural revival including the resuscitation of an ancient language. Herzl discerned a wide gap between the tangible results of this revival and the enormous artistic hopes it had inspired throughout the world. From his perspective, the new Hellenistic culture did not succeed in enhancing the Greek's standing in the eyes of critical, cultured Europeans.[46] How could he be sure that the new "Jewish culture" would be a source of pride and respect, rather than testimony to the Wagnerian accusation that Jews possessed no unique, creative spirit? Herzl concluded that organized Zionism's most prudent cultural strategy might be to wait for a national literature to develop organically on the national soil. Did not the cultural Zionists themselves claim this as a prerequisite for genuine cultural products?[47]

Above all, Herzl saw the goals of the *Kulturisten* as premature, rather than fundamentally undesirable. Nahum Sokolow reported that Herzl once admonished him that

> You, with your cultural banner, are upsetting rather than building. About what are you quarreling? First there has to be a home and peace for the Jews, then let them choose the culture they want. They will, of course, bring along with them many cultures, like bees who suck honey from different flowers and bring it all with them to one beehive; precisely this mixture will be far more interesting than one monotonous culture.[48]

In addition, Herzl may well have sensed that a focus on Hebrew culture was not the best means for nationalizing the Jews of his day – that Hebraization was too esoteric a concept to activate a national consciousness among the Jewish masses. He was not alone in this – even some cultural Zionists drew similar conclusions. For example, Shai Hurwitz, the Berlin Hebraist, wrote that "in the final analysis, modern Hebrew is mainly the concern of its authors themselves," and the preeminent Hebraist and educator in the *Yishuv*, David Yellin, admitted that "[t]he lot of the Hebrew language in the *Golus* resembles the fate of a date-tree, which has been plucked up from its roots and replanted high on the Alps, without glass-covering above and without artificial warmth below."[49]

A major theme in the platform of cultural Zionism which Ehrenpreis' address did not cover was the relationship of Zionism to Yiddish. This subject was a focal point for a second major cultural speech at the 1897 Congress delivered by Nathan Birnbaum, later known under the pen-name Mathias Acher. Birnbaum, publisher of *Selbst-Emanzipation*, and a founder of the Viennese Jewish-nationalist student society *Kadimah*, was one of the most prominent figures in pre-Herzl Jewish-national movement.[50] Even more so than Ehrenpreis, he attended the Congress as a disgruntled delegate because he had hoped for a more substantial role.[51] In his speech entitled "Zionism as a Cultural Movement" he echoed a basic position of Ahad Ha-Am, asserting that "the great wave of Yiddish literature and theater" was too interconnected with European culture to be representative of a unique Jewish culture. The new Hebrew literature, on the other hand, exemplified such a distinct culture. Birnbaum used the dichotomy of "culture" versus "civilization," current in Germany, to distinguish his preferred variety of Jewish national expression.[52] The fruits of Yiddish were wedded to European civilization, according to Birnbaum. This implied that Yiddish was weighed down by materialistic concerns, rather than suffused with spirituality. In contrast, "men of Hebrew letters, inspired by Zionism, were increasing in number," and they had begun to transcend European civilization and culture to forge their own national identity.[53] The Hebraists, Birnbaum suggested, were far more capable of developing an authentic Jewish national ethic than the Yiddishists, since their goal was a complete, new national life for Jews on an equal footing with that of other nations. To countless Jews living west of the Pale of Settlement, Birnbaum's disparaging remarks about Yiddish may well have struck a familiar chord. In many respects, they characterized middle-class Jewry's attitude towards the language of their parents and grandparents, or what they themselves had spoken in their childhood. "Jargon," or *juedische-Jargon* as they sometimes called it, was best left to the world of the *shtetl*. Herzl, too, had originally written that Yiddish was a mark of the Jews' "imprisonment" which would be swept away when Jews gained complete autonomy. Yet Birnbaum did not simply destroy; he wished to build up an entirely new, thoroughly dignified cultural edifice.

Through the establishment of Jewish autonomy in Palestine "the Jews would ultimately regain their national creativity by liberating themselves from the bondage of alien ideologies and anti-Semitism." "True freedom and Jewish culture" would thus prevail "through the final triumph of the Zionist ideal, a Jewish State." Ultimately Birnbaum arrived at a compelling variant of the broader Zionist synthesis. He clearly affirmed that the concepts of freedom, culture, and political autonomy were inextricably linked for the Jews.[54]

Despite what reads as a skilled polemic, Birnbaum received only polite applause, and his address was rarely mentioned in the numerous reminiscences of the First Congress. Unlike Ehrenpreis, his talk did not lead to any formal proposals. The relative neglect was partially due to the fact that Birnbaum's speech largely summarized the well-known views of his journal. It was also true that most secondary speakers at the 1897 Congress were overshadowed by the euphoric exaltation surrounding Herzl and Nordau. The tepid response to Birnbaum should not be taken as evidence that his concerns lacked importance in the evolving program of Zionism. On the contrary, as we shall see, within a few years the growing stress on Hebraism by the *Kulturisten* would evoke some of the most acrimonious prewar Zionist polemics in defense of the Jewish masses and Yiddish culture. Ironically, Birnbaum himself soon came to be *persona non grata* in the cultural Zionist camp. After a complete falling out with Herzl in 1898, he disavowed the Zionist Movement and gravitated toward diaspora nationalism, Yiddishism, and eventually an orthodox party, the *Agudat Israel*. Alienated by difficulties in getting along with his contemporaries, in many respects Birnbaum was a casualty of the new life which had been breathed into his brainchild.[55] He would witness how many students originally inspired by his views became the loyal cadre of day-to-day workers in the Zionist office under Herzl.[56]

In addition to the cultural addresses on the official First Congress agenda, there was an informal evening meeting at a hotel near the Congress hall on the subject of "Jewish Folk-literature as a Means of Elevating the People." The gathering commenced with remarks in German and Russian by Leo Motzkin and Eliahu Davidson, who had been colleagues in the proto-Zionist Russian-Jewish Academic Society at the University of Berlin.[57] Readings from a variety of Hebrew pieces from lyric poetry to popular science followed, ending with a discussion in Hebrew.[58] Taking place as it did outside the confines of the Congress protocol, the meeting was cited by some *Kulturisten*, such as Ehrenpreis, as evidence of Zionism's lack of commitment to culture. Nevertheless, get-togethers such as this continued to be held during the first few Zionist Congresses and provided cultural Zionists with a wider forum than any in which they had previously participated. Despite exceptions, a great amount of personal satisfaction and mutual support appears to have been derived from these events, even if their business was not recorded in the *Stenographisches Protokoll*.[59]

Mutual support was particularly needed at this time in view of the massive difficulties that hindered the work of the early Zionist culture committees. While Ehrenpreis was inclined to blame Herzl for the initial ineffectiveness of these organizations – "Herzl, solely from his own will, did not want it – and it did not happen"[60] – the main reason for the failure of the committees was logistical in nature. The committees' membership was widely dispersed. Ehrenpreis lived in Diakovar, Croatia, Kaminka in Prague, Ahad Ha-Am in Odessa, Sokolow in Warsaw, and Ben-Yehuda in Jerusalem. Moreover, as nearly every letter that passed between the cultural Zionists pointed out, their budgets were very limited.[61] It was impossible for members to meet regularly for committee work, and the movement could not afford to subsidize periodic meetings. Most Zionist leaders considered themselves fortunate to be able to attend the Congress itself every one or two years.[62]

The culture committees did hand out assignments, but these could rarely be completed on a timely basis. In later years, the cultural committee work became even more problematic when American or Canadian delegates were included. After noticing his name on the culture commission at the Fourth Zionist Congress, New York-based Richard Gottheil wrote the Zionist office in Vienna that he "was too busy with the publication of the *Maccabean* [the organ of the American Zionist Movement] and with the work of the American Zionist Federation to contribute substantially, and he did not think that the committee would in any case accomplish anything significant."[63] Gottheil's attitude may have been fairly widespread among those named to the culture committees. Most delegates were too busy with cultural projects in their own personal bailiwicks to tend to the cultural business of the movement as a whole. Therefore the newspapers *Maccabean, Hashiloach,* and *Hamelitz* were more pressing to Gottheil, Ahad Ha-Am, and Nahum Sokolow respectively than the brainstorming of large-scale cultural measures for a movement which as yet lacked the institutional means to enact them. The same applies to Ben Yehuda's concentration on his pioneering linguistic project in the development of Hebrew, and Kaminka's preoccupation with his academic and popular scientific works.

There were, to be sure, Zionists who sought to overcome the obstacles in the way of implementing cultural programs from the movement's center. This was one theme which Ehrenpreis, for example, emphasized in his address to the Second Zionist Congress (Basel, 1898). Ehrenpreis devoted a portion of this speech to the elaboration of his earlier proposals. Attempting to bridge the gap between the personal efforts of Zionists involved in cultural work and the official policy of the movement, he proposed the founding of a "General Hebrew Speaking Union" to influence Jewish youth throughout Europe. He also urged the appointment of a fifteen-member education committee, whose expenses for travel, and policy implementation would be defrayed from Zionist Organization membership dues.[64] Despite constructive suggestions, such as these, however, the logistical difficulties plaguing the cultural committees and the absence of a centrally coordinated Zionist cultural policy persisted throughout the prewar period. Early Zionist cultural endeavors would continue largely dependent on personal initiatives of committed individuals and the ambitious projects of relatively small, informal groups. Ironically, in the long run, the diversity of effort which this decentralized, polycentrist approach permitted may have proven more fruitful than the strict centralized coordination of policy and may have enabled the movement to extend its influence to a far greater audience.

At the Second Zionist Congress of 1898, the most persistent challenge to the prewar efforts of cultural Zionism also made a vocal appearance. This was the critique by orthodox Judaism. Whereas the inaugural Congress witnessed no programmatic attack on the cultural theses of Ehrenpreis and Birnbaum, the former's address one year later encountered a stinging rebuttal. Interestingly, Ehrenpreis had anticipated such repercussions. With the growth of political Zionism, the issue of the movement's relationship to orthodox Judaism had come to greater prominence and was widely debated in the Jewish press of Eastern Europe. To a large extent, the first objective of Ehrenpreis's 1898 address was to quell the notion that the *Kulturisten* wished to supersede orthodox Judaism. Assuring the delegates that this was not the case, Ehrenpreis claimed that Zionist cultural work would in no way interfere with religious matters and he inserted a declaration of "non-interference" into the resolutions of the culture committee.[65] "The culture that we desire and are striving towards," Ehrenpreis maintained,

> is neither religious nor anti-religious, but national . . . why do the sons and daughters of other nationalities take delight and pride in the heroes of their people? Is there not a deep sorrow in your hearts when you ask: Where are

our heroes, our poets, our champions, who certainly exist, but we simply do not know them? . . . We seek a unique content for our own spiritual life, and we must give this to our people.

Ehrenpreis asserted that the Congress must inspire a deep moral commitment from all Zionists; Zionists must therefore do more than "pay the *shekel* [the minimum dues contribution] and notice the symbols on the shares of the Jewish Colonial Trust;" they must "acquaint themselves with the spiritual treasures of their people." Every Jew who wants to work openly for the cause should "not only send his children to gatherings where Zionist speeches are made, but send them to schools where they will learn Hebrew" and integrate it into their lives. While conceding that this "was simply impossible in many communities," Ehrenpreis argued that a mass Hebraization could be achieved through the implementation of his plan for a General Hebrew Speaking Society and the realization of his cultural committee, which to this point had been "a stillborn child." Ehrenpreis proposed that the commission be reconstituted as an autonomous body, with its chairman given a seat and vote in the Zionist Central Committee in Vienna. The main functions of the committee would include oversight of the Hebraization effort, along with the coordination of support for Jewish-national education in Palestine.[66]

Despite the contention that Zionist cultural efforts did not conflict with traditional religious affairs, Ehrenpreis was obviously concerned with the promotion of secular Hebrew education, which the religious viewed as a threat. Furthermore, like many *Kulturisten*, he sought to provide a secularized mythology which would serve as a spiritual rallying point for the new Jewish nation. All assurances notwithstanding, his elaboration of the cultural Zionist platform was likely to arouse suspicion and mistrust in the orthodox camp. Within the Congress setting, the first rebuttal to the *Kulturisten* program was delivered in 1898 by Rabbi S. Y. Rabbinowitsch, a delegate from Poltawa, who would participate in several successive Congresses.[67] As an orthodox rabbi, Rabbinowitsch asserted that all talk of secular culture was unnecessary because traditional Judaism offered a complete way of life. Moreover, from his point of view, Zionism's implicit tolerance and glorification of the varieties of modern Judaism could not be condoned. Talmudic Judaism simply did not allow for pluralism. Assurances that orthodoxy would not be compromised were not enough; what would a secular national culture be, if not something to replace or compete with Judaism, like the nationalisms current in the Western

European states? If Hebrew became popularized, it would be just another vulgar tongue, if not worse because it was Jewry's God-given tongue.[68] Rabbinowitsch concluded that the movement, and especially the Congress, should confine its efforts to securing a charter from the Sultan for Palestine. Although the speaker would not have put it in such terms, his dismissal of the cultural Zionist program represented the theocratic rejection of another version of Enlightenment ideals which menaced the orthodox way of life. It was quite typical in this regard. Indeed, the number of orthodox who joined Herzl made up a minute group; those who viewed Zionism as a heresy far outweighed those sympathetic to its aims.

That further orthodox attacks on the *Kulturisten* were not forthcoming in 1898 was mainly due to the timing of the Congress agenda. As in the preceding year, Herzl had relegated debate on cultural matters to the final hours of the Congress. When these issues were afforded more time, the prospect of prolonged strife was evident. Rabbi Moses Gaster, the Chief Sephardic rabbi of London, was far more sensitive than Ehrenpreis, Ahad Ha-Am, and nearly all of his contemporaries deeply engaged in cultural matters in recognizing that Zionism was a threat not only to the theological foundations of talmudic Judaism, but also to its material and especially financial basis. He privately expressed the view that the movement's "interference" in the established Jewish educational institutions "might do great harm and engender bitter animosities." Gaster suggested that Zionists might have to content themselves with something supplementary and innocuous where the orthodox were dominant, like providing "historical readers" from a Zionist perspective.[69]

Such attempts to promote an "understanding" were of little initial value. Responding to the customary speeches promoting secular Hebrew culture at the Third Zionist Congress (1899), Rabbi I. J. Reines, who would in 1902 found *Mizrahi*, the orthodox party within the Zionist Movement, quickly mounted a counter-offensive. He reiterated the points made by his colleague, R. Rabbinowitsch at the Second Congress, and labeled the *Kulturisten* as "dissidents." This sparked a "debate," which was actually more of an exchange of world views. In this instance, Herzl forcefully mediated between the orthodox and the equally strident cultural Zionists, always pressing for unity, which was apparently in accordance with the feelings of the bulk of the delegates. He argued that the matters of theory raised in the cultural debates were far too intricate to be decided on the

Congress floor. They were not issues that could be simply amended and voted on. No doubt Herzl realized that the more such questions were discussed, the more discord would be sown.[70]

This fear that any discussion of the *Kulturfrage* would incite acrimony was realized by the exchange at the Fourth Congress, which ended with a dispute over a statement by Leopold Kahn, a Viennese lawyer and *Kulturist*, on the issue of whether or not to include the word "religious" in a call for Zionism to work towards "religious, moral, and national education." Herzl supported Leo Motzkin's proposal to strike "religious" from the proclamation, so as not to invite a misunderstanding of Zionism's preference for any variety of Judiasm over another, and especially to dispel the idea that it was aligned with orthodoxy; this won the enthusiastic approval of the assembly.[71] Although he was cautious about not offending the orthodox, Herzl tried to balance the perception of the movement as one that was wedded to tradition with the notion that many aspects of that tradition had ceased to be meaningful for a great number of Jews, especially in the West.

Rabbinowitsch challenged what he saw to be the attempted supplanting of Judaism by cultural Zionism, exemplified by Martin Buber's appeal in a talk on "Propaganda and Agitation" for all to uphold the Zionist cultural program.

> He said, parenthetically, that until now there has been the religion; now Zionism reigns. That is a false principle; the religion has not ceased to exist, and it will not cease to exist. I maintain that a Jew who is not a Zionist is still a Jew. He is not logical, then, but he may still be an upright and honest Jew.[72]

Reines added that the cultural program served little purpose for the Jews with whom Zionism was supposedly most concerned, the poor of the Pale of Settlement. Although the members of the Democratic Faction, such as Buber, professed to champion democracy in Zionism by making the administration of the colonial bank and *Die Welt* less autocratic, what was their relation to the masses of impoverished, religious Jews? Reines asked.[73] In the most trenchant terms, he argued that "The *Kulturfrage* is a disaster for us. Culture will ruin everything. Our region is entirely orthodox. It is lost through [this insistence on] culture." Reines appealed for the assembly to heed the Basel Program, which he believed did not allow for pursuing the secular cultural indoctrination.[74] The effort to include social and class issues in the *Kulturfrage* would prove to be more effective later from the spokesmen for *Poale-Zion*.

The artist E. M. Lilien tried to bridge the widening gap; he seems to have been best suited for this role. Appearing closer to the world of Eastern Jewry, or at least less antagonistic to it than his colleagues in the Democratic Faction, Lilien was reputed to be an observant Jew, and he usually spoke Yiddish, not German. He admitted that once he shared the reservations of the rabbis; he too had called "the Jewishness of Zionism into question;" still, he predicted that the advocates of *Kultur* and the orthodox would eventually discover that they were not at cross purposes. Lilien's conclusion was that cultural Zionism "will make us complete Jews, and it will enrich our Judaism. In an earlier time, if a Jew was a man of culture, it meant that he belonged to a foreign nation." "Since the appearance of Zionism, a Zionist knows that as a Jew, there is a history or an aesthetic of significance belonging to his own people."[75] Lilien interwove the worlds of the ghetto and modern secularism in his art, but his response could not mend the rift between religious and secular on the floor of the Congress.

At the Eighth Congress (the Hague, 1907), Ehrenpreis recounted that the efforts of the *Kulturisten* had been confounded for nearly two years as a consequence of the Uganda controversy. They marshalled their energies to urge Zionism's refusal of the British offer on the grounds of its incompatibility with a cultural renewal which depended on a Palestine-centered Hebrew movement. Now they were ready to resume the cultural endeavors that were dear to them. However, there was a new direction taken by Zionists that Ehrenpreis saw as diminishing the movement's drive to nationalize European Jewry; some had become involved in parliamentary politics, as Zionists, especially in Russia and Austria-Hungary. "It is the nature of parliamentary work that the entire power of the Jewish nation is being absorbed in it," Ehrenpreis insisted. It was "a significant drain on purely Zionist work." But "as long as Zionism remains committed to a single domain and a single platform, it has few enemies. If it begins, though, to spread out in all directions, it will create enemies in every camp."[76] To be sure, it was presumptuous for Ehrenpreis to assume that the Zionist-leftist political efforts expended in the European states would otherwise have been devoted to cultural Zionism.

Also underlying his plea was a goal earlier expressed by Herzl and Nordau, that Zionism should aim to avert Jews from revolutionary socialism and radicalism because these movements portended an unknown future at best, and at worst, inestimably harsh repercussions for the masses of Jewry. Of course, the argument was made that the

Zionists were the most radical wing of Jewish politics in trying to completely overcome the Jewish condition of marginality.[77] Although many if not most Zionists sympathized to some degree with the demands of revolutionary socialism, there were serious, fundamental objections from those coming from a typically bourgeois European perspective. They saw the workers' movement as a symptom of a deeply problematic or weak social order, which threatened to completely rend the bonds that held European society together; Jewry stood to lose the precarious footholds it had painstakingly attained.[78] Revolutionary socialism defied the conventions of moderation, the balance of past and future, and the positive concept of rootedness that tenaciously prevailed in Zionist culture; such was probably the prevalent view among middle-class Zionists in Central and Western Europe.

Revising his earlier pleas for the immediate dissemination of Hebrew in his 1907 address, Ehrenpreis then demanded that the movement's message be spread beyond Europe to the 50,000 Jews in Morocco, and the one-half million scattered throughout the Ottoman Empire; there were more than a million Spanish-speaking Jews, he informed the delegates. This was a call for a more conventional model of mass political participation. Although Ehrenpreis never gave up the banner of cultural Zionism, he modified his stance in an attempt to reach out to contemporary Jewry; to a substantial degree, he had further internalized Herzl's call for accommodating the whole of Jewry.[79] Furthermore, this reasoning represented an acknowledgement of the Herculean demographic obstacles in the way of forging a Jewish national culture. There were not only "party interests" at stake, Ehrenpreis pleaded, taking another stab at the Zionists in European politics, but "profound Jewish national interests," by which he meant the end-goal of a unified culture through Hebrew.[80]

Despite this turn to "populism," for the first time Ehrenpreis invoked the hearty disapproval of a group other than the orthodox or their supporters: he was attacked from the left, by Daniel Pasmanik, whose career spanned a broad range of Zionist and European politics. Pasmanik was not a member of the *Poale-Zion*, but he shared many of their sentiments at this point in his career. He objected to the idea that some Zionists' engagement in leftist politics might be detrimental to the overall cause; if Zionism did not penetrate politics on all levels, Pasmanik argued, it would surely lose any hope of attracting the masses of Jewry. He then charged that cultural Zionism was exclusive and elitist: this was the first occasion that the *Kulturisten* were condemned in a Zionist Congress from a secular standpoint. Pasmanik stated that Ehrenpreis represented "an artistocratic movement of cultural Zionists which had inadvertently pushed itself to the wall." Pasmanik's admonition raised shouts of "Bravo!" "When one speaks of regeneration," the speaker continued, "it means more than just changing one's tastes in aesthetics and literature – sociologists call regeneration something different: a socioeconomic rebirth. Here the cultural Zionists are completely out of touch. They are in error to blame the Sixth and Seventh Congress," which were largely concerned with the Uganda controversy, "for not being more concerned with culture. If a people is hungry, it does not think about literature; above all, it thinks about satisfying its hunger." Here Pasmanik was in accordance with Max Nordau's "pragmatic" critique of cultural Zionism. Nordau had insisted that a cultural renewal was meaningless without a change in the material basis of Jewish life.

Ehrenpreis defended cultural Zionism as "an ideology which gives a hungry, suffering people a language and a culture. What had Zionism done, what have any of the Congresses done to satisfy hunger?" Ehrenpreis asked. "Zionism did not comprise an organisation to alleviate hunger," he continued; "it was a movement of national rebirth that would eventually, eternally stave off hunger." The final question, as Ehrenpreis framed it for the Congress, was "are we a national or an economic movement?"[81] Whereas earlier they had been accused of being biased against lower classes due to their anti-orthodoxy, the *Kulturisten* were now painted as narrow, inflexible, and chauvinistic towards the secularized, Yiddish-speaking, Jewish working classes. Most likely, Pasmanik's criticisms were shared by a number of Zionists. It was significant that Zionism was struggling with the idea of how the Jew was to survive in the modern world and remain a Jew, Pasmanik implied, but its methods might be more relevant to the plight of the majority of the Jews.[82] This line of opposition to cultural Zionism would be continued and developed in response to an even more urgent demand for Hebraization.

In 1899, Leopold Kahn had challenged the Third Zionist Congress to become a Hebrew-speaking assembly within the next twenty years. He was not far off the mark; by the Ninth Congress (1909), there would be a number of Hebrew speeches, as well as some Congress business conducted in Hebrew. This was precipitated by a proposal from Nahum Sokolow at the Eighth Congress, which again revealed very mixed sentiments concerning Hebrew. The floor was supposed to belong to Ehrenpreis, but on the eve of his main address on the *Kulturfrage* he fell ill. "It is the luck [*Masel*] of our *Kultur*," Nahum Sokolow began in Ehrenpreis' place, "that when we have a speaker, he becomes sick."[83] The laughter of the delegates, in part, was due to the acrimony in the previous years over the *Kulturfrage*. Sokolow proposed that Hebrew be adopted as the official language of the movement, and that it be instituted as the language for correspondence, speeches, conferences, and the Congresses. If the Congress recognized a language other than Hebrew in light of the progress of Hebraization, "that would be assimilation," Sokolow claimed; then Zionism would no longer be national, and no longer Zionism. Furthermore, this should be enacted so that the movement in the diaspora was consistent with the growing use of Hebrew in Palestine, which the Zionists were ardently cultivating. Sokolow equated the use of, or learning of Hebrew with the legitimacy of one's place in the movement, and the adherence of Zionism to its professed goals. There were bursts of applause and calls of "Objection!" as Sokolow spoke; at the conclusion the applause was interrupted with loud objections and general tumult on the floor.

When Sokolow's resolution was reread to be voted on at the conclusion of the Congress, it elicited approval, humor, and anger. In summing up, Sokolow claimed that Hebrew was a language held in common by the greatest number of delegates; "some sixty percent understand Hebrew." His statistic was probably an exaggeration. "The others will learn it. Two years is enough. (Laughter.)" One delegate complained that Sokolow's plan would eliminate the most important addresses of the Congress, such as those of the current President, David Wolffsohn, and its preeminent orator, Nordau; it was simply impractical. After Heinrich Loewe read a short endorsement of Sokolow's proposal in Hebrew, Wolffsohn (who did know Hebrew) asked: "Herr Loewe – what did you say?" prompting uproarious laughter. Eventually, Sokolow's proposal, which in fact allowed the Congress to proceed in German, read that

> the Congress resolves in principle to adopt the Hebrew language as the official language of the Zionist Movement for its Congresses and conferences, and to introduce it in practice gradually. Our national tongue will thus become obligatory for Zionism. But noting the necessity of popularizing this idea, the organization has the right to use languages besides Hebrew.[84]

The Congress report of the Actions Committee of 1909 amendment to the *Stenographisches Protokoll* was even more strident about the compulsory nature of Hebrew culture's place in Zionism:

> Without national culture, Zionism has no purpose, and no connection with history. It would become superficial, cowardly, and quickly die out in a time of distress. In Zionism lies the seeds and essence of all national, moral, intellectual, and spiritual development for the Jews . . . Mark it well: not as agitation, but as instruction; not simply as politics, but as a loving commitment to tradition and history, and as a living progenitor of the Hebrew language.[85]

What began as a fringe element, however it may have shared the ultimate aims of the ideology, seems to have inundated Zionism to the point that it now prevailed as the movement's standard.[86] Hebrew's ascension may be traced to a number of factors: certainly the language became a more important unifying symbol after Herzl's death. Concurrently, the persistence of anti-Semitism in many parts of Western and Central Europe, though not in the virulent form of the interwar period, possibly provided an edge of tension that helped feed interest in Hebraism. Assimilated Jews who identified with the crumbling atmosphere of liberal tolerance perhaps were attracted to Hebrew culture as a positive affirmation of their identity in a Christian environment that increasingly began to question whether they belonged. Furthermore, individual efforts, such as the work of the members of the Democratic Faction had a definite impact – the result was the dissemination of Zionist literature in reading rooms, the growth of the Zionist press, and respect accorded projects of the *Juedischer Verlag*. The decentralized diversity of the *Kulturisten* actually may have aided the cause of Hebrew more than would have been the case if cultural policy had been strictly centralized from the start.

A very significant reason why an official culture policy that was influential and coherent did not emerge as quickly as other aspects of the movement is revealed in an unpublished comment of Moses Gaster, concerning his work for the cultural committee, that "I have scarcely any breathing time."[87] It was "not of an elevating character" to be on the forefront of a marginal, but at the same time vehemently attacked political movement. Added to the notion that most *Kulturisten* were too immersed in their personal cultural work to devote much effort to the movement in an explicitly "official" capacity, engaging in Zionist politics consumed a great deal of their time and energy, especially if it had to be divorced from one's livelihood. It is doubtful that any of the most active Zionists could have made a living chiefly from their Zionist-related work, especially in the movement's earliest years. Simply put, it did not pay, and they were always hard up for money. In contrast to the mythologies that they were trying to activate, Jews did not constitute a country, and there was no substantial bureaucratic apparatus with a treasury from which to draw funds. If Herzl, Herzl's parents, David Wolffsohn, and Johann Kremenezky had not donated the bulk of their personal fortunes to the movement, at least until the Jewish National Fund was firmly established, the basis of support for cultural activities would have been even more limited.[88]

In December 1898, Leopold Kahn wrote the members of the Culture Commission that their geographic dispersion was chiefly responsible for the lack of progress in cultural matters. Kahn proposed to reconstitute the committee without a chairman, which would communicate through the post, with himself as coordinator responsible for distributing the information to all the members; it was a rigid structure in which "all the suggestions had to be passed around and voted on before the activities could commence."[89]

Reporting on the committee at the 1899 Congress, Kahn refrained from detailing the organizational muddle to which the committee succumbed; he emphasized instead the resistance to the program by the orthodox as the reason for its failure to produce concrete results.[90] There was some truth to his allegation that obstructionist tactics by the orthodox were troublesome, but Kahn exaggerated the role of this opposition in accounting for the commission's meager results. Intimating that the *Kulturisten* were all to the good for the movement, while the orthodox were harmful, was far better suited to Congress rhetoric than admitting the real obstacles in the way of bringing the committee together. Kahn labeled the culture issue the "pitiful child" of the Congress.[91]

Martin Buber, as a representative of the Democratic Faction, introduced what proved to be one of Zionism's more successful cultural creations in his speech on Zionist art to the Fifth Congress (1901), which ended with the centerpiece of his plan: that the movement "loan" the necessary funds so the *Juedischer Verlag* could intensify its work, and that the movement take responsibility for publicizing the company.[92] The *Juedischer Verlag*, founded earlier in 1902 by Buber, Feiwel, Lilien, Davis Trietsch, and Alfred Nossig, was styled as the chief means of disseminating a Zionist national culture to Central and West European Jewry through publishing the works of Hebrew and

Yiddish writers in German, and by reproducing (in books and on postcards) the products of Jewish artists. Buber also called for increased support for the Jewish national library in Jerusalem; a more structured cultural commission, that the Actions Committee request the Nobel Institute in Stockholm to accord modern Hebrew and Yiddish literature its rightful place in the library of the Institute and prize competition, and to establish a bureau to compile and analyze statistical data about world Jewry. One might imagine that there was an earlier debate about whether to include Yiddish in the appeal to the Nobel committee; it most likely was included because a number of *Kulturisten*, including Berthold Feiwel, greatly respected Yiddish.[93] Chaim Weizmann, largely echoing the recommendations of Hermann Schapira from the First Congress, proposed the need to investigate the founding of a Jewish university under the auspices of Zionism; at this point it was not altogether clear if there would be some type of transitional institution in the diaspora, although the goal was decidedly a university in Palestine.[94]

In contrast to their other resolutions which were speedily passed at the Fifth Congress, the component of the Faction's program in which the members had the most at stake personally – the *Juedischer Verlag* – was not expedited by Herzl. Perhaps he rejected the project because it was a financial risk the movement could ill afford; possibly, though, it was a way of punishing the members of the Faction, especially Buber, for disrupting the façade of unanimity of the Congress when they staged their famous walk-out to bring attention to their program. Nevertheless, Herzl did encourage the delegates to support the *Juedischer Verlag* on their own.[95] Ironically, it was Herzl's successor as President of the Zionist Organization, David Wolffsohn, who privately supplied the critical funding for the *Juedischer Verlag*, and also gave one of the largest donations towards the purchase of property for the Jewish university.[96] After Herzl, Wolffsohn and Nordau were perceived as the leading proponents of "political" Zionism.

Through the election of a culture committee at the Fifth Congress that included such recognized figures as Ahad Ha-Am and Israel Zangwill, along with several members of the Democratic Faction – including Weizmann, Buber, Feiwel, and Lilien – it seemed that effective policies would finally be initiated. From its inception, though, this committee too was hampered by an untenable geographic mix; representatives' homes ranged from Baltimore to South Africa to

Russia.[97] No one could imagine assembling the entire committee at once, and the least amount of foresight could predict that communications would be troublesome. Yet this was undeniably the chance for the *Kulturisten* to prove what they could accomplish in positions of leadership, with so many loyalists to their cause on the board. Despite an official push from Herzl, the culture commission was slow to respond.[98]

The transcripts of two meetings of culture commission members from Russia indicate that Ahad Ha-Am proceeded rather cynically in his new role as an officially designated leader of the movement.[99] The two men who attended the first session with Ahad Ha-Am, Jacob Bernstein-Kohan and J. Rawnitzky, basically concerned themselves with matters similar to those which had occupied the earlier committees: planning for national literary projects, schools, and libraries. In the sessions held on February 28 and March 13, 1902, the discussion barely moved beyond questions of funding, publicity, and the relationship of the commission to the Actions Committee and the regional organizations.[100] The second meeting, held in response to the constitution of another cultural commission by the All-Russian Zionist Conference in Minsk (October 4–10, 1902), included two of the same members from the earlier assembly – Ahad Ha-Am and Bernstein-Kohan, this time joined by J. Klausner, I. Idelsohn, and the poet C. N. Bailik. The minutes and consequences of the second meeting did not differ substantially from those of the first, with the exception that commitments for continued work were pledged on specific topics (which were not followed up), and an extensive questionnaire concerning cultural matters was drafted, to be answered by local organizations. It is not known whether the questionnaire was ever distributed, its responses recorded, analyzed, and acted on. Indeed, the myth that the political Zionist leadership was directly responsible for stunting the promotion of cultural work may be adjusted by recognizing that the commission set up by the Minsk Conference, which approached the *Kulturfrage* in a more deliberate and committed manner, failed to make "any significant contribution" to cultural endeavors beyond discussion of the issues.[101]

Despite the perception of Hebraism's slow progress which was distressing to the *Kulturisten*, by the end of Zionism's first decade they were on sure enough ground to proffer terse polemics against Yiddish, which noted the success of the *Bund* in sparking a Yiddish cultural revival.

> In the Jewish literature and in the Jewish press in Russia a certain turnabout has taken place. In many circles Yiddish has replaced Hebrew; the national has lost ground to the popular. From our standpoint Yiddish has never been dismissed as having little value or been demeaned. It has existed among the great masses as a living language of the people and has, in the course of the last decade, developed a thoroughly wonderful literature. But it is entirely different and signifies something completely opposed to Hebrew. Hebrew is the ancient spirit; Yiddish, the reality; Hebrew, the language of Zion; Yiddish, the language of the *Galut*.

The *Bund*, which stressed the legitimacy and dignity of Yiddish culture in their quest for national autonomy in the Pale of Settlement, and its estranged brother Zionism, espousing Hebrew, had by 1907 both grown strong enough to become the focus of identity or foil for the other.[102]

This juxtaposition implicitly emerged in the debates at the Tenth Zionist Congress (Basel, 1911), in which a core group of delegates were resolute in abiding by the Congress's new language regulation. Interestingly, Ehrenpreis was not in attendance. He had forsaken Zionism, coming to the conclusion that Hebrew was "incapable of creating a 'redeeming synthesis between Judaism and Europeanism,'"[103] which foreshadowed the rise of Zionist resistance to the Hebrew revival. At the end of the Congress' opening address, President Wolffsohn praised "one God, one people, one language, one country, one Zionism!," affirming the intensified attention to Hebrew.[104] For the first time, entire debates were conducted in Hebrew during the official proceedings. This constituted one of the most drastic changes at the Congress, which many Zionists agreed was all to the good. Such a view, however, would not have been seconded by scores of delegates. Significant discord at the Tenth Congress was sown by the insistence on Hebrew.

In his address to the 1911 Congress, Sokolow testified to the great success of Hebrew in inculcating a Zionist national consciousness – although much more needed to be done, in the way of institutional support. He remarked that several non-Jewish civilizations had used Hebrew to add luster to their own cultures, and that a few particularly admirable cultural movements had embraced Hebrew. It was, Sokolow professed, a cultured national tongue, of the most noble spirit. Repeating proposals from the first two Congresses, Sokolow proposed the establishment of a General Hebrew Speaking Society, and a Language

Academy to serve as an enlightened guardian of Hebrew.[105] The Academy was no doubt modeled on those of the European states, which would introduce new words into the language, and attempt to mollify the adoption of foreign words and phrases.

Also at the 1911 Congress a speaker for the *Mizrahi* objected to what he perceived as the particularly insidious trend in the Hebraist movement. Contrary to Sokolow's claim of the Hebrew revival's "nobility," he charged that Hebrew literature had sunk to the lowest depths of vulgar popular culture. Referring to a controversy that had erupted in the Hebrew press between the Ninth and Tenth Congresses, he announced that "Brenner's ideas compel the strongest repudiation." The writer C. J. Brenner had argued that it was possible "to be a good Jew, and at the same time to be thrilled by the Christian legend of the son-of-God."[106] Understandably, the religious found the entire topic disrespectful to the faith, which seemed to be symptomatic of the bellicose manner in which the *Kulturisten* handled their affairs. To the orthodox, many of the new Hebrew writers flaunted their doubts about the veracity of sacred texts and the sanctity of traditions, while exuding a desire to stretch the limits of respectable behavior. "We are prepared to tolerate Jewish epicureanism, but not of Brenner's variety," the delegate asserted.[107]

In addition to the *Mizrahi*'s disapproval, the objections to the *Kulturist* drive for a broader compulsory commitment to Hebrew at the 1911 Congress revolved around two main points, which were interrelated. The first was that the use of Hebrew at the Congress was simply an unwise strategy, if one was intent on mobilizing the masses of Jewry.[108] The second, more weighty allegation, was that Hebrew was not the true language of the people – the masses spoke and had a profound attachment to Yiddish and Yiddish culture. On behalf of the *Poale-Zion* party, which had recently held its own conference in Vienna, Leon Chasanowitsch protested against the primacy of Hebrew. Chasanowitsch was a Labor Zionist emissary to England, the United States, and Canada, and served as the Party Secretary in Vienna from 1913 to 1919.[109] "Everyone must have the right to freedom of thought, political and cultural," he urged, invoking the spirit of toleration exemplified by the founder; "that is the old tradition of Herzl: Zionism must not concern itself with personal political matters." Sokolow's "archaic tendencies," Chasanowitsch charged, "did not represent the thought and interests of all Zionist circles, above all not the organizations of workers, and at the very least, not the masses to whom Zionism should be addressing itself. The language question was not yet closed," he warned.[110]

Indeed, the Zionist Movement had been deeply ambivalent about Yiddish. A Yiddish edition of *Die Welt* had existed for several years; a number of Yiddish stories were published in the featured product of the *Juedischer Verlag*, the *Juedischer Almanach*; and several of that press's books promoted as Jewish cultural treasures, such as *Jung Harfen*, were originally Yiddish.[111] The Fifth Congress had even pledged to ask the Nobel committee to have Yiddish considered for their literature prize along with Hebrew. The official Zionist Movement, therefore, had both scorned and proudly appropriated *Yiddishkeit*.

Chasanowitsch's comments are particulary worthy of analysis because they are the most strident attacks on Hebrew in the context of the prewar *Kulturdebatte*. To a certain extent, his criticisms played out the tension between the diaspora nationalism of the *Bund* versus Zionism – albeit Chasanowitsch was in the Zionist camp. This outpouring, which elicited numerous objections, bursts of applause, and jeers, embodied at least as significant a cultural conflict as that between political and cultural Zionists, or the divisions between the *Mizrahi* and *Kulturisten*.

"We Labor Zionists revere Hebrew," Chasanowitsch declared; "we also work in the spirit that a complete Jew must master Hebrew culture and language." They had, in fact, established their own schools and Hebrew courses, he explained. "But it is not the language of the people. We cannot accept the extreme standpoint that the language of the people is excluded. That requires the most profound contempt for the people. (Great unrest, angry shouts.)" The speaker claimed familiarity with "the work of Hebraists from different countries," and found "a tinge of distaste for the masses, through which, there is a tinge of contempt for the people."[112] Chasanowitsch's diatribe was much more harsh than that of Pasmanik at the previous Congress. Whereas Pasmanik criticized the *Kulturisten* for not going far enough in their program to alleviate the economic misery of the Jews in the Palė, and incidentally labelled them aristocratic, he did not fundamentally question their concept of culture – but its relative weight in the whole scheme. Chasanowitsch, on the other hand, cut to a central paradox of Zionist culture. Zionism styled itself as a movement of the Jewish people – but was it not a marginal element, that was trying to elevate the "unenlightened" to its own level of national consciousness? Was this not a danger, especially if the movement intended to inspire youth? Zionism wished to restore Jewish pride and dignity; but reaching that stage implied that one had to recognize that certain aspects of Jewish life were somehow terribly flawed or corrupted, and in need of transcendence.

Chasanowitsch conceded that

> the Jewish nation is in danger, that we are losing our youth, that we must have a connection to our past – and that bond is the Hebrew language. I see that for Germany, for France, and for the cultured [*gebildete*] circles. But in the democratic strata of the people the only means of cohesion is the language that they speak. We cannot renounce this bond. You can have Hebrew culture, but you must leave Yiddish. You are building a wall, and the "Jewish aristocracy" is depriving itself of having an impact on the people. (Unrest. Shout: socialist!) Hebrew created antagonism between the people and the nation. Hebrew unites [the Jews] of Germany, France, and some of Turkey – but not the lower classes of the people. The masses are repulsed by this national movement.[113]

"It has been said from the tribune," Chasanowitsch alleged, directly challenging Sokolow, that Yiddish is a "language of lies." "All the proposals concerning Hebrew will not advance the Jews. Words of a resolution will not elevate the speech of the masses, and the reality of the people from their level of culture. If culture will indeed be created, we need equality of rights; here that is in short supply;" again, the cultural progress was joined to autonomy and equal rights, which had originally been annunciated in the Congress setting by Birnbaum. What then, Chasanowitsch asked, was the role of *Kultur* for the Congress, and the primary place for Hebrew? "In *eretz Israel* it is an entirely different question; there it can be the colloquial speech." "Concentrate your efforts there, where the question is closed; but don't bring any *Kulturfragen* into the politics!"[114]

How then, was a Zionist from Central or Western Europe to assimilate such criticism? What remained to be done, in terms of diaspora cultural work, if the field of Hebrew was doomed where it seemed to have been most hospitable, where the Jews lived in the mass? In addition to focusing efforts on Palestine, Chasanowitsch urged the delegates to strengthen some of the notions that had been championed by the Democratic Faction: "Deepen Zionism! Make it scientific! Do research and statistical work on the history of assimilation, which Jewry has corrupted! Put it in the hands of the true, national, professional men. Such work should be used as the basis of a

Jewish science and Jewish history – then Zionism will certainly profit. Cultural development will then be set into motion." Chasanowitsch articulated the canon that science and history were a fruitful means to discern the essence of the people, representing the embrace of technology and scientific knowledge that the *Kulturisten* and political Zionists hailed as a messianic force that would help redeem the Jews.[115]

Recalling the academic orientation of the Faction, the speaker contended that "the way to win the Jewish youth is through nurturing Jewish scholarship. Create stipends for Jewish history and research; on that we can agree with our whole hearts."[116] Indeed, probably no one in the assembly of hundreds would have voted down that part of his plan. On the whole, however, Chasanowitsch's appeal was a retreat from the growing intoxication with Hebrew culture;[117] he wished to cast Zionist culture as a more generalized concern for using learning, self-cultivation, and science on a voluntary basis, to ameliorate the condition of the Jews. Chasanowitsch, speaking for the furthest left-wing of the movement at that time, wanted something every Zionist could agree on: Judaized *Bildung*, imbued with the notion that all Jews are mutually accountable to each other. He qualified that they must also be mutually respectful of each other, regardless of class. In addition to appropriating part of the Democratic Faction's program,[118] he had reoccupied a space initially carved out by Ahad Ha-Am: that of a de-mythologizer and skeptic within the camp of believers.

Chasanowitsch admitted that the proponents of Sokolow's plan comprised the Congress' majority; "but the majority of the Jewish masses you are not." The speaker was in the minority at that Congress, but substantial sympathy for his point of view was evident from the shouts and applause from the floor, and by the assembly's permission for him to hold forth for such a long time. The Congress was not that generous with ideas it considered outrageous or heretical.[119] "If the Zionist Organization wanted to include the broad masses, it needs other means to make this possible," Chasanowitsch implored the Congress not to "rely on its fortuitous majority;" "that would be fatal for the Zionist Organization. I believe that this is the price Zionism must pay in the wake of Czernowitz."[120]

Chasanowitsch was referring to the Czernowitz [Bukovina] Yiddish Language Conference, the first international, interparty assembly to deal with the role of Yiddish in Jewish life (August 30 to September 4,

1908). Its organizer was Nathan Birnbaum, who was now an ardent Yiddishist. Approximately seventy delegates attended the convention to discuss problems of grammar, literature, translation, theater, translation of the Bible into Yiddish, and other issues, but above all, to formally sanction Yiddish as the national language of the Jews. Predictably, the Zionist Hebraists and militant Bundists argued vociferously. After tedious debates, which probably changed few if any opinions, a compromise resolution was adopted proclaiming Yiddish as "a national language" and asking for its political, cultural, and social equality with other languages. By using the phrase "a national language," as opposed to "the national language," the conference intended to make the use of Hebrew a matter of personal conviction. Despite its ridicule by many leading Zionists, including Ahad Ha-Am who labeled Czernowitz "a Purim spectacle [*Purimspiel*]," it heightened the prestige of Yiddish at the expense of Hebrew and Zionism. To Chasanowitsch, the "revenge" of the masses for the Zionists' belligerence and disdain toward Yiddish at Czernowitz was a fact that the Zionist Congress was compelled to confront.[121]

Finally, Chasanowitsch offered his own resolution: "that the cultural activity in the lands of the *Galut* be the autonomous concern of the federations and national organizations, and that the regulation of such affairs be determined by the needs of different organizations." Quite correctly, someone from the floor shouted: "that's what the *Mizrahi* wants!" "Yes, exactly the same as the *Mizrahi* resolution," Chasanowitsch retorted sardonically:

> I am sorry that we should agree with the *Mizrahi*. (Laughter.) But opposites attract! The anti-Semites also want us to go to Zion, and we would therefore agree with them, as well. (Great unrest among the *Mizrahi* – shout: Insult!) I have the greatest respect for the *Mizrahi* when they support Jewish culture or work in the national Congress. Moreover, I think that among the orthodox there are many more national elements than among the Jews who refer to themselves as a nation . . . As long as Hebrew culture possesses an inner truth, we will be compelled toward the goal, even if it is through different means.[122]

Chasanowitsch expressed one of the vital myths which held the Zionists together. After the death of Herzl, there was a broad consensus that Hebrew culture had a transcendent value which should be actively sought; yet this was inextricably linked to national symbols which political Zionism had activated – especially as it was exhibited for the Jews of Central and Western Europe.

In other exchanges, the Tenth Congress also proved to be a forum for illuminating the intransigence of the cultural debate since its inception, while simultaneously demonstrating the extent to which Hebraism had been at least passively accepted by the "right wing" of the movement. A delegate moved to reassert the declaration from the Second Congress (1898) that Zionism "intended no infringement on the religious laws of Judaism." Angry that the motion had seemingly carried little weight for more than a decade, and at their feeling of second-class citizenship in the unborn state, some of the *Mizrahi* threatened to leave the organization. R. Rabbinowitsch pledged, however, that if all the other *Mizrahi* left, he would remain. "If we want to leave Zionism, where would we go? Perhaps to the camp of the anti-Zionists? Will one find better Jews there?"[123]

The subtext of Rabbinowitsch's remark was that Zionism had become in many ways a microcosm of the Jewish world; one might also read it as a Jewish-national confession being stressed over Judaism, that even the non-orthodox *Kulturisten* were better Jews than their anti-Zionist orthodox brethren by virtue of Zionism. This was in the same spirit as Shmarya Levin's assertion earlier in the Congress that the streets of Tel-Aviv were "more Jewish" than an orthodox synagogue in Frankfurt.[124] Indeed, only thirteen years earlier such an evaluation from an East European rabbi like Rabbinowitsch would have been unthinkable. This type of cross-fertilization of the secular-national and the religious was now an established feature of Zionist culture, as was especially evident in Zionist art and in presentations of Zionist Palestine. Simultaneously, though, Zionists also used the tools of Zionist culture for self-criticism and de-mythologizing the movement.

Symbolic of Zionist culture coming full circle, the alleged countercurrent of the movement in its first few years – "Ahad Ha-Am-ism" – was assailed as a stifling, domineering ideology of Zionism at the last Zionist Congress before the First World War (1913). The defenders of Ahad Ha-Am, however, held the floor much longer than the detractors. In any case, "Ahad Ha-Am-ism" was specifically reproached as narrow-minded and a form of national chauvinism. In response to a call for a vote approving of the Actions Committee report, Morris Rosenfeld, a celebrated Yiddish poet and member of *Poale-Zion* called "the Hebraization of the movement . . . a one-sided plea for Ahad Ha-Am-ism, that we consider pernicious."[125] Rosenfeld's *Lieder des Ghetto*, illustrated by Lilien, had also been a highly publicized volume of the *Juedischer Verlag*. Ahad Ha-Am, who had admonished the Congress for living through myths that were absurdly or even destructively detached from reality, had now become the object of similar accusations.[126] The immediate cause for Rosenfeld's ire was an article by Ahad Ha-Am in his newspaper *Hashiloach* in which he allegedly described the literati working expressly toward creating a "cultural center" in Palestine as being more significant to the *Yishuv* than the farmers and workers.[127]

Similar attitudes, Rosenfeld charged, were being disseminated by the chief organ of the movement, *Die Welt*, which had consistently espoused that Eastern Jewry's legitimate tongues were "either Russian or Hebrew." He countered that in a work considered to be a Zionist classic, Arthur Ruppin's *Die Juden der Gegenwart*, the author – a linguist – wrote that "Yiddish was the single bulwark of Jewish nationalism in the East." The Actions Committee seemed to be driving the *Poale-Zionisten* out of the movement, declared Rosenfeld; *Die Welt* had printed an article against Yiddish culture, without allowing for a response, and had refused to print the *Poale-Zion* resolutions concerning procedural matters in the pre-Congress issue. Was this the position of a Zionist Organization which accommodated all of its groups? The *Poale-Zionisten* believed that "this theory," 'Ahad Ha-Am-ism,' was progressively eroding the potential following of the movement." Rosenfeld stated that many Western Zionists mistakenly believed that "the Hebrew movement was a driving force among Eastern Jews;" this was a grave error.[128]

Several outcries against the speaker at that point testifed that he had stripped away some of the movement's heartfelt mythologies. In 1897 Ahad Ha-Am had denounced the Western Zionists who were inactive in the Hebrew revival for pursuing Zionism, because he perceived that they were not aware of their essentially selfish motivations: it made them feel as if they were doing something useful for their people, and moreover, it made them self-satisfied. The possibility was now aired that the *Kulturisten* had become so enamored of their own designs that they too had grown alien to the essence of the people, and were operating from primarily self-interested motives.

There were now voices in the mainstream expressing sentiments similar to Rosenfeld; Ehrenpreis had resigned, and the "Prague Circle," which included some of the most brilliant minds in the movement, were asking for a reevaluation of the role of Hebrew.[129] Even some self-proclaimed "lovers of Hebrew" felt that this had become so much a part of the movement that Zionism might be hopelessly adrift in an abstract realm, detached from politics and Jewish realities, except for those in *eretz Israel*.[130] Even there the focus on Hebrew culture was beginning to come under scrutiny; there was more credence given to the view that Jewish life in the *Yishuv* was quite complex, and Hebrew textbooks were no longer a panacea.[131]

Toward the conclusion of the Eleventh Congress in 1913, Gaster summarized what he saw as the cultural route on which Zionism had embarked: "When I stood here for the first time, fifteen years ago as the speaker on the *Kulturfrage*, the men shook their heads and did not understand what culture was. The answer is [what is happening] here today. We are the representatives of Jewish culture."[132] To be sure, the majority of delegates agreed with Gaster and were enthusiastic, to varying degrees, that the movement had assumed such a character. Many affirmed that the Tenth Congress "was the most impressive and effective Jewish gathering ever held,"[133] with the accent on culture largely responsible. Yet this was not a unanimous verdict. "Because only ten or perhaps five percent of the audience knew Hebrew, the Hebrew speeches – which delegates kept insisting on – had to be translated into German," wrote one frustrated observer. "They were not always the most clever ones, and this business took a great deal of time. Although I am myself a [British] lover of Hebrew and a Hebrew writer, I must confess that the Hebrew speaking at the Congress made a most sad impression."[134] Indeed, the reality was that Hebrew had developed tremendously, but it was still at a relatively embryonic stage which necessitated numerous improvisations, vague references, and recourse to languages other than Hebrew. Nevertheless, by 1913, the myth of the regenerative power of Hebrew to nationalize the Jews had become firmly entrenched in Zionist culture, albeit with dissent that became assimilated into the patterns of Zionist cultural pronouncements. After all, was it not normal to have a *Kulturkampf*, and demands for better treatment by workers in a modern state?

Apart from the consensus that formed around the Hebrew idea, the emerging Zionist ideology displayed other philosophical underpinnings and myths which made it attractive to Central and West European Jews in a time of growing uncertainty, and which served to bridge many of the national, class, linguistic, and religious differences that were apparent in the cultural debate. How this reinforced the cohesion of the movement and at the same time reflected the education and cultural values of the members it recruited is the subject of the next chapter.

CHAPTER THREE

CARRYING OUT THE CULTURAL PROGRAM

The Hebraization of the Zionist Movement consumed a great deal of the energy devoted to the problem of culture at the Zionist Congresses. Within the realm of the *Kulturfrage*, in discussions that were not necessarily focused on Hebrew, Zionism was fitted with a humanistic and cosmopolitan countenance corresponding to the biases of middle-class Central and West European Jewry. This part of Zionist culture became another significant source of cohesion for the movement's faithful. The polemics concerning the creation of a new national mythology for the Jews usually deemphasized the theology and ritual practices of Judaism, recasting Judaism primarily as the story of the Jews as a nation – conceived in terms of history, and of the corporeal people and Land of Israel. It was hoped that this would engender the consolidation and secularized idealization of the Jewish people. Furthermore, such discussions facilitated programs and policies to strengthen and disseminate Zionist nationalism, including Hebraism; the very forms that this cultural transmission assumed revealed a specific cultural vision of early Zionism for Western Jewry. The self-conscious myths adopted by the movement and public declarations of their philosophical bases show both why the movement was as attractive as it was and further indicate the influence of Western, liberal education and a distinctly humanistic nationalism in its content.

After the First Congress, most of the movement's political symbolism seems to have been taken for granted; Herzl had indeed "cast the mold."[1] But many dimensions of the national culture to suit Zionism and the Jews were yet to be determined, especially its specific mythological content beyond the revived Hebrew language. Moses

Gaster, the chief Sephardic rabbi of London, addressed this issue at the Second Zionist Congress (Basel, 1898). Gaster was one of many who cut an appealing, anti-stereotypical figure at the rostrum; he was relatively young, had a spirited following in London, and quickly gained admirers among the Zionists; like many of the delegates, he had fled from East to West. Originally from Rumania, Gaster was known as a modern rabbi and scholar who was well versed in secular affairs. It would be difficult to find a more appropriate figure to speak for the creation of new Jewish myths; indeed, Gaster was the choice of a number of Zionists to succeed Herzl when the leader died in 1904. Still, the movement did not favor having a rabbi, no matter how free-thinking, as its head, and among Zionist intimates, Gaster was thought to be excessively irritable and "prone to quarreling irreconcilably with persons of all types."[2] It is interesting to note, however, that such characteristics did not seem to hinder his grand Congress performances.

"When the first Jewish colonies were established in Palestine," Gaster recalled, "the initial question asked was not 'where will we live,' but 'is there a schoolhouse for our children?'" This elicited an emotional response from the floor. "The schoolhouse should exist not simply for the children in the individual colonies, but as the school for all of the Children of Israel." Even more enthusiastic applause greeted Gaster's affirmation of education as the priority of the movement. "Therefore," he continued, "culture is identified with Zionism, and we say that Zionism is inseparably bound to cultural advancement: we Zionists do not relinquish the things which are good from the intellectual achievements of this or past centuries, but accept them with the provision that they be assimilated completely in our own way, and that they merge fully with our flesh and blood, in a Jewish manner, adapted in a Jewish spirit."[3] Although Gaster did not detail the processes by which non-Jewish culture was to be Judaized, he reiterated Herzl's pledge that Zionism would never renounce the fruits of the secular culture which Jews valued. However, these were to be subordinate, and always subject to adjustment to what Gaster called "a Jewish spirit," which was most likely in accordance with Herzl's formulation of "justice, truth, liberty, progress, humanity, beauty, and Jewish solidarity, in the service of enlightenment," as the essence of Judaism.[4] Perhaps more than any other segment of the *Kulturdebatte*, Gaster articulated what most Zionists felt to be the main signpost for Zionist culture: it was to serve an educative and edifying function.

The basis of the cohesion of this culture and its teleology, Gaster asserted, were not simply a bolstering of national sovereignty and nationalism for their own sake, which coalesced most nations, but the idea that Jews constituted a religious community, and that their religious traditions were a constant source of inspiration. Hence, their quest toward national grandeur or honor would never overwhelm the religious imperatives of the Zionists' faith. This was, he qualified, not to say that they all held the same view of Judaism; but "the depths of their souls responded to the same impulse, to return from exile to redemption;" redemption was only attained by pursuing justice. Gaster's view of Judaism was anything but dogmatic or exclusive; "as a ray of light is made up of many colors along the spectrum, so Judiasm exists naturally as a pluralistic entity;" he held this view as representative of Zionism's comprehension of Judaism. It was one of the most beautiful and glorious aspects of the movement to Gaster, which he claimed was a manifestation of Zionism's indebtedness to a broadly conceived cultural nationalism. Under no condition would the movement restrict the life of the individual; this he held as fundamental.[5]

The watchword, for Gaster, was tolerance – again echoing the sentiments of Herzl. He declared that the movement would "not have a religious character foisted on it;" here he was referring to the leadership's refusal to accede to the demands of some East European orthodox leaders prior to the Second Congress as a condition for their participation. Zionism was "neither the expression of a single party, nor an individual's point of view, nor a specific religious orientation, but an expression of the entirety of Judaism and Jewry."[6] Zionist culture for Gaster was therefore the preeminent framework which could include all of Judaism and Jewry in a pragmatic program. Indeed, there would even be some members of the *Mizrahi* in later years who would repeat such assertions as articles of their Zionist faith.[7] The dominant code was for there to be absolute, mutual toleration and respect between Jews. Even though the spiritual rebirth of Zionism resided in the realm of modern culture, it intended "no harm to Jewish religious principles."[8] Given the fact that Zionists tended to exaggerate the movement's all-inclusive character, it is nonetheless important to remember that no other Jewish institution, organization, or sect so magnanimously embraced the whole of the people. The next year, Gaster likened Zionist national culture to the beams from a lighthouse which would guide "the Jewish Ship of State" to its destination, the shores of the Promised Land; it would "steer the movement clear of the treacherous rocks of ignorance, fanaticism, and intolerance."[9]

Gaster, who would later recall the philosophes by proposing a new Jewish encyclopaedia as an urgent national project for Zionism, sounded warnings similar to those of Voltaire's "Mohammed the Prophet" and Lessing's "Nathan the Wise" in his quest for enlightenment over superstition. Indeed, the archetype of antiquated Jewish fanaticism, as opposed to the pervasive calm and rationality exhibited in Zionist culture was the orthodox community of Jerusalem – which seemed to exist completely disconnected from reality.[10] To a less extent, however, here Gaster was speaking of the anti-Zionist religious masses of Jewry in Eastern Europe as being in the throes of such an unenlightened existence, a view with which most Western Zionists concurred.

Further setting the tone for Zionist culture at the Second Congress, Osaias Thon of Cracow, the speaker who followed Gaster, affirmed his enthusiastic support for Gaster's message. Thon, as well, was a "modern" (not Reform) rabbi, who had been a student of the sociologist Georg Simmel. He furthermore regarded himself as a disciple of Ahad Ha-Am and simultaneously revered Herzl as "a magnificent man," exemplary of "the most aristocratic manliness."[11] Fulfilling a vision of Ahad Ha-Am, he established a number of *Tarbut* (Culture) Hebrew academies in Poland and Galicia; he also wrote a lengthy study of Herbert Spencer, along with a number of scholarly works. Later, he flagrantly violated the canon of Ahad Ha-Am-ist gradualism by participating, as a Zionist, in Austrian politics as a representative of Eastern Galicia, and in the Polish *Sejm*. Indeed, Thon was a Zionist in whom the various facets of *Kultur* in Zionism were decidedly pronounced; he, like Gaster, seemed to embody the ideal Zionist man. "The immense value of Zionism," said Thon, was in the very fact that it provided an opportunity to unite "all of Jewry from a broad base of nationalism" – not just from something smaller in its conception, which was actually losing power – that is, Judaism as a confession. Moreover, "modern culture is nationalism," Thon continued, and "Zionism represents the great culmination of modern culture for Jewry."[12] For Thon and many other Western Zionists, it was impossible to separate *Kultur, Zionismus,* and *Nationalismus* from one another, without removing essential features of the others.

Also seconding Gaster by fusing the concept of culture with tolerance, as opposed to fanaticism, Fabius Schach, a German Zionist leader claimed that "every honorable Zionist keeps his religion to himself, and lets others do the same. Every cultured [*gebildete*] Zionist knows that to be imbued with *Bildung* means that one would never injure religious feelings, but at the same time, it would be an error to allow orthodox religious sentiments to dominate the movement," as appeared to be the aspiration of some of those present at the Second Congress.[13] Schach had illuminated a theme which was rife throughout the debates on language, concerning the extent to which Zionism should compel its membership to adopt cultural perspectives which were beyond their personal preferences or convictions. Again, the ambivalence of a Zionist's ideal attachment to the movement emerged as a motif in the *Kulturdebatte*. This issue of Zionism's involvement in the private life of the individual would rarely ebb in the movement, and perhaps reach its greatest peak during Herzl's lifetime through the rise of the Democratic Faction.

Between the Second and Third Congresses, in correspondence with his fellow members of the cultural commission, Gaster revealed the extent to which these early Zionist leaders saw themselves as modern philosophes; his thought indicates that Zionist nationalism was not only beholden to ideals of the early nineteenth century, but also to the eighteenth-century concept of inaugurating a new order through the rationalization of academic disciplines. The creation of an encyclopaedia, which especially interested Gaster (and was fulfilled in its most successful incarnation under Nahum Goldmann), occupied a substantial share of the discourse on culture. The Zionists aspired to correct and augment the cultural possessions of Western civilization by providing a secularized, scholarly record of Jewish history and thought, and to consolidate a body of systematic knowledge from a Jewish national perspective; their objectives were indeed similar to those of the *Wissenschaft des Judentums* of the early nineteenth century.[14]

For "our great encylopaedic Dictionary," Gaster wrote, "we must select the best men and try to formulate a systematic plan . . . the work in this line of 'Kultur' will be of everlasting value and we must not allow dilettante and superficial writers to spoil the work by their own ignorance. We must not budge an inch on this. Either the work is to be done in a manner of which we all shall be proud, or it is not to be done at all! We cannot make any compromises . . ."[15] Gaster obviously shared the concern of Herzl, that not all of the new Hebrew literature, or writers, were of sufficient quality to be presented before the world as the best fruits of the Jewish nation. In reference to projected concessions, Gaster might have been thinking of the inclusion of certain Yiddish texts and writers, given the generally disparaging view of Yiddish among Zionists. Gaster's insistence on quality also points to a central problem facing the organization's cultural work: if this was supposed to represent the glory and eternal values of the nation, could it be accomplished with so few funds? In the face of constant designs for large-scale cultural projects, the meager finances of the Zionist Movement were a substantial impediment.

The Zionists equated such a scholarly endeavor with winning acceptability and honor in the eyes of the Western academic world, which was of paramount importance to them. Along with a Jewish encyclopaedia as a source of pride and living knowledge to Jews, and as a symbol and practical reference for Jews and non-Jews, the Zionists also felt compelled to establish a Jewish national library. Besides serving to hold the cultural, especially the literary and scientific products of the Jews, a national library was also symbolic of the existence of a worthy cultural heritage. As strange as it sounds in retrospect, the mention of the national library elicited a great emotional response at the Congresses. At this point Gaster was considering libraries located in the diaspora as a temporary means, but even these had to be treated with great care. Entrusting the selection of its holdings only to "experts," he proposed "the formation of a nucleus of such books and periodicals which we consider indispensable for a Zionist library." "If we work in unity I have no doubt that our recommendations will carry great weight with the local organizations."[16] There was tremendous confidence, on the part of these early *Kulturisten,* that voluntary educational efforts – on the weight of their authority – such as the establishment and selective supplying of reading rooms, would be one of the most effective means of instilling a national spirit among the Jews; Zionists heard about the success of such projects in reports on activities in the Zionist press and at the following Congresses. This was carried out mainly by stocking the existing university and community reading rooms with Zionist materials, as well as by establishing specifically Zionist reading rooms. These did indeed serve as national-libraries in miniature.[17] The issue of supporting a central national library in Jerusalem, which had actually already begun independently of the Zionist Movement, would become a regular order of business in the next year's Congress.

Martin Buber introduced some of the most ambitious of early

Zionism's programs for the transmission of Zionist culture to European Jewry. At the Third Zionist Congress (1899), under the aegis of the "Agitation" committee, Buber proposed stimulating the spread of national history and literature toward the education of the Jews in a national spirit. In large part, he hoped that this could be prompted through the democratization of the operation of the movement's organ, *Die Welt*, which he believed was too narrowly conceived. Buber appealed to have the affairs of the paper overseen by a committee outside of the Actions-Committee, so that it could be a vehicle for cultural Zionism, and he spoke in general terms for a more systematic attempt to reach the masses of Jewry through periodical literature and lectures. In addition, the movement should actively promote more propaganda organizations, scientific and cultural Zionist societies, organizations for women and children, gymnastic, sport, and song clubs, organizations among professionals and workers, and dramatic performances in a Zionist spirit. Along with its existing official publications, Buber requested that the movement provide songbooks, an "A-B-C Book" (to explain, in brief format, aspects of the movement), and an inexpensive series of books for children. To strengthen awareness of Palestine, the committee was called on to encourage presentations of products from the *Yishuv* in European exhibitions, and to promote trips to Palestine. Buber also suggested that the movement adopt a national holiday, possibly the Sabbath during the Chanukah festival, to instill unity and national pride among the Jews – to link the victory of the Maccabees to the new Jewish national movement for all the generations of Jews to come.[18] He barely could have been closer to Herzl's earlier prescriptions.

Indeed, despite Buber's feeling that the movement was not committed enough to culture, he was cognizant that "agitation and propaganda" might complement the creation of a national culture, and that in themselves these activities fulfilled a role similar to *Kultur*. At the 1899 Congress Buber's ideas were seconded by a number of speakers, including Gaster, and this motif was articulated in later Congresses by Alfred Nossig and Sammy Gronemann, among others.[19]

With the young Buber as one of its leaders, the Democratic Faction played a most significant role in establishing certain Zionist myths as well as a style of youthful vigor and robustness. Its members aroused a good deal of controversy but also appealed to many Central European Jews who witnessed or participated in burgeoning, idealistic middle-class youth movements of the era.

Buber elaborated on the concept of the all-inclusive character of Zionism which had been introduced by Herzl, and expounded by Gaster, Thon and others at the Third Congress (1899). Zionism was not, Buber declared, simply the orientation of a political party; it comprised a complete view of the world [*Weltanschauung*]. The development of this world view was the province of what he referred to as "inner agitation." Zionism should not approach its potential adherents as one would a "liberal" or a "conservative," Buber asserted, but it should gear itself to be assimilated totally, as a person thinks of himself as a "man" or an "artist."[20] Buber was among the *Kulturisten* who wished to launch a forceful, official cultural program, which coalesced as the Democratic Faction at the Fifth Zionist Congress. At the Fourth Zionist Congress (London, 1900), he and his colleagues put forward many of the ideas that animated their program in that Congress's *Kulturdebatte*. In addition, other Zionists, such as the Viennese lawyer and writer Leopold Kahn, elaborated similar designs for the movement, which seemed to a large degree representative of the views of Western Jews who identified with Zionism.

At the Third Congress (1899) Kahn had defined Jewish culture as "the progress of man's knowledge of himself as an individual, and as a member of the nation to which he belongs." Kahn's canon echoed Fichte's *Addresses to the German Nation* (1807–8). "It is the process of the development of his faculties, accompanied by the cultivation of the means by which he may improve himself, towards the perfection of his spirit. National culture is the distinctive coloration of these ideas with the qualities of the national community, the acquisition of a special national signature." Such a signature was the Jewish religion, which Kahn said "comprised the greatest share of our culture. It informs our morality, and the requisites of human society and civilization." Kahn conceded that cultural work would have to be tailored to meet the needs of different communities, but at the same time it should meet the requirements of all Jews, especially to educate children in a unified national spirit.[21] In summation, stressing the cosmopolitan nature of Jewish culture as conceived by Zionism, the speaker equated their cultural labors as Zionists with work for the general cultural elevation of mankind. Kahn's speech made a tremendous impression, eliciting an emotional response from the floor; his talk was praised and expounded upon by other speakers.[22]

At the next Congress (1900) the ideal of Zionist *Kultur* was drawn in contrast to orthodox Judaism, prompting further elucidations of the underlying philosophies of the *Kulturist* perspective. "Zionism need not encroach on one's private life," Chaim Weizmann asserted, following the lead of Schach and others; he added that "we have concluded that for us, the religious question is a private matter."[23] Zionism, to Weizmann, was a means to fulfill oneself as a Jew, while personally abandoning those aspects of the tradition he considered archaic. The religious Zionists were especially bemused that Weizmann and his cohorts could advocate the deepening of Zionism, to shape the inner and communal lives of Jews, while declaring an aversion to religious practice. Such an ideology appeared to them to be following the path of the Reform movement, which Zionists routinely chided for selecting the elements of Judaism it retained as a matter of expedience. To the orthodox, Weizmann had provocatively trodden on the sanctity of Judaism through his rigid separation of the public and the private – and he saw this as integral to Zionism. For most Western Zionists, who would have agreed with Weizmann, while possibly believing his presentation of such ideas in that setting unwise, one of the movement's chief attractions lay in its contention that Jewry constituted a nation whose members were mutually accountable to each other, toward the benefit of all. The orthodox in the movement primarily saw Zionism, though, as the best means of safeguarding their way of life.[24] Weizmann had clearly articulated a rejection of the world of the orthodox, which he saw as synonymous with the repression of the *shtetl*, and proclaimed that he would not tolerate its institution in Zionism for the sake of appeasing or attracting the orthodox. Liberalism was to take precedence over Jewish orthodoxy in his Zionist culture.

In the same vein, Leo Motzkin declared that "our intention is a pure, unsullied assurance that our idealistic convictions will not be impugned." He added that the demands of the orthodox rabbis were no less than "an insult to the intelligence" of himself and his colleagues. Motzkin saw an affinity between the issue of culture and the agitation of the masses – which was also intertwined in the language debate, and later taken up by the orthodox as a rationale for rejecting the *Kulturfrage* for Eastern Europe. Signifying the relationship between the debates on culture and the realities of the Jewish world, the orthodox as well as the *Kulturisten* – in this case, against the gradualist spirit of Ahad Ha-Am – sought to legitimate their "idealism" as the best means of immediately reaching the Eastern Jews. If Zionist culture prepared the way for "a homeland of freedom," Motzkin insisted, then the possibility existed that the masses of Jews would turn to "our side."[25] To be sure, "freedom" for Motzkin meant throwing off the shackles of the *shtetl*; it was the ultimate realization of individual and communal emancipation. This dimension of the *Kulturdebatte* reveals how fluid the demarcation was between culture, propaganda, and agitation. The Zionists' positions on culture must therefore be seen in light of their strategies of Jewish nationalization and integration, not just as an argument over the purest means to attain the Jewish national ethic; in the next Congresses this would become a dominant issue in the debate.

As their earlier speeches in the Congresses intimated, Buber, Motzkin, and Weizmann perceived themselves as expressing the will of Jewish youth, whose rightful place was at the helm of the movement. Indeed, the contemporary European nationalisms comprised elements that may be characterized as rebellions of youth, and, simultaneously, "bourgeois anti-bourgeois revolts;" that is, young people who sought to distance themselves from the older generation, but nevertheless clung to many of its core values.[26] Similarly, these young Zionists – who championed the reconstitution of a Jewish sovereignty, the revival of Hebrew, and a Jewish totality – advocated what may be seen as a "traditional anti-traditional revolution."[27] Much of their frustration and ire was directed at the world of their elders, along with parts of the non-Jewish and anti-Jewish societies of which they were a part. Nevertheless, they consciously appropriated and exalted aspects of each. There can be little doubt that a main impetus driving these young people to Zionism, rather than, say, a more leftist political orientation, was their desire for acceptance in the European society at large and the connection of Zionism to *Kultur*: to simultaneously be a proud Jew, respectable, and a conscious participant in the creation of Western culture, if not its very vanguard.[28]

Although they demanded discipline, in the form of an obligatory commitment to the Zionist cultural project – by every Zionist – the Faction members also required that Judaism and Zionism not impinge on what they considered the manners and morals of their private lives. In this, they were responding to primarily East European concerns. They had rejected the *shtetl* in large part because they wished to escape the allegedly suffocating influence of their families and teachers, and they did not want this replicated in Zionism. Their own sense of moral rigor was epitomized by independent advanced scholarship and personal growth, as well as sacrifice, exemplified by a devotion to Zionism in the face of humiliation and material hardship. To be sure, they were ambivalent about their desire for Zionist culture's pervasive influence in their lives.[29] Modern rabbis, such as Gaster, Thon, and Ehrenpreis, also condoned a greater separation of the public and private, accompanied by new national commitment, as part of Zionism's legacy. The orthodox of Eastern Europe, however, could not simply resign themselves to the mandates of youth, and strove to impart their convictions to the movement.[30] This dynamic would at times be amplified or diminished, but it was always present.

Perhaps the most poignant statement of the convergence between Zionist culture and the Jewish generational conflict is found in Weizmann's extensive memorandum to Herzl of May 1903, after the Congress in which the Democratic Faction was formally constituted. Weizmann wrote that contrary to the view of many West European Zionists, "the larger part of the contemporary younger generation [in the East] is anti-Zionist, not from a desire to assimilate as in Western Europe, but through revolutionary conviction" epitomized by the *Bund*.[31] Indeed, the *Bund* had been far more successful than Zionism in capturing the loyalty of Jewish youth in Eastern Europe around the turn of the century. Before a program explicitly fusing Zionism and socialism was articulated by the Labor Zionists around 1906, the Jewish nationalism of the *Bund* would have significantly greater appeal for the Eastern Jews who literally lived a world apart from the Western counterparts.

"Saddest and most lamentable is the fact that although [the *Bund*] consumes much Jewish energy and heroism, and it is located within the Jewish fold, the attitude it evidences . . . is one of antipathy, swelling at times to fanatical hatred" toward parts of the traditional Jewish world, Weizmann continued. There was, to be sure, no such virulence in Zionism at this early stage. The most extreme elements of the movement, which were only recently organized into parties, hoped to persuade all the other members to accept or at least tolerate their own variety of Zionism, while many Zionists were opposed to the very notion of parties within the movement.[32] In the Pale of Settlement, Weizmann wrote, "Jewish children are in open revolt against their parents." "The elders are confined within tradition and Orthodox inflexibility; the young make their first step a search for freedom from everything Jewish. In one small town near Pinsk, for example, youngsters tore the Torah Scrolls to shreds. This speaks volumes."[33] It seems that Weizmann did not differentiate between those involved in the *Bund* versus those in more overtly revolutionary and anarchistic movements. Most Zionists could never accept behaviour so blatantly disrespectful of the traditional faith.

Weizmann asserted that Jewish youth in the East were attracted by "the revolutionaries with their powerful arguments drawn from tragic day-to-day realities, their ideal of personal heroism, and the magnetism inherent in martyrdom." Zionism, on the other hand, was perceived as being dominated by the *Mizrahi*, according to Weizmann, due to the profusion of their propaganda in Eastern Europe. It certainly did not help that Weizmann and his non-orthodox contemporaries were located mostly in Central Europe. At any rate, the *Mizrahi* was, to Weizmann, the main reason for Zionism's failure to compete with revolutionary socialism and the *Bund*. In Eastern Europe, further confounding the issue, the perspective of the *Mizrahi* had become misidentified with the proposals of the *Kulturisten*. What was needed was a strong affirmation of a secular national ideology, to color all of Zionism, which Weizmann saw as epitomized by the Democratic Faction.

The Faction "forms the connecting link between the older and the younger generation," Weizmann presumptuously proclaimed.

> It alone is assuming the struggle against the revolutionaries, which indeed it does. *It alone is freedom loving and socially enlightened. It extracts the Jewish essence from among the masses and pours it into a European mold.* But what that Jewish essence is, the European Zionists refuse to comprehend; even the leadership has still to recognize it . . . What we regard as Jewish culture has til lately been confused with Jewish religious worship, and when culture in the literal sense was discussed, the Zionists of Western Europe thought that it referred [only] to the improvement of educational facilities in Eastern Europe. Perhaps it is now understood, because of the specific activities of [Faction] members, that *the totality of Jewish national achievement is intended – particularly that literature, art, scientific research, should all be synthesized into Europeanism, translated into modern creativity, and expressed in institutions bearing their own individual character.*[34]

Weizmann maintained that the Faction's articulation of "*a loftier view of life, with scope for enthusiastic action*" could move the Jewish masses. He imagined, in agreement with Herzl, that Jewry longed for existence on a higher, and more autonomous cultural plane, with youth as its avant-garde.[35] "Perhaps [this] is the only reply that we can make to our opponents," Weizmann conceded, since Zionism could not yet guarantee the masses a clear enough social and economic vision of the future.[36] Despite this admission of the movement's limitations, Weizmann avoided a painful cultural dilemma: that in seeking the higher plateau, the existing culture of the Jews was sometimes neglected and occasionally disparaged, as we have seen in the language debate between orthodox, socialists, and the *Kulturisten*. When he announced or implied his desire "to convey some Jewish content to the Western Jew and some refinement of his Judaism to the Eastern Jew, and thereby create an opportunity for a bridge between the two," it was often taken as a patronizing, assimilationist, bourgeois mentality.[37] At any rate, according to Weizmann and his friends, this bridge was to be built by Zionist youth. Clearly, the youthful wing of the party was beholden to most of the biases which characterized the Western leadership's cultural pronouncements.

With the movement still in its infancy, Zionism struggled with the problem of divining its essence in ever more diverse ways. The Fifth Zionist Congress (1901) was a paradoxical event, with respect to the problem of culture in early Zionism. This was the forum in which Weizmann and his colleagues attempted to broaden their impact on the Zionist mainstream. Even though this Congress devoted far more time and energy to the agenda of the *Kulturisten* than any Zionist gathering to date, simultaneously, there was intense criticism of the movement for not being as committed as it should be to culture.[38] This culminated in the Democratic Faction's "walkout" to bring attention to their cause. Indeed, many of the Faction's ideas, including stepping up the dissemination of Hebrew, support for Zionist libraries, statistical studies of Jewry, and intensifying research on Jewish colonization in Palestine were already taken up by the movement, and were liberally cited in the addresses of delegates not associated with the Democratic Faction.[39] Sometimes these cultural references were part of regional or national reports, or interspersed with calls for hygiene and attention to physical training and fitness, such as in the speeches of Nordau and Oscar Marmorek.[40] Furthermore, the spread of *Kulturist* notions was also shown by the support for Hebrew and Zionist literature which was evident to any reader of *Die Welt*, and the movement's founding of Zionist *chadarim*, conferences, and lectures. Individuals now were receiving stipends to coordinate these activities.[41] All things considered, the Faction simply was not representative of that radical a deviation from the flow of the movement.

Nahum Sokolow, who was significantly older than the Faction members, publicly expressed his sympathy with their aims at the 1901 Congress. Similar to Ehrenpreis' appropriation of Hebrew literature for Zionist culture at the First Congress, at the Fifth Congress Sokolow made an appeal to bring the *Wissenschaft des Judentums* into the fold of Zionism, as the central national body of scholarship. This was quite understandable, since Zionism and the *Wissenschaft des Judentums* held many characteristics and goals in common, along the lines of secularizing the Jewish experience. In the mid-nineteenth century, the founders of the *Wissenschaft des Judentums* intended that a scientific inquiry into Judaism and Jewry assume a role commensurate with its contributions to civilization, within the body of German scholarship and universities, and in the general Jewish and even non-Jewish consciousness. Sokolow implied that although it attracted some facile minds, it made limited progress towards its goals, and that most Jews considered it moribund; such assumptions on the speaker's part were questionable, at best.[42] The work of the *Wissenschaft des Judentums*, Sokolow asserted, could be revived and made to flourish with an infusion of Zionist ideology – to turn it from an "archaeological" pursuit into a living organ in the Jewish national body.[43] As Sokolow proposed a massive Jewish academic project, encompassing history, philosophy, and all levels of literature to be enlisted in the service of Zionism, so Martin Buber at the 1901 Congress recast what he saw as distinctively Jewish efforts in art, literature, poetry, and music into the mold of a national regeneration through Zionism; his subject traversed the boundaries between the creation of culture and cultural transmission.

Buber's talk was an enumeration of the achievements of Jews in the arts, emphasizing those whose works were definite expressions of their Jewish self-consciousness. He began by voicing his dismay over a comment of Max Nordau that the priority of the movement should be more material matters, as opposed to art.[44] The development of the soul of the people, best manifested through art, deserved equal attention, Buber contended. It must not and need not wait for surer material grounding; the "aesthetic education of the people" had to be tended to immediately. He asserted that artistic endeavours were of the utmost significance in furthering the cause of Zionism, while holding that genuine Jewish creative expression would be attained when Jews had their own soil under their feet, in Palestine.[45] Like Gaster, Buber was immediately concerned with the erection of an alternative secular culture as a basis of the Jewish nation, which could also have an immediate impact on diaspora Jewry; "the most magnificent cultural document," testifying to the unfolding Zionist culture, "will be our art."[46]

Although Buber was disconcerted that the Zionist Organization had not assumed a more forceful leading role in Zionist culture, he proclaimed the continuity between the political undertakings of the movement and the aesthetic agenda he articulated. Buber himself described the project as "propaganda in a grand style." Up to the moment of his address, though, Zionism had endeavoured to win Jewish minds and souls only by the way of "the word."[47] Certainly, Buber took for granted the national edifice – namely, the Congress, myths, symbols, and ceremonies – in which his own speech, and an artistic exhibition of the Congress were encased. To have given credit to Herzl and Nordau for portending a Jewish totality would have detracted from what Buber and his colleagues saw as the great distinctiveness of their message.[48] Indeed, Buber's ideas about the power of art and aesthetics to move men were not nearly as removed from Herzl's predilections, as one would infer from some of Buber's writings about his estrangement from the movement's leader.[49]

Later Buber presented a cultural resolution which proved very controversial, despite its non-binding nature: "The Congress declares that the cultural improvement, namely, the education of the Jewish people in the national spirit, is one of the most essential elements of the Zionist program, and it is the duty of all of Zionism's adherents to participate in it."[50] Herzl quite correctly perceived that this Congress, too, had not come any closer to reconciling the orthodox and the *Kulturisten*. Therefore, in order not to inflame the delegates' passions, he moved to postpone this, and the other discussions on the cultural resolutions until nearly the end of the Congress. The motion of the President elicited a response which had never been heard by Herzl in the Congress hall: a laugh of derision from Leo Motzkin. An argument ensued, in which Motzkin and Buber challenged the authority of Herzl, which was no doubt seen by the leader as an ill-mannered insurrection of sorts. Herzl held his ground, supported by a clear majority of the nearly three hundred delegates – and the thirty-seven members of the Democratic Faction walked out, for an hour, in protest.[51]

The Faction returned when their agenda reached the floor. All of their proposals, with the exception of support for the *Juedischer Verlag*, were accepted by the Congress; the fact that these resolutions were passed was less a product of the pressure wielded by the group, than the reality that their project was well within the realm of political Zionism. Even their credo of "each Zionist's obligation to partake in cultural work" was sufficiently vague, so that it might be seen as a logical extension of the Basel Program's call for strengthening national consciousness. Herzl was visibly enthusiastic about almost all of the committee's resolutions.[52] And, whatever their differences, none of the Faction members missed the opportunity to be photographed with the leader.

The quarrel with the rambunctious youth (who actually ranged from their mid-twenties to late thirties, while Herzl was forty), quickly patched over with each of the individual Faction members, was at least as much a consequence of Herzl's displeasure with their manners as it was a serious disagreement over ideology and policy. Nonetheless, Herzl was sensitive to the rabbis' fears that the official alignment of the movement within the strictures of Ahad Ha-Am might turn Zionism into an even smaller sect. In his comments before the vote on the cultural resolutions, and in his closing comments, Herzl stressed the role that Zionism had played in uniting Jewry's diverse views of the world, and his affirmations of the movement's unity automatically called forth roars of approval.[53]

The Democratic Faction, as a group, did not become a permanent force for the advancement of a Zionist national culture. The chief reasons for the failure of the Faction to execute its program were due more to personal conflicts between the members; for instance, relations between Weizmann and Leo Motzkin were especially problematic.[54] As individuals, though, the men tended to their projects with zeal: Buber, Feiwel, and Lilien to the *Juedischer Verlag;* Weizmann and Feiwel to agitation for the Jewish university; and Motzkin to political writing, and the collection and analysis of data on European Jewry and the colonization of Palestine.[55] They were all much more adept at living their program than administering it.

Partly motivated by a desire to alter what it perceived as a detrimental image and myth of the movement, the Faction wished to supplant the perception of Zionism's close affinity to orthodoxy with that of Zionism's affinity to a youthful, Judaized intelligentsia. In some respects similar to the challenge the Faction posed to the movement's founding elites, the role of women also began to be rethought in the prewar era. One sign of this was the speech of Miriam Schach at the Tenth Zionist Congress in 1911. She attempted to impart a counter-myth against what she saw as Zionism's perception and self-apprehension as a society of men, and against its portrayal and placement of women in subordinate roles to men. The sister of Fabius Schach and a co-founder of the French Zionist organ *L'Echo Sioniste*, she felt representative of a group which had been overlooked as leading proponents for the advancement of *Kultur* in the Zionist program, and as the subject for the fabrication of constructive myths.[56] There had, however, been speeches in some of the earlier Congresses by women, thoughtful articles had appeared about women in Zionism in *Die Welt*, and numerous women's Zionist organizations had been founded, probably the best known of which was the *Juedisch-Nationale Frauenvereinigung* in Germany, established in 1900.[57] For the most part, Schach's analysis was imaginative, perceptive, and consistent with the liberal confession of the movement's culture.

Symbolically, when women were represented as "the personification of Zionism," such as in Fredrich Beer's medal given to delegates at the First and Second Zionist Congresses, they were shown as indistinct, passive figures, pointing the way to Zion.[58] In some other Zionist artistic products, though, such as in the *Juedischer Almanach* (1902) and *Juedischer Kuenstler* (1903), biblical women were frequently shown as commanding figures. Nevertheless, the pictures of contemporary women in the same volumes, usually in domestic scenes, were closer to their assigned role in European society and Zionism until this time, depicted as a solid support for their husband and children.

In any event, their particular presence in the context of the Congresses or the *Kulturfrage*, for Western Jewry, was not sharply thrown into relief until Schach's speech at the Tenth Congress. It was probably the first time that the matriarchs were presented as Zionist heroines; Sarah, Rebecca, Rachel, and Leah could be cited as great national figures, as models for Jewish women, new Zionist Women. Furthermore, Schach announced that it was time for Zionists to "call their women from the kitchen," and allow them to embark on serious cultural work; hitherto they had been asked to dispense "*tsimmes*" and "sweetness." The German adage extolling "Kinder, Kirche, und Kueche" ["children, the Church, and the kitchen"] as the province of women's work should not be taken to heart in Zionism. After all, if the priority was to educate children in a national spirit, how could they expect to accomplish such a goal without the active support of the mothers of Israel? From whom did children learn to speak? Who told them bedtime stories which they would remember their entire lives? Who allayed fears and frustrations, and instilled dreams and hopes? Who determined the atmosphere of the home, and made it Jewish? The same Zionist culture must be imbued in women as men; and when meaningful, rather than symbolic roles were assigned to women, the movement could expect far greater success. The most significant spadework for a national culture resided in the realm of women, Schach asserted.[59]

To be sure, as it was practiced and received at this time by Central and West European Jews Zionism was a self-consciously male bastion. The myth of female equality in Zionist culture would largely arise from the images of Jewish life in Palestine accompanying the growth of the *Yishuv*, and would assume a prominent place in Zionist imagery after the First World War.

Typical of Zionist Congress proceedings, especially during the debates on culture, Schach, too, mediated her disagreements with the movement through a generous dose of humor. Serious problems concerning the sexual division of labor within the movement were nonetheless underscored, but for the most part the image which remained as she left the dais was one of strong backing of the Zionist project on the part of women. Jewish solidarity was always the key. Indeed, the *Kulturdebatte* often provided an opportunity for the factions to profess the unanimity of Jewry within the movement as their most profound creed, while indicating what they sensed as their common bonds beyond Judaism: the notion of ongoing emancipation, to supersede the European emancipation of the Jews.

At the Ninth Congress (1909), five years after Herzl's death, a *Mizrahi* delegate sprinkled his polemic with quotations from "two poets, Herzl and Heine," both of whom nearly every Zionist regarded as the greatest of heroes. "The latter means more to us than a poet, although his greatness also derives from the fact that he was a poet." The delegate, Professor R. Weyl from Frankfurt, acknowledged that Herzl's stature was due in part to his accomplishments in the secular realm, where he was a celebrated writer. Indeed, that is how Herzl had often described himself; he had written that "the worst that one can say about me," regarding his plans for the Jewish State, "is that I am a poet."[60] Weyl showed himself to be as accomplished as his non-religious couterparts, in that they had appropriated images associated with orthodoxy. The *Mizrahi*, too, sometimes found symbolic common ground in *Kultur*. Weyl "called on a Christian poet – who might even be called a Hedonist – namely, Goethe. You might not have considered him a man in the mold of the *Mizrahi*! (Laughter.) Goethe proclaimed that no nation had ever attained greatness without satisfying its religious spirituality, and moreover, no nation had ever attained greatness which had stifled the religious spirit."[61] The speaker could not have picked a triumvirate more amenable to Zionist culture than that of Goethe, a humanistic prophet of German nationalism; Heine, who had challenged some early manifestations and excesses of that nationalism, while actively cultivating his adopted Germanic and genetic Jewish heritage; and Herzl, who, through a Goethe-like vision, had applied the critical insight of Heine to the contemporary Jewish scene, and founded a new orientation to Jewry; and each had done so as a widely recognized *litterateur*. Weyl was truly attempting to tap the cultural sensibilities that dominated the movement for Western Jews.

Along the same lines, a *Mizrahi* delegate from Budapest assured the Ninth Congress that if by the term *Kultur*, "one meant consideration of Jewish history, character, attitudes, feelings, ideals, and a general way of comprehending the world, then the *Mizrahi* had no objection. It was an error to take for granted the notion that the *Mizrahi* were opposed to culture; they had no wish to be hostile, contentious, or abusive. While they held their religious convictions and appealed for religious interests, they were in principle not opposed to *Bildung*."[62] The Zionists were neither unanimous in their support of the Hebrew language, nor on a specific variety of Judaism, nor a specific vision of an ideal Jewish polity; but they seemed to agree, for the most part, on the value of a Judaized *Bildung* as a vital force to build a Jewish nation. It is from this assumption that most of the work to convey this new language and national culture would proceed; the stress would be on the cultivation of the individual.

Still, more updated methods of nationalization were also adopted by the movement in the prewar years. Sammy Gronemann delivered an address on "Propaganda and Agitation" at the Seventh Zionist Congress (1905) in which many of the ideas of the *Kulturisten* were represented. But in addition to these now familiar notions, he suggested that the efforts to nationalize the Jews should concentrate more on visual images and symbols as a source of cohesion, and as a means of increasing the Zionists' following. This talk was important not only because some of Gronemann's suggestions were accepted, but because his view was a summary of the orientation to which the movement had already committed itself concerning the acculturation of Zionist ideals, especially for Western Jews. Gronemann was an important contributor himself to Zionist culture. Originally trained as a lawyer in Berlin, he devoted most of his efforts to journalism, before he turned to writing plays and novels from a Zionist perspective; he was one of the main contributors to a short-lived Zionist satirical magazine, *Shlemiel*.

Showing his awareness of the interrelatedness of diverse layers of cultural activity, Gronemann stated that "the best *Gegenwartsarbeit* is the agitation and propaganda for our idea!" He intentionally borrowed Buber's expression for immediate, day-to-day work to found a Jewish national culture. This had usually been used to imply the efficacy of small-scale projects, dedicated to Hebrew culture, in Palestine. Indeed, *Gegenwartsarbeit* was seen as the chief means of enacting a program of cultural Zionism which was often referred to as "practical" Zionism. In the speaker's view, the movement must recognize that a renaissance in Jewish art and culture was inexorably linked to fundraising, increasing membership, and even purchasing olive trees for the Jewish National Fund. Those who argued that there was a large "moral" price to pay for such "low" cultural activity were blind to the reality of the connections between the various planes of the movement. The consequence of relegating these phenomena to distinct areas meant the greater possibility that Zionism "would be degraded to the superficial level of a charitable institution." Not surprisingly, Gronemann insisted that the movement must represent itself as an indivisible whole.[63]

Gronemann further warned that a Zionism characterized primarily by erudite or idiosyncratic lectures and highbrow literature would also diminish the movement, a warning seconded several times at this and later Congresses.[64] The greatest need was to develop a form of nationalism with which the entirety of Jewry could identify. This had been accomplished, Gronemann declared, to a great extent by the Zionist Congress; yet more was needed to sustain interest in the movement between Congresses. Again recalling Buber, the speaker pressed for the institution of a Zionist national holiday – "not just a tasteless spectacle" – but an event that would assure the public of the permanence and continuity of the movement. "The most beautiful speech or the most insightful book is useless," Gronemann maintained, "unless it is read or heard." Such cultural products were indeed being spawned by Zionism; but it was also the movement's task to get the books into people's hands, or to have them go to a meeting; more individuals simply had to be drawn into the movement.[65]

Jewish art, such as that reproduced and discussed in the monthly *Ost und West*, which was not an official Zionist publication, but shared some of the movement's goals and had numerous Zionist contributors, could be more deliberately infused into the movement's propaganda, Gronemann claimed. *Ost und West* had been very successful in making Jewish art accessible, recognized, and appreciated by Western Jews; the speaker might have added that the *Juedischer Verlag* had also distinguished itself in this regard. Furthermore, he proposed the publication of a new Zionist daily newspaper, separate from *Die Welt*, featuring numerous photographs which testified to the new Jewish life being created through Zionism.[66] Indeed, the stepped-up presentation of images of Palestine accompanied the enlarged place of Jewish culture in Palestine in the Congresses' debates on culture. Gronemann's plan of having Jews from different corners of the world, with their vastly different world views united through common images, did to a certain extent come about. This was surely one of the most important bases of unity for the movement. At that time, an archive of Zionist photography, especially focused on the Jewish colonies in Palestine, was emerging in various Zionist books, pamphlets, and newspapers, which provided a uniform and comprehensive treatment of the Zionist colonization project.[67] Specifically, though, Gronemann declared that Zionism needed a single grand, national painting; "it should be bestowed upon the Congress, and display an image of Herzl in the center, surrounded by his colleagues and friends."[68] The painting described by Gronemann never did emerge, and the pictures of Herzl with other Zionists did not seem to be as popular as pictures of the leader by himself. Nevertheless, Herzl's was the most recognized countenance in Zionism, and probably the most recognized in prewar European Jewry.

Indeed, Gronemann's prescription to imitate German and other nationalisms by asserting a greater sensitivity to visual images came to be an increasingly important sphere of Zionist cultural activity. In addition to this revitalized support for the movement's appropriation of tried and true methods of nationalization, Zionist theory and praxis, as articulated in its cultural debates, exhibited the movement's myths and philosophical assumptions which derived from the early nineteenth century. Furthermore, the self-perception of many *Kulturisten* that they were latter-day philosophes reflected the cosmopolitan orientation of the assimilated middle-class Jews filtered through a century of rising nationalism. But the discussions on culture also testified to an understanding of organizational forms, techniques of disseminating nationalist ideas, and an idealism and vigor characteristic of the "non-revolutionary revolt" promoted by the emerging youth movements.

CHAPTER FOUR

ZIONIST HEROES AND NEW MEN

The theory and polemics intended to engender new Jewish myths were accompanied by specific efforts, in the context of the Zionist Congresses, to provide examples of "a New Jewish Man" for Central and West European Jewry. This concept sometimes coincided with the ceremonial presentations of the movement's leadership, especially its idealization of Herzl, and it lionization of its living symbols throughout this period, David Wolffsohn and Max Nordau. In addition, the Zionist sports and gymnastic clubs, which assumed a highly visible role in the Congress days, constituted a significant means of displaying a new Jewish male type; the members of these societies were seen as the heirs of Nordau's credo of *Muskeljudentum* [muscular Jewry]. Exhibitions of the *Turnvereine*, ostensible signs of Zionism's manliness, strength, and vigor, became a greatly anticipated and prideful aspect of the festivities which complemented the Congresses' proceedings. But perhaps the most important "new Jews" perceived through the Zionist Congresses were those growing up in the Jewish settlement of Palestine; this subject will also be dealt with in the final three chapters, in the context of the imagery of the Zionist project. Such images and themes, however, were rooted in the discussions of education in Palestine and displays of the "new Jewish life" in the *Yishuv* at the Congresses. New Zionist Men would arise, above all, from Zionist educational institutions in Palestine. The ultimate product of this process was a new Jewish man bound to his ancestral home of *eretz Israel*, cultivated by a specifically Zionist form of *Bildung*.

To be sure, the advent of Theodor Herzl in political Zionism was accompanied by the creation of a myth that the founder was the embodiment of the New Zionist Man.[1] After Herzl's death in 1904 at the age of forty-four, the significance of his life was presented in increasingly epic proportions within the context of the Zionist Congresses, and through the promotions of the Jewish National Fund.[2] The myth of Herzl was articulated most explicitly in the Seventh Congress (1905), which was the first Congress held after his death, and at the Eleventh Congress (1913), which was the last major Zionist convocation before the First World War. Although the formal ceremonies dedicated to Herzl were few in number, his was a constant presence; rarely would more than a quarter of an hour pass at any of the five post-Herzl Zionist Congresses before 1914 without at least one reference to the founder.

The Seventh Zionist Congress was draped in black. Black bunting trimmed the balcony, and a black band was placed across the right corner of the Zionist flag.[3] Although the proceedings were in large part an extension of the fiery East Africa debate, the tenor of the Congress contributed towards the fashioning of Herzl into an infallible myth. Max Nordau's opening oration envisioned Herzl as a tortured Messiah for Zionism. The leader, Herzl, had so internalized the failings of his flock and the Jewish people as a whole, Nordau admonished, that he could no longer go on living; the Jews' misguided selfishness, lack of discipline, and paucity of true devotion to their people were arrows in the leader's body – but Herzl's indefatigable spirit never faltered.[4] Indeed, the Congress never tolerated serious criticism of the founder.[5] And, to a certain extent, Herzl's death helped exonerate Nordau from his role as a staunch defender of the Uganda scheme, by those who held him in contempt of Zionism for this stance. They were reminded that Nordau was the most important leader next to Herzl, and his trusted friend and colleague.[6]

A portrait of Herzl by Leopold Pilichowski, "a well-known painter of Jewish subjects,"[7] was placed at the head of the Ninth Congress (Hamburg, 1909); this fulfilled the resolution of the Eighth Zionist Congress (the Hague, 1907) to memorialize the leader in such a way.[8] It had commissioned "a beautiful, appropriate picture of our late Herzl, to be placed over the podium during the proceedings of the Congress, so that his gaze, even though it may be subdued, will always, as before, look over us."[9] The next Congress was presented with "a full-length picture of Herzl, his hands in black gloves, holding a walking stick, bowler, and a black cape draped over his arm, while standing on a mount overlooking the Holy Land" [Figure 8]. Max Bodenheimer

8. Portrait of Herzl by Leopold Pilichowsky.

later wrote that even though it showed Herzl as a "powerful" figure, it was a disappointing representation of the leader.

> Why Pilichowsky did not represent Herzl as president of the Congress was inexplicable to me. Whether it was artistically justified to represent him as wearing dark gloves and carrying a cloak over his arm can be left undecided. The explanation that Pilichowsky gave me was that he wished to direct the entire attention of the onlooker to the head, which stands out brilliantly highlighted. But I rather think that the gloves are an artist's trick. Pilichowsky had never seen Herzl. To paint the fine, slender, expressive hands of Herzl from imagination was repugnant to him – hence the gloves.[10]

The gravity with which Bodenheimer evaluated the portrait of Herzl was not unusual for the movement. Another Zionist critic of Pilichowsky's Herzl portrait thought that the accentuation of tokens of "elegance" were "superficialities" that detracted from "the elegance that naturally belonged to Herzl."[11] To be sure, the Congress' portrait of Herzl was a sacred symbol of Zionism which demanded the strictest attention to detail. Whatever the failings of the picture, it was indicative of the primacy of Herzl's image as a cohesive force of the Congress and in the movement overall.[12] Now that he was no longer alive, all the factions of the movement could embrace the image and reputation of Herzl for their various purposes, emphasizing his ability to compromise, and his watchword of toleration. Above all, he embodied the principle that Zionism must include the entirety of Jewry.[13]

After Herzl's death and even in the wake of the Uganda debacle, the Congresses continued to grow; still, the leader's countenance was one of the guiding threads of the movement. The number of participants and spectators increased steadily, while the agenda and length of time for meeting were extended as well. The Eleventh Congress (Vienna, September 1913) was by far the largest prewar Zionist Congress, and to a great number of delegates and observers the most unwieldy and ill-defined of the lot. Especially compared to Basel, where the most recent Congress had been held, Vienna was felt to be "disharmonious with the mood and movement of Zionism" – the normal hectic life of the city overwhelmed the Congress, whereas in Basel the Zionists were always the center of attention. One reporter wrote that in Vienna the notes of the "Merry Widow" drowned out the wail of "Zion's daughter," alluding to the lyric of "Hatikvah." Whatever spirit of unity reigned at the Congress, though, could be traced to the fact that Vienna had been Herzl's city. "It is vast and vague and visionary – it could perhaps produce only such a visionary as Herzl."[14] On the Sunday morning there was no session held, so that the delegates and visitors could join in "A Visit to Herzl's Grave" in the Doebling Cemetery.[15] It would be the most profound Zionist demonstration in Europe before the First World War; the procession and graveside ceremony was perhaps the zenith of the movement's appropriation of its own early history.[16] Such an event was critical in the increasingly positive reception accorded Zionism by Central and West European Jewry, especially through the mediation of the Congresses.

Over 10,000 persons were present, including representatives of Zionist federations from many countries, women's organizations, Jewish gymnastic and sport societies, scouts, university students, Jewish mercantile bodies, and workmen's organizations. Wolffsohn and the Greater Actions Committee led the slow double-file procession. Many wept as they passed before Herzl's tomb. Jewish students' organizations from Vienna laid wreaths on the grave; delegates to the Congress from Palestine and others with standards lowered their banners before the tomb. One delegate wrote that "it was beautiful and touching to the point of magnificence." The graveside visit gave rise to comparing Herzl to the patriach Joseph, insofar as Herzl's remains were awaiting their transplantation to Jewish soil in Palestine.[17] To commemorate the event, there were postcards and pins produced with images of Herzl's grave [Figure 9].[18]

The procession had at its head David Wolffsohn. As Herzl's reluctant successor to the presidency of the Zionist Organization, Wolffsohn had been a subdued yet effective living symbol of the movement. To be sure, doing anything more than "keeping the movement going" during his presidency may have been "beyond him;" this was no small feat, however.[19] There was far from open rejoicing among Zionists about Wolffsohn taking over the reins of the movement upon the leader's death in 1904, in part because he was not overtly a man of *Kultur*. Wolffsohn hailed from the Pale of the Settlement, was self-educated, and had made his fortune as a timber merchant in Cologne. David Vital writes that because of this, he was "looked at askance by a great many of his colleagues who wanted someone of more distinguished intellectual and academic attainment to lead and represent them."[20] The paradox – that most who denigrated Wolffsohn were themselves originally Eastern Jews – was not lost on the movement.[21] Yet his role in sustaining the image of a leader who seemed to be a bridge between the various Jewries and visions of Zionism, while being an acceptable

9. Postcard of Herzl's grave from the Eleventh Zionist Congress (1913).

emissary to the gentile world should not be underestimated. He could be quite eloquent and witty, although he never approached Herzl's mystery or elegance. Wolffsohn too became a venerated bearded icon of Zionism, enshrined on postcards and Jewish National Fund stamps [Figure 10].[22] Moreover, on the dais of the Congress he was truly loyal to Herzl's penchant for finding common ground between the delegates, and he looked the part of a leader; he was calm and manly.[23]

The other great living symbol of Zionism in the prewar years, especially during the Congresses, was Nordau. While Herzl was continually recalled and memorialized at the Eleventh Congress, Nordau's conspicuous absence allowed for an unusually candid assessment by the delegates of what he meant to the movement. Officially, Nordau was absent due to illness. His decision not to attend, however, was probably more due to his feeling of alienation from the movement. After receiving a telegram from Nordau which was harshly critical of the reduction of Zionism's scope and goals since the movement was launched by Herzl, the delegates were pressed to formulate a response; it aroused tempestuous scenes. Apparently Nordau disagreed with the mainstream of the movement regarding the thrust of the Zionist "cultural" project – which he saw as narrow and ineffectual. Yet at the same time there was no denying that he was one of the movement's most significant symbols, who could only be depreciated at the expense of the movement as a whole: Nordau did indeed represent the movement. "A vote of no confidence" for Nordau would be castastrophic for Zionism, a delegate asserted:

> I have heard, from those in the upper echelon of our movement, that Max Nordau is a myth. I believe that Nordau is a symbol of Zionism. For the entire movement, and for the whole Jewish people Nordau is one of the creators of the Zionist idea. Whether that is true or not I will not argue; but it is enough that people believe it. The instant that it is declared that Nordau does not have a place in our organization, then it may be said that contemporary Zionism is not a modification, or a further development from the same ideas which Herzl and Nordau put forward. We have a completely different Zionism if Nordau cannot participate.[24]

Certainly Nordau was no longer the paramount figure that he had been in the earliest years of the movement. Yet his Congress oratory and countenance were among the seminal organizing principles of early Zionism. In particular he was seen as the leading advocate of *Muskeljudentum*, or the creation of a "muscular Jewry." Although Jewish sports clubs and even the term *Muskeljudentum* predate Nordau,

10. David Wolffsohn.

he was the preeminent figure to popularize this idea.[25] The notion that the state of one's body, mind, character, and moral sentiments are interrelated permeated all of his thought.[26] The worship of Nordau as a Zionist hero, in the propaganda and polemics of the movement, was constantly referred to when the new male type was shown or discussed. Quotes from Nordau and allusions to his thought appear repeatedly in this component of the movement.

In one of the most reprinted articles of the movement, "Muskeljudentum" (1900), Nordau wrote that persecution had "destroyed the bodies of the Jews" through the ages. Even Western Jews bore the scars of their former ghettoization: "In the narrowness of the Jewish streets our poor limbs forgot how to move joyfully; in the dimness of our sunless homes our eyes developed a nervous blink . . . But now the oppression is broken. We are allowed the space to, at least physically, live out our lives."[27] He exhorted the Jews to "revive an old tradition," and "let us once again become deep-chested, taut-limbed, steely-eyed men."[28] Gymnastics would help instill "calm confidence in his own strength" for the New Jew. A muscular Jewry would help win Jewish honor; respect and pride in one's Jewishness became a matter of public display through athletics.[29]

As early as the Second Zionist Congress (1898) the idea that a robust national spirit could only reside in a healthy physical body was proclaimed during the *Kulturdebatte*; a Russian delegate pressed the Congress to consider the creation of Jewish-national gymnastic societies as a means of strengthening national consciousness under the rubric of national culture.[30] Although this particular talk made little impression, the subject of Jewish gymnastics as a way of nationalizing the Jews was taken up in earnest by Zionism, and figured prominently in its presentation to Central and West European Jewry.[31] Similar to the Zionist student societies with their nationalistic fetes, as discussed in relation to the *Commers*, the Jewish gymnastic movement borrowed extensively from its German and Slavic national counterparts. Rather than requiring a special effort to create such organizations, the Jewish-national athletic societies that already existed quickly attached themselves to Zionism; to be sure, the publicity accorded the movement and its Congresses helped swell their membership, and inspired the establishment of more groups.[32] Above all, these provided another vehicle for the assertion of Jewish manliness through Zionism.[33] Among their conscious attempts to mitigate the alleged Jewish characteristics that spurred anti-Semitism were their efforts to calm the nerves of Jewish youth through sport, exercise, and hygiene.[34]

This branch of the movement had its own monthly, *Juedische Turnzeitung*, which featured one of Nordau's tracts on "The Significance of Gymnastics to Jewry" in one of its early issues, and it consistently claimed him as a mentor of the movement.[35] A show by local and visiting Zionist gymnastic societies became a great attraction of the Congress days.[36] Most Zionists perceived Jewish gymnastics, along with more traditional forms of aesthetics and education, as a legitimate and prideful component of Zionist *Kultur*.

Predictably, following their motto that "a healthy mind lives in a healthy body" in fashioning the New Zionist Man, the Jewish gymnasts' preeminent concern was with physical fitness.[37] While such ideas could be found in most "German national" student societies, the Zionists quite consciously attempted to distance themselves from the gentile German groups. Their Jewishness was said to be manifested in a variety of nationalism that was anti-chauvinist and more broad-minded in outlook, compared with the self-styled Aryan groups.[38] Similar to the fraternities, with which their membership significantly overlapped, the Zionists' use of Hebrew set them off from the gentiles. They employed Hebrew in exercise drills, and sang Hebrew songs as a sign of their distinctiveness. Jewish gymnasts also liked to show themselves as operating within a Jewish tradition; their heroes were Judah Maccabee and Bar Kochba, and they also adopted the Star of David and Lion of Judah as their symbols. Although Heinrich Heine had mocked Father Jahn (the founder of the German gymnastic societies), the young men of Bar Kochba, the Berlin Jewish gymnastic group, regarded Heine as one of their champions, and maintained that the poet would have admired them for their humanism and cosmopolitanism. After all, they claimed, Heine was a proponent of progress and harmony.[39] Furthermore, they prominently supported the literary and aesthetic dimensions of the movement, and a number of the leaders in this area, including Martin Buber, saw fit to contribute to *Juedische Turnzeitung*.[40] The Jewishness of the Zionist gymnasts did not prevent them, though, from appropriating aspects of the so-called "pure" German gymnastic movement, such as the writings of Father Jahn which they deemed useful. Indeed, the Jewish gymnast's symbiosis of *Deutschtum*, *Judentum*, and liberalism, mixing exercises with Heine's jabs at the vaingloriousness of German nationalism, was a critical transmitter of Zionist national culture especially to the Jews of Central Europe.

Ironically, Nordau was not a witness to the most grand display to date – and the most grand before the State of Israel would be established – of *Muskeljudentum*. An immense celebration and gymnastic exhibition took place the afternoon of the memorial service for

Herzl at the Eleventh Congress in 1913, on the grounds of the Vienna football club. This was probably the largest non-religious prewar gathering of Jews in Central and Western Europe. Over 25,000 spectators filled the stands, which were decorated with banners showing Stars of David and menorahs, and blue and white Zionist flags; more than 2,000 Jewish performers participated. An Austrian military band played "Hatikvah" as the student groups filed in. With the crowd's enthusiasm at a fever pitch, the Chairman of the Committee for Jewish Gymnasts from Berlin gave a short welcoming address "expressing his pleasure at being able to afford the Jewish and non-Jewish world a demonstration of gymnastic and athletic skills." At the conclusion, spectators threw flowers to the athletes.[41] The *Turnverein* Chairman was also invited to the evening session of the Congress; he thanked the delegates for their efforts, and recited the gymnasts' motto: "We fight for Judah's honor/ Full strength in youth/ So when we reach manhood/ Still fighting ten times better."[42]

The Jewish gymnasts implicitly showed that Europe could serve as a training ground for a new type of Jew. Yet the complete transformation of the Jewish people, according to Zionist ideology, could only take place in Palestine. The first cells of "a modern natural Jew" were said to be brought to life in Palestine; it was seen as "a focal point of immeasurable moral value for the entire Diaspora."[43] Despite their best intentions in the movement's first few years, the Zionists were simply not yet in a position to effect a substantial change in the cultural life of Jewish Palestine. Although interest in the Jewish presence there was intensified in this period, Zionist cultural work did not make significant headway until a few years after Herzl's death. In the context of the Congresses, Western Zionists were in large part connected to the formation of the New Man in Palestine through discussions of the institutions that would propagate this type. Therefore, the concept of the New Man was inextricably linked to the subject of Jewish national education in Palestine. These discussions usually centered on the strengthening of the existing non-religious Jewish schools, especially those in the colonies; sponsorship of the Bezalel Art Institute and the Jewish National Library in Jerusalem; support for the Hebrew (later Herzl or Herzliya) Gymnasium in Tel Aviv; and agitation for a Jewish university. These were all seen as crucial institutions which would foster a new Jewish type. The most "pure" Zionists would be those who had been trained in the movement's own educational institutions.

At first, the Zionist efforts at influencing Jewish cultural life in Palestine, and thereby shaping the New Man, meant providing funds for textbooks, and partially funding the institutions which were concerned with imparting a Jewish national education.[44] The movement was chiefly interested in making modern Hebrew the language of tuition in Palestine; Zionist enthusiasm for this aspect of its project reached its peak during the so-called "Language War," which occurred at the close of the period under discussion.[45] Such activities were tied directly to the polemics on the Hebrew revival; indeed, this was portrayed as its very heart.[46] As early as the First Zionist Congress in 1897, specific forms of education in Palestine were deemed necessary progenitors of the New Jew; these closely reflected the cultural predispositions of Zionism's constituency in Central and Western Europe.[47]

It is not surprising that in Zionist polemics, an ideal Zionist man would be one educated at a Zionist university. It is true that Jews had always studied, and even distinguished themselves in European secular education once they gained admission. But the notion that an ideal Jew was one educated in secular and scientific subjects, in an environment which was both modern and predominantly Jewish, was a unique contribution of Zionism. The Jewish university would emerge as a chief institution designed to represent and develop the new Zionist man; to most Western Zionists, universities implicitly trained men for national liberation.[48] Hence, a Jewish university would pave the way for the national liberation of the Jews.

At the First Congress, in addition to the speeches linking the potential for Jews to develop their own autonomous culture to the acquisition of a national homeland, an explicit plea was voiced by Professor Hermann Schapira of Heidelberg for the creation of a Jewish national university in Palestine. The notion that a university should be the cornerstone of a revived Jewish polity remained prominent in Zionism; it would be championed by several figures, but the actual project leading to the foundation of the Hebrew University in Jerusalem derived from the efforts of Chaim Weizmann and Berthold Feiwel's *juedische Hochschulebureau*.[49] Still, several years earlier Schapira proposed an institution of higher learning which spanned religious and secular realms; it would comprise schools of theology, theoretical sciences, and technological and agricultural fields. Furthermore, it was to serve as the midpoint of the religious, moral, and spiritual development of Jewish youth. "What we lack most of all," said Schapira, "is a center for our culture; we require the creation of such a center for the working out of all the problems of culture encountered by Jews."[50]

The actual foundation-stone for a Jewish university in Palestine would not be laid until the interwar years; still, the pronouncements that the establishment of a Jewish university was one of the principal objectives of Zionism, and notice that the project was indeed underway produced stirring moments in the Congresses. At the Fifth Zionist Congress Chaim Weizmann elaborated his own proposals for a Jewish university, and from that point reportage about the progress of this plan was firmly entrenched and highlighted as part of the Zionist discourse.[51] The next instance when news of the university project proved to be a source of great inspiration for Zionists was at the Eleventh Congress (1913). Menahem Ussischkin, perhaps the greatest Zionist orator at that Congress announced that a substantial sum had been donated for "the crown of our cultural work," a Jewish university. "It has been 2,500 years since the destruction of the First Temple on Mount Moriah," he reminded the delegates – which prompted the body to rise *en masse*. "And today we stand, ready to breathe life into a courageous plan. Let us build a temple of culture and knowledge on Mount Zion."[52]

Weizmann elaborated on Ussischkin's call; he proposed a Temple to *Bildung*, quoting from Fichte: "What man of noble thought would not, through deed or idea, wish to scatter seeds, eternally progressing toward the perfection of his race? These are something new, that have never before existed, cast into time – which will remain in time – as an unlimited source of new creations."[53] Ussischkin and Weizmann urged the construction of "a new holy place" enshrining "true knowledge and true science."[54] Heinrich Loewe placed the matter in a secularized context which had been obvious to most Zionists from the outset of the movement: "Universities are the birthplace of culture and *Bildung*: the European states have understood their value. Now Central Europe is celebrating the hundredth anniversary of the War of Liberation, in which the universities played such an important role. From where was the liberation of Prussia led? From the founding of the University of Berlin!"[55] The Congress expressed overwhelming jubilation at the nearly unanimous decision to go ahead with the university project.[56] The rapture over the university was perhaps the great summary of Zionist culture and, to a large extent, the Zionist movement before 1914. As Herzl had wished to make use of the "ribbons and fantasies" he saw so deftly used by Bismarck in order to animate the Jewish nation, Weizmann and Loewe saw their Jewish nationalism through the prism of German nationalism of the War of Liberation. Herzl had shared their conviction, from this era, that nationalism need not be exclusive and chauvinistic – but could lead to brotherly bonds with the men of other nations, and the flowering of culture and knowledge.

A Zionist institution which ostensibly realized the movement's goal of producing New Men in the prewar years was the Hebrew *Gymnasium*; by 1914 it was the tangible pinnacle of Zionist achievement in Palestine.[57] The inspiration for the *Gymnasium*, too, emanated from early nineteenth-century German national ideals. It stood at the forefront of the effort to nationalize Jewish education in Palestine in Zionism's presentation to European Jewry. A *Gymnasium* was a quintessential bourgeois Central European symbol; it was an obligatory crucible of middle-class virtues, a well-rounded education, and respectability. Therefore it became a preeminent locus for the acculturation of *Bildung* in an ideal Zionist world. Perhaps due to the spectacular nature of the founding of the Hebrew University in Jerusalem between the wars, the place of the Hebrew *Gymnasium* in the discourse of early Zionism seems to be undervalued. In the last three Congresses before the First World War, and in the images and texts of the movement from 1907 to 1914, the *Gymnasium* was shown as one of the most glorious manifestations of Zionist culture. To most Zionists who visited or reported on Jewish Palestine, nothing was more impressive than the children being turned into "national Jews" at the *Gymnasium*.

The subject of Zionist sponsorship for the Jaffa *Gymnasium* was introduced at the Eighth Congress (1907) by one of the more colorful personalities in the movement, Shmarya Levin, who delivered a long address summarizing the state of "National Education in Palestine." The speaker was most adept at "making the few green spots in Zion look like the beginnings of great forests;" his analysis made a strong impact on the delegates.[58] It was time, Levin asserted, to commence serious work if Zionists wanted to institute an educational system based on the ideals of the movement. Repeating a point that had been raised at earlier Congresses, the speaker related that numerous countries and sects had significant influence on the educational life of Jews in Palestine; "there were not enough Jewish schools, and they were generally not as good as some of the missionary schools. Even at the American University in Beirut, which did not discriminate on the basis of nationality or religion, all students were required to attend church twice daily; and one could predict that the religious obligations were more stringent at the denominational institutions." Zionists owed a special debt to the Jewish youth of Palestine, Levin asserted: "many who had grown up in the Jewish colonies felt compelled to leave in order to complete their education. How could one expect the youth to stay, with an incomplete and deficient educational system?"[59]

Jewish schools, where the main language of tuition was Hebrew, existed in the colonies; but obstacles to the further adoption of Hebrew were present even there, Levin explained. The New Man required fluency and acculturation in the old/new language, modern Hebrew. Most likely, the language spoken in the pupils' homes was something other than Hebrew, probably Yiddish, Russian, Arabic, or Ladino. Multi-lingualism, the speaker maintained, was the province of the wealthy; among the masses – from which the immigrants invariably hailed – only one language must prevail; and the only spot on earth which could nourish Hebrew as a living language was Palestine. Furthermore, due to the composition of Jewish Palestine – a population that now included Yemenite, Ashkenazic, and Sephardic Jews – a common tongue was necessary to unify the children. New Men could not exist in isolation, and it would be pointless if pre-Zionist divisions were allowed to continue; if Hebrew was not pressed, English or French might eventually serve that function. Indeed, vastly different conditions ruled in the various systems and individual schools. In the schools run by the *Hilfsverein der deutschen Juden*, for example, more Hebrew than German was used; in the Rothschild schools, the students studied English twenty hours a week, versus ten of Hebrew. Levin found their English to be terrible, but their Hebrew exemplary. At the schools sponsored by the *Alliance Israélite Universelle*, the extent of Hebrew use and quality was dependent on the teachers; otherwise French was the main language.[60]

On the other hand, continued Levin, the schools supported by the Odessa Committee of the *Chovevei Zion* provided the model which the other schools should follow. The main school at that time was the *Bet HaSefer Lebanoth* in Jaffa, for approximately three hundred Jewish girls. To Levin, it was not extraordinary just to hear Hebrew spoken – he had not anticipated the degree to which it was used, and had developed. "I cannot say that the school is complete," Levin admitted. "But in any case, we have set a solid course." "A healthy orientation in Palestine need not be overtly national, in the sense that one might say that such was a prerequisite in America, Russia, or Germany. In Palestine one only had to be natural; thus, the task of the teachers was much lighter." In addition to accomplishing an automatic nationalization of the Jewish students, the cultivation of schools along the lines of the Odessa Committee's example would supposedly prevent the Arabs in Palestine from becoming anti-Semitic. In Levin's view, the Jews would be wise to open their schools to the native Arabs; this supposedly afforded physical and spiritual protection for the New Men. He reasoned that because Hebrew was closer to Arabic than French, the Arabs would be attracted to the Hebrew schools. Insofar as these schools were dominated by Jews and had their roots in Jewish culture, it would not be possible for the Arabs to assimilate anti-Semitic notions.[61] Despite Levin's willingness to acknowledge the existence of the native Arabs, he did not reach the same conclusions of some Zionist writers on the issue, who contended that the only way for the New Jews to survive in Palestine was to learn Arabic as their second language.[62] At the next Congress (1907), Moses Gaster expressed a hope that the burgeoning culture of the *Yishuv* should draw on the attainments of Islamic, as well as Western civilization, in the building of a new society.[63] This, however, was a lonely voice.

There was a movement afoot, Levin continued, on the part of parents in Palestine who "were not satisfied with the education available to their children." They wanted a way for their children to be educated and remain in the country; they desired "an academic secondary school [*Mittleschule*]. To this end, almost nothing had been attempted until only quite recently." Now, "we have the founding of a *Gymnasium*," formally inaugurated in the fall of 1906. Levin confessed that when he first heard the idea, he was very skeptical – but his visit to Palestine proved the contrary. His fears that the project was a result of presumptuousness or pious delusions were allayed when he sensed the genuinely unselfish motives of the administrators. A truly good school could be nurtured in Jaffa, Levin asserted, "which would allow the parents not to forsake the country by sending their children abroad, and portended even greater possibilities for Palestine." Negating his earlier reservations, Levin concluded that "it was the appropriate moment for the establishment of at least one such institution."[64] Even the *Mizrahi* were moved to support the *Gymnasium* with a sizeable donation for each of its first three years.[65] The coeducational *Gymnasium* in Jaffa, located in the new Jewish quarter of Tel Aviv (named after the Hebrew title of Theodor Herzl's *Altneuland*), was referred to as the Hebrew *Gymnasium* [*ha-Gymnasia ha-Ivrit*, in Hebrew], and later as the Theodor Herzl or Herzliya *Gymnasium*. Near the end of the Eighth Congress (1907), Jacob Moser of Bradford, England, contributed a tremendous sum (by Zionist standards) towards a new building for the Hebrew *Gymnasium* in Jaffa, with the condition that the school should be named after Theodor Herzl. This move stimulated great enthusiasm and numerous pledges of financial support.[66]

Levin also praised the work of the Bezalel Art Institute in Jerusalem, and introduced its founder, sculptor Boris Schatz, which ignited a storm of applause. Bezalel would also be acclaimed as a monumental institution in which a new Jewish type was being prepared. Perhaps no other aspect of the Zionist vision so profoundly and directly contradicted the anti-Semitic myth that Jews were unproductive, and incapable of skilled, prideful manual labor. "The Society for the Establishment of Jewish Cottage Industries and Handicrafts in Palestine," commonly referred to as "Bezalel" had been described in an earlier speech at the Seventh Congress as having already made a colossal influence on the economic life and morale of Palestinian Jewry.[67] Bezalel was officially founded in 1906, but the project of Boris Schatz was underway, at least in part, by 1904. Bezalel was an ultraconservative arts and crafts school, inspired by the theories of Walter Crane and John Ruskin, which intended to produce an artist-craftsman type that had long been pushed to the margins of industrial society. The main task of the institute was to train workers and thus activate a nucleus for a community of artisans in Jerusalem. It constituted a specific romantic vision of Jewish manual labor, and a Jewish working class in a reborn Zion. In the eight years from its inception to the First World War, Bezalel played a magnanimous role in providing a visual dimension to Zionism for European Jewry.[68]

It would become a routine part of the Congresses to extol the virtues of the Bezalel Institute, despite the fact that it repeatedly came close to bankruptcy and that it encountered fierce enmity in Jerusalem from the orthodox inhabitants.[69] Only rarely would allusions to its limitations or problems with Schatz or Bezalel be brought to the attention of Congress delegates.[70] In the words of Otto Warburg (who succeeded David Wolffsohn as the president of the World Zionist Organization) Bezalel was part of "a systematic founding and building up" of institutions which comprised "the creation of a center of Jewish culture in Palestine."[71] Bezalel also spawned the nascent national museum, which comprised artistic, archaeological, and natural-historical sections.

The Eighth Congress witnessed a well-attended Shabbat afternoon address by Schatz. The speaker "described the objects of the school, which by means of the promotion of art industries among the Jewish population in Palestine, gave them an opportunity of earning a livelihood, and at the same time raised them morally and economically." By the midpoint of its three-year probationary period, Schatz insisted that Bezalel was on a sound footing, "though several investigations would have to be conducted in order that the foundations might be firmly laid and the future line of work clearly defined." Carpet weaving and stone carving were said to be the most profitable parts of the enterprise, and the instructional division "was very important for the numerous native children whose future it assured." After Schatz thanked the audience and the members of the Palestine committee, "a number of speakers from various countries spoke in support of the school." This presentation complemented an exhibition of Jewish art, including a display of Bezalel products, that was open throughout the Congress.[72] A more spectacular Bezalel exhibition and sale accompanied the Ninth Congress.[73] The testimony and memoirs of Zionists such as Moses Gaster and Chaim Weizmann indicate that Schatz achieved his desired effect: it appeared that a new, native Jewish art form was being cultivated in Palestine, through an institution directly related to the Zionist Organization and the mechanisms of the Congress.[74] The New Man claimed and provided evidence of possession of a new aesthetic.

Even though Jewish education in Palestine was in an embryonic stage, at best, Levin set up a mythical dichotomy at his speech to the Seventh Congress. World Jewry could be divided into two categories, Levin maintained: there were "cash Jews" [*bare Juden*] and "credit Jews [*Wechseljuden*]. The latter are "credit Jews, in the sense that they do not know if in two or three generations there will still be Jews," implying that they were not actively concerning themselves with the survival of Jews as Jews. Credit Jews exist throughout the world; pure Jews exist only in Palestine." He left the delegates with the observation that "everything we plant in Palestine grows and flourishes there as in no other land."[75]

The Tenth Congress in 1911 was the setting for a view of the new Jewish man through a radically different medium: film. In 1909, during the Ninth Congress there was a well-received slide presentation by Heinrich Loewe, emphasizing the achievements of the Jewish National Fund in Palestine.[76] The film had been shot by Murray Rosenberg of London, during his journey to Palestine; it was dedicated to the memory of Herzl. A publicity announcement (when it was shown at the next Congress) promised the spectators a "Sensational!" and "Powerful!" show which was simultaneously an "historic document," and the "first product of the most advanced technology" in the service of Zionism.[77] For the first showing, a 1200-seat theater was filled to capacity. After seeing scenes of the Pyramids and the Sphinx, and a Cairo bazaar, the locale shifted to Palestine. The first, and longest segment displaying Jewish life in Palestine was of the Bezalel Institute in Jerusalem, to which the action came back several times. The moving pictures were not very different from the still photographs of the workrooms and studios that were widely disseminated by that time. Shots of the Wailing Wall and the Old City were difficult to distinguish, perhaps due to insufficient lighting and general commotion which the photographer could not control. But the New Jewish Man was not entirely absent, or restricted to the confines of Bezalel. Stonemasons hewing the stones for the *Technikum* (the Jewish technical institute), laborers draining a marsh, building roads, and plowing fields were intended to inspire the crowd with examples of Jews engaged in manual labor. It is not clear, however, if the film achieved its desired effect of attaining "the highest propaganda value."[78] Nevertheless, the overall impact of the Palestine displays at the Tenth Congress left some with the feeling of "living in the Land of Israel for a week."[79]

There are few, if any references to the Rosenberg film in delegates' memoirs. Possibly, the unavoidable presence of many non-Jews in the majority of scenes, especially Arabs (and some Turks), did not quite meld with the pictures with which they were familiar; New Men lose their power when they are lost in a crowd. In addition, Palestine appeared less than aesthetically breathtaking. At any rate, the organizers decided to show it again for the Eleventh Congress, after which they received several invitations to present it throughout Europe. Whatever the show's imperfections, there was a clear sense among the delegates that "seeing" the work in progress sparked their desire to press on with the work of building up a Hebrew culture in Palestine, peopled by new Jewish men.[80]

The focus on the human material of Palestine as Hebraized *gebildete Menschen* did not receive a totally unqualified sanction during the Congress days. Predictably, the new Zionist man was not Jewish enough for the orthodox in the movement, and they struggled to make the institutions of Palestine, especially the *Gymnasium*, more attuned to orthodoxy.[81] Eventually the orthodox founded their own secondary school in Palestine, the *Tachkemoni-Schule*. There was also weighty criticism of the attempt to activate this vision from other quarters: some admonished the movement for emphasizing intellectualism and *Kultur* in the *Yishuv*.[82] Such an argument ran that the Zionist Movement would be wiser to support more practical professional training – such as in agronomy, medicine, and engineering – to foster self-sufficiency.[83] Perhaps the most devastating critique of the stress on Hebrew and cultural institutions for Palestinian Jewry came from Arthur Ruppin, the head of the Palestine Development Company. What the colonists needed above all, Ruppin declared, was "more neighbors," that is, more Jewish colonists, and land for the new colonies with colonists to settle it.[84] A more thoroughly planned, centralized, far-sighted, and labor-oriented view should take precedence over the requirements of a cultural and linguistic center. Despite these objections, which signaled a complicated reality underlying the attempted Jewish regeneration, overall the Congresses succeeded in announcing the arrival of new Jewish types – which would be elaborated and painstakingly visualized and personalized by the Zionist Movement. It was a crucial part of the effort of building up Jewish Palestine, in image and reality; the *Yishuv* seemed to be in the process of becoming more normal and idyllic.

CHAPTER FIVE

ART AND ZIONIST POPULAR CULTURE

Zionism was born into a highly visual age, when advances in graphic technology, coupled with the rise of the popular press made possible a profusion of photographic and artistic representations.[1] The development of photography coincided with the increasing prevalence of cartoon and caricature; this extended visualized politics into the personal realm at an unprecedented level. At least in urban populations, great masses of people could have access to similar depictions of places, policies, and personalities – which ranged from realistic photographs to images exaggerated toward the beautiful or grotesque.[2] Even if we assume that Jews tended to be more literate than their surrounding populations, it is still crucial to examine not only what European Jews read and heard about Zionism, but also what they saw as Zionism.[3]

Artistic images in Zionist popular culture assisted in establishing paradigms for Western Jewish perceptions of the Zionist project. Most important, these construed a mythical Palestinian homeland and national landscape in the mind of European Jewry; it provided the movement with images of recognizable and admirable leaders, and recast traditional Jewish images in a national context, as an alternative or supplement to those of the familiar European nationalist ideologies.

Herzl had held and practised very firm ideas about the role of myths and symbols in Zionism, and he recognized the need for an aesthetic dimension to the novel mass movement he wished to forge. "There is a wall," he wrote in June 1895, "namely, the demoralization of the Jews. I know that beyond it lies freedom and greatness."[4] For Herzl, art and aesthetics would be a vehicle for the Jewish acculturation of

11. Postcard and delegate-card from the First Zionist Congress (1897), drawn by Carl Pollak and designed by Heinrich York-Steiner.

national ideals, using "the simple and moving form of symbols" as means to breach that wall.[5] Herzl believed it crucial to "think in images," because people were moved largely by "imponderables, such as music and pictures." But this was not just to agitate the unwashed masses – Herzl wished to facilitate the processes by which middle-class people, such as himself, found exhilaration in Wagnerian opera.[6] Concurrently, he recognized the tremendous efficacy of traditional Jewish symbols that were held in common by all Jews – that "dreams, songs, and fantasies" which were "floating in the air" must be harnessed to practical politics.[7] "In all of this," Herzl wrote, prescribing a Jewish national festival with an elaborate backdrop and costumes, "I am still the dramatist;" art was to be part of the stage setting for the theater of politics he hoped would internally transform the Jewish world.[8]

The first products of political Zionism that used Jewish art to arouse Zionist sentiments were the postcards, delegates' and visitors' cards designed for the First Zionist Congress [Figure 11].[9] The quality of this work is amateurish; indeed, they were drawn by a university student, Carl Pollak, who helped run the daily operations of the Zionist office in Vienna.[10] The poor grade of the pictures, however, did not seem to diminish the delegates' enthusiasm in seeing and possessing their first

Jewish national artifacts. The London *Jewish Chronicle* made special note of the appearance of the Congress postcard, and included a reproduction of it in its report. At the final session, the concluding scenes included "a brisk sale of commemorative postcards."[11]

Pollak's design has two framed narrow images at the ends, with the heading "Zionisten-Congress 1897" and a Star of David in the center. Beneath is the Hebrew proclamation: "Who will bring from Zion the redemption of Israel?"[12] The left scene shows three pious Jewish men, and one woman praying at the Wailing Wall in Jerusalem. The right panel has a bearded man in peasant garb, dropping seed out of his hand. This duality of religious, traditional Jews, and pioneer, peasant-farmer Jews persisted as the most frequently employed generic Zionist images, often within the same medium. Thus the proclamation infers that both the religious Jews at the Wall and the farmer will be the vehicles of redemption. The farmer had little significance in the historical memory of Western Jews, but it portended a future order where true emancipation would be attained through the Jews' labor on their own soil. This was an appropriate illustration for nearly every variety of Zionist thought at that time. Each faction of the movement shared the notion that the regeneration of the Jews could only be attained "by the sweat of their brow," or physical labor tied to agriculture or crafts.[13]

In addition to these pictures, the delegates also brought home postcards of the *Stadtcasino*, a lapel pin in the shape of the Lion and Star of David (which was on the flag), and a gold pin surrounded by a blue and white ribbon.[14] Most Zionist Congresses issued pins, ribbons, or medals; all had distinctive postcards. The medal for the First Congress had a round medallion mounted in the center of a gold Star of David. It depicted a biblical-type scene with a prominent female figure, "the embodiment of the Jewish ideal, Zionism." She was pointing the way to the Promised Land for a wandering Jewish family. Crafted by Herzl's friend, the Viennese sculptor Friedrich Beer, this image was also used as a commemorative medal for the Second Congress. Prior to that Congress, *Die Welt* reproduced a photograph of the medal and explained the symbolism in great detail.[15]

Similar to Germania, Britannia, and Marianne, this female symbol reappeared in Zionist postcards – usually with pictures of Theodor Herzl, after Herzl's death in 1904, as a bridge between the founder and the Jews' march to Zion [Figure 12].[16] A more distinct female image was featured in the postcard for the Sixth Congress (1903) rising out of the ground before a farmer, accompanied by the Biblical injunction: "Those who sow in tears will reap in joy" [Figure 13].[17] The generic female symbol, as an agent of change from the wretched Jewish past to the happy, healthy future, did not persist past 1914 as a Zionist motif, possibly due to its lack of grounding in Jewish mythology. While she existed, though, she was always respectably clad, and simply showing the way Eastward; "Zion" was no close relation to some of the aggressive Mariannes.

The official postcard from the Second Zionist Congress (1898), drawn by Menahem Okin, repeated the main representations of praying Jews at the Wailing Wall and an agricultural scene [Figure 14].[18] A Star of David enclosing a Lion of Judah is near the center, and a quote from Ezekiel, in large Hebrew characters, occupies the bottom right corner: "Behold: I will take the Children from amongst the nations and bring them to their land."[19] Presumably to symbolize the universal relevance of Zionism, a Moorish arch, classical column, and a nun (reading the bible) are included. Erwin Rosenberger, a young delegate to the Congress who also helped staff the Zionist Organization office in Vienna, believed that around the traditional Jews at the Wailing Wall, the pictures displayed "the new life burgeoning out of the ruins – workers in the field, a man sowing seed who vaguely resembled Herzl, dancing children, peacefully grazing cattle and, in the background . . . a hill . . . intended to suggest Mount Zion."[20] Reinforcing the image from the First Congress postcard, the top illustration showed "Jewish" Palestine in a pastoral, Central European, pre-industrial setting. The symbol of the sun's rays emanating from the horizon was meant to intimate the divine presence in the land which was called forth by the Jews' return. Zionism was not, in its polemics, an anti-modern movement; nonetheless, this did not prevent Zionists from expressing their ideals with such romantic imagery.[21]

The scenes of Jewish farmers, working in open sunlight on a vast expanse were a conspicuous attempt to parry the stereotype of Jews as an innately urban people, averse to nature and agricultural pursuits.[22] Yet this was more than a defensive posture: it idealized Zionism's emphasis on the development of a "normal," agrarian-based society. It was not, however, a complete retreat into a utopian future: it is crucial that this shared the medium with mourning or praying Jews in a somewhat more realistic setting. In this way, it recognized religious Jewry as a potential mass of followers for Zionism. But at the

12. Herzl postcard, with female "Zion," by S. Rovkhomovsky.

13. Postcard from the Sixth Zionist Congress (1903).

14. Postcard from the Second Zionist Congress (1898), by Menahem Okin.

same time it presented orthodoxy as a condition of the past, to be transcended to a new ideal, which was illustrated in the contrasting scene. It was also possible that in this utopia, the worlds of secular and religious Jews could peacefully and fruitfully coexist. The national landscape visualized for the Jews of Europe almost always contained Jews farming and praying.

After the Second Zionist Congress, reproductions of a number of pen and ink drawings by Menahem Okin appeared in *Die Welt*.[23] The very fact that these were published coincided with the Zionists' contention that they had initiated a new historical epoch, and that its principals deserved to be immortalized simultaneously with the Congress. Okin also contributed to the institutionalized memory of the event by painting a scene from the opening ceremony of Theodor Herzl shaking hands with Max Nordau. This was distributed to Zionist reading rooms as a frameable picture, and made into a postcard.[24] It shows the leaders surrounded by the delegates, whose eyes are transfixed on them. All of the men are clad in the obligatory white tie, starched shirt, and black formal wear, highlighting the quintessentially bourgeois and respectable tenor of the Congress. The painting was intended to be the equivalent of European and American state-founding portraits, but its low artistic value made it less popular than other pictures shortly after it was introduced. Probably the most

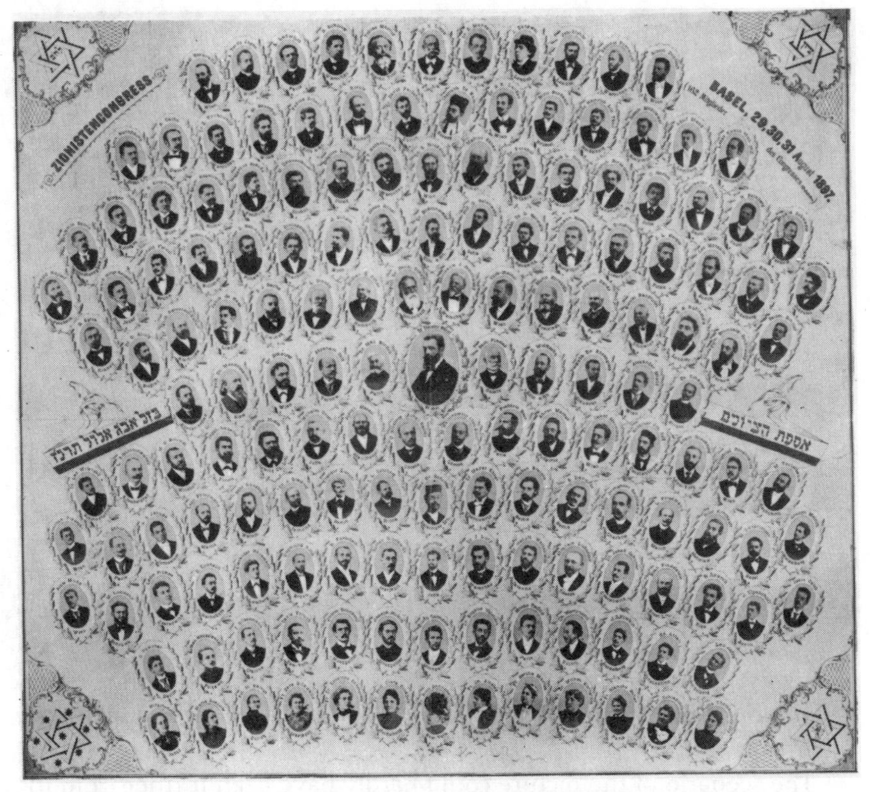

15. Group portrait of the First Zionist Congress.

popular group representation from the earliest years of Zionism was the portrait of participants in the First Zionist Congress, done in cameos, with an enlarged Herzl in the center [Figure 15].[25]

The commemorative postcard from the Third Zionist Congress (1899) is notable because it combines, in a single scene, motifs from the formerly distinct pictures [Figure 16]. Okin's drawing shows an old, white-bearded, *talit*-clad man, his pious wife in back of him, with his arms outstretched. He is blessing two pioneer-farmers, one of whom has his arm around his youthful son.[26] This is a clear portrayal of unanimity between generations in the Zionist vision; it was a means of mitigating the real-life revolts of Jewish youth. A trend that would continue, especially in drawings and etchings of Jewish Palestine, is the depiction of religious Jews belonging to the older generation. It is a manifestation of what may be termed a division of labor in the imagery of early Zionism: the elderly do the praying, the youth, the

16. Entrance card from the Third Zionist Congress (1899) by Menahem Okin.

plowing. Young, religious Jews appeared only rarely in Zionist representations; religious Jews usually recalled sages or grandfatherly figures.

The scenario of the picture could hardly have been further from the Jewish-Palestinian reality. An accommodation of sorts between orthodox Jews and Zionist immigrants did not occur until after the period under consideration, when Abraham Isaac Kook assumed the post of chief rabbi to the Ashkenazi Jews of Jerusalem in 1919.[27] At the very least, such scenes obfuscated the orthodox Jews' vehement opposition to the Zionist project. Contrary to the bitter enmity aroused by Zionism in religious quarters, the images represented a harmonious totality encompassing past and future, youth and old age, and secular and religious Jewry.

The youth/old-age dichotomy is again employed for the official picture of the Fourth Zionist Congress (1900), but in this case the "exilic" state of the elderly is emphasized [Figure 17]. Recalling the notion of the wandering Jew, a small bundle and a cane lie on the ground near the central figure, who wears a *shtraimel* (Chasidic fur hat); behind him is a trail of *shtetl* Jews. Directly in back of him is a weary or despondent woman, with her head resting on her hand. The counter image to the right is a group of small, indistinct darkish figures

17. Postcard from the Fourth Zionist Congress (1899).

placing bushel baskets into a cart; a tropical tree is in the background, before what appears to be the walls of the Old City of Jerusalem. Mediating between these scenes is a hazily drawn woman, "Zion," in a flowing white robe and angel's wings, with a Star of David as her halo, hovering above the Eastern Jews. She points to the Palestinian harvest scene, directing the old Jews to the new Jewish society.

The souvenir postcard of the Fifth Zionist Congress (1901) was a qualitative leap from its predecessors; it introduced E. M. Lilien as a leading artist in the Zionist camp [Figure 18]. Up to this point, the choice of pictures to be used seems to have been made in the Vienna office by the university students with the guidance of Herzl.[28] Before the Congress, *Die Welt* had lavishly praised the books *Juda* and *Lieder des Ghetto*, poetry anthologies that were illustrated by Lilien. Zionists enthusiastically greeted these works that showed previously disparaged Jewish characteristics and characters in a proudly defiant fashion.[29] Illustrations from *Juda* and *Lieder des Ghetto* were used repeatedly in Zionist promotions; indeed, Lilien's work constituted a significant share of Zionist popular culture. Israel Zangwill praised the accessibility of Lilien's pictures, noting that "by contributing not to galleries but to books, magazines, and bookplates, [he] has brought art nearer to everyday life. Restricting himself to black and white he has minimised

18. Postcard from the Fifth Zionist Congress.

the difference between his original touch and its mechanical reproduction." Hence, for Zangwill, a writer who geared his novels to the Jewish masses of London's East End, "a Lilien postcard was more valuable than many a pretentious oil painting." Zangwill was typical among Zionists, in becoming acquainted and impressed with Lilien through his Congress postcard.[30]

Lilien was an exemplar of the *Jugendstil* or art nouveau style, which was frequently used in Zionist media; this was predictable, considering the vogue of art nouveau in Central Europe at this time.[31] Surrounded by a floral pattern, Lilien's pen and ink drawing recalls the dichotomies of youth and old age, exile and redemption, the Diaspora and Palestine. Similar to the now customary depictions, the figure on the left bottom corner is an old, stooped, white-bearded Jew, leaning on his cane; the man is encircled by barbed wire – a further example of his bondage. Above him, standing sturdy and upright, is a male angel with huge finely feathered wings, who wears a large Star of David on the front of his white robe. The angel's right hand grasps the shoulder of the old man; his left hand points to the image on the right: against the background of a radiant sun, a man furrows a field behind a team of oxen. Disproportionately large stalks of wheat are in the right corner, below the man and oxen. The Hebrew inscription beneath the picture, flanked by a Star of David is: "Let our eyes witness Your

Loving return to Zion;" it is a verse from the *Amidah*, a central prayer in Jewish liturgy.[32] This became one of the most reproduced Zionist works, adorning, for example, the Jewish National Fund's appeal pamphlets for the Purim and Chanukah holidays.[33]

Unlike his forerunners, Lilien was a formidable member of the Zionist Organization. The Zionists' admiration of Lilien's work was undoubtedly influenced by the respect accorded the artist. Lilien embodied a strange blend of *fin-de siècle* anti-types: his art resembled that of Aubrey Beardsley, whom most Zionists would classify as a model of degeneracy, but Lilien's goal was Jewish national health and regeneration.[34] Further, he came from Galicia, and he emerged as an apparently wholesome product of that environment – he seemed to be a model anti-type of the stereotypical pale, sickly, unkempt, unaesthetic Eastern Jew – while maintaining a commitment to many elements of traditional Judaism.[35] The fact that Lilien primarily spoke Yiddish and seemed to remain "a Jew through and through" lent integrity to his overtly sentimental drawings.[36]

Ten of Lilien's works were featured together with the works of Josef Israels, Jehuda Epstein, Alfred Nossig, Hermann Struck, and Lesser Ury, among others, in an exhibition concurrent with the Fifth Congress held in the Congress hall.[37] The First Zionist Congress had hung portraits of proto-Zionists in the hallway of the Basel *Stadtcasino*, but this exhibition of Jewish art, under the auspices of the Zionist Movement, was clearly the first time that the works of Jewish artists were being presented in a Jewish national context in Central Europe.[38] At the very least, most delegates probably shared the impression of Weizmann (commenting on a similar show at the Eighth Congress in 1907), that the exhibition was "modest but promising" and it portended "the beginnings of a national art."[39] These and other shows during the Congresses were open to the public, and they usually ran several days prior to or after the Congress dates.

The exhibition was marginal, in a sense, but it was a prominent manifestation of Zionist ideals upon which nearly every Zionist could agree. The show stressed biblical heroism, and the appearance of such works affirmed Jewry's place as a contributor to European high culture. Complementing the exhibition, Martin Buber delivered a long speech on "Jewish Art."[40] Although he began with a note of confrontation by challenging Max Nordau, it is likely that the delegates found Buber's speech more boring than controversial.[41] The talk focused on the plastic arts, but included developments in Jewish literature and music, within the framework of the speaker's theory of Jewish national regeneration.[42] Exemplifying his stress on the leading role of youth in Zionism, Buber introduced Lilien as one of the younger artists, but the most self-consciously Jewish of the group; this ignited a tremendous ovation by the delegates.[43] The tribute to Lilien was part of Buber's attempt to trace the course of the Jewish revival, emphasizing that this was a prelude to a full-fledged cultural flowering that could only take place after the attainment of Jewish sovereignty in Palestine.

Buber referred to a recently published article by Nordau in which he mentioned a possible role for art in Zionism. He had asserted that art could only be used for didactic purposes towards Zionism's political aims, and did not comment on the role of art in fashioning a "national soul" for Jewry, which was Buber's theme.[44] This relatively minor conflict between Buber and Nordau was not a particularly efficacious encounter. The fact remained that Zionism simply had no central policy on art and aesthetics; individuals in the organization continued to pursue their own dogmas and designs. There was never any dominant program with power to influence all that was produced or promoted in the name of the movement. Buber, despite feeling that he was out of line with the recognized leadership of Zionism, had already established himself as a *de facto* head of the movement concerned with the advancement of Jewish art.

This was due to Buber's participation in the Democratic Faction, whose chief enterprise, the *Juedischer Verlag*, was one of the most effective means of invigorating and spreading their concept of Jewish culture; Buber, along with Lilien and Feiwel, was a founding editor of this venture. After Herzl, these men were among the principal shapers of the aesthetic dimension of Zionism. But it should not be forgotten that along with their sincere intent of cultivating the national soul of the Jews, the Zionist political program was ever present. Art also fell into the realm of propaganda and constituted "a beautiful and valuable means of agitation."[45]

In the first group of works published by the *Juedischer Verlag* in 1902 was the *Juedischer Almanach*, consisting of poetry, prose, and artistic reproductions; the artistic section was edited by Lilien, with Feiwel as the general editor.[46] Feiwel hoped that the *Juedischer Almanach* would become a "noble document" of the cultural awakening of Jewry under Zionism; the reviews of the book indicate that it impressed its audience very favorably, proving convincingly that there was now an incipient but positive relationship between Jewry, culture, and art.[47] The very name was meant to be revolutionary and provocative – to show pride in Jewry and Jewishness – which was reminiscent of Herzl's attempt to turn the phrase *Juden-Blatt* into a badge of honor for *Die Welt*.[48] Indeed, the fact that the Faction saw a work such as the *Juedischer Almanach* as a primary instrument for nation-building, with its success or failure to be gauged by its evaluation in the arts and literary section of the press, speaks volumes about its variety of nationalism. A national language, literature, and art were at least as important as the physical attainment of sovereignty. The *Juedischer Verlag* was far from an ornament; it was an integral part of their program. Their quest for recognition and respectability was greatly abetted because they were able to include works by Jewish artists who were well known in Europe, especially Josef Israels and Max Liebermann – mingled with much less celebrated and more overtly Jewish and Zionist subjects and artists.

A number of Old Testament scenes were pictured, most of which attested to the imagined heroism, vitality, and romance of ancient Israel, while many of the contemporary subjects reflected everyday bourgeois life – with which their Central and West European readers could easily identify. Consistent with the postcard pictures, however, there are numerous depictions of traditional Jews; the division of Zionist labor cited earlier is paralleled in this product of "higher" culture. Most often, Eastern or traditional Jewry is represented by etchings of old men removed from any landscape; they possess an air of wisdom and rich character, with a significant touch of misery [Figure 19].[49] Only rarely are there younger men or women in religious garb. Yet the religious youth in this medium are also passive and non-threatening, belonging more to the past. The *Almanach*'s treatment of the Zionists' vision of their future home in Palestine was of a higher quality than the earliest postcards, but similar sentiments were aroused. Palestine was usually shown through etchings; the antiquity of the Land of the Bible was the point of emphasis.

One of the artists who contributed a number of the Palestine pictures, Hermann Struck, also drew what proved to be the most popular and enduring single image of Zionism from 1897 to 1914: a side portrait etching of Theodor Herzl [Figure 20].[50] It is interesting to recall that Struck, who was one of the most prominent artists in the

19. "Polnischer Jude" by Hermann Struck.

attempt to define a Zionist aesthetic, was a loyal and outspoken member of the *Mizrahi*. Evidently, Struck had no problem filling these ostensibly dissonant roles.[51]

Struck, though mentioned by Martin Buber in his Fifth Congress address, did not merit a place in *Juedische Kuenstler*, which Buber edited for the *Juedischer Verlag* in 1903. Similar to his Congress speech, in the introduction to this volume Buber begins his summary of

20. Etching of Herzl by Hermann Struck, postcard from the Eleventh Zionist Congress (1913).

Jewish artistic accomplishments in a defensive manner. In this instance, though, his adversary is a genuinely bitter foe – Richard Wagner. Even *Juedische Kuenstler*, a product of the so-called cultural regeneration of Zionism, took anti-Semitic assertions as its starting point.[52] Wagner's theory was well known: that Jews did not possess an inner life that was capable of original, creative artistic expression. Buber's response is part apologia; how could Jews be expected to attain the cultural level of other peoples if they live on soil that is inherently alien or even hostile to them, where they are excluded from national traditions and history? Buber concluded that the current work represented a beginning, which was quite admirable, given the only recently rescinded limitations of the ghetto that gave Jews access to the world of Western art.[53]

Before appearing in the gallery at the Seventh Zionist Congress (1907), Josef Israels was repeatedly appropriated in the displays of Jewish art through Zionism [Figure 21].[54] For Israels, as with the other five artists in *Juedische Kuenstler*, the author attempted to discern the particularly Jewish aspects or motivations of his work.[55] On the whole, *Juedische Kuenstler* was as unsuccessful at coming to a concise definition of "Jewish art" as nearly every attempt following it to encapsulate the

21. "Der Thoraschreiber" by Josef Israels.

concept.[56] Israels was unusual in the group of artists used in the *Almanach* and Buber's anthology, because he did, eventually, publicly express sympathy for the Zionist Movement. Ironically, it was Max Nordau who delivered the brief eulogy for Israels at the Tenth Zionist Congress in 1911. "Israels showed a Jewish artist's temperament, whether or not he himself was aware of it," claimed Nordau, whom Buber and others had accused of extreme insensitivity to the need to nurture Jewish national creativity. "We find in his drawings the intensity of feeling, the energy of expression, the high moral dedication, and the emotional nature that embodied the greater characteristics of his people."[57]

Most of the Jewish artists chose not to say anything about their feelings about Zionism; the only member of the group to place himself squarely in the category of "Zionist art" was Lilien. The text of *Juedischer Kuenstler* never went as far as to claim that the others were Zionists, yet, clearly, they allowed their works to be seen and reproduced in the framework of a Zionist project. At some level, the artists acknowledged and permitted the perception of their works within the domain of Jewish culture, as delineated by the movement. This was similar to the appropriation of Jewish literature by the *Almanach* and the *Juedischer Verlag*; most of the writers were not Zionists, but they authorized their works to be included under the banner of the movement.

Until the First World War, the *Juedischer Verlag*, along with the "Libanon" and "Phoenix" companies, was a main producer and distributor of Zionist pictures and postcards.[58] Although the *Juedischer Verlag* styled itself as the custodian and disseminator of "high" culture in Zionism, it was not averse to this function. The vast majority of these postcards could be classified as *fin-de-siècle* iconography; overwhelmingly, Theodor Herzl was the most popular Zionist subject. It is almost impossible to overestimate the extent to which the image of Herzl figured in the self-definition of Zionism, and in the media concerning Zionism that was presented to the Jewish world. The profusion of Herzl portraits, in many cases copies or imitations of the Struck etching, is startling. Besides existing as pictures which could be framed or simply tacked to walls, it adorned the trademarks of candy made in Palestine, canned milk, cigarette boxes, rugs, Jewish ceremonial objects, and numerous household articles.[59] From 1897 to 1914, a photograph of a Zionist office, meeting hall, or reading room without the Struck etching or a picture of Herzl was simply not to be found.

For most Zionists, the representations of Herzl were much more than a matter of kitsch for the masses; this was something to be taken very seriously, especially after Herzl's death in 1904.[60] To almost everyone who wrote on early Zionism, including Herzl's chief critic, Ahad Ha-am, Theodor Herzl was the consummate personification of the incipient Jewish State.[61] Herzl's physiognomy to most Zionists was the purest symbol of Zionism's aspirations. On might say his was the specific countenance of the movement. Herzl's looks were professed to be serious, proud, intelligent, noble, attractive, unique, and at the same time – recognizably Jewish. He was ultimately respectable and manly. Summarizing the whole of Zionist imagery, the Herzl portraits were both forward and backward looking: his beard and visage placed him squarely in the recollection and idealization of traditional Judaism, while his gaze was directed toward the future.[62] His manliness and handsome looks consciously rebuked the anti-Semitic stereotype of Jewish effeminacy and ugliness; simultaneously, though, his dark complexion and face were perceived and extolled as exemplary Jewish features, in which the Zionist Movement and the Jews could take great pride.[63] In this way, as shown with the *Juedischer Almanach*, part of the anti-Semitic stereotype was retained, in order to be inverted as an auspicious aspect of Jewry and Zionism.

22. Postcard of Herzl looking out from the Rhine Bridge in Basel, photograph by E. M. Lilien.

One of the most reproduced pictures of Herzl was a photograph taken by E. M. Lilien. It shows Herzl leaning over the balcony of his hotel room in Basel, overlooking the Rhine [Figure 22]. It placed Herzl in the present – in Basel, the site of the early Zionist Congresses, the temporary hub of the national life of the Jews – but he was undoubtedly fixed on the future.[64] Herzl himself expressed great satisfaction with the picture.[65] After his death, this image was imposed on a

Jerusalem scene, with Herzl looking towards the Tower of David rising above the walls of the Old City, as a team of Jewish pioneers march to work in the valley between Herzl and the walls [Figure 23]. This variation was used for pictures and Jewish National Fund stamps, which along with photographs from Herzl's journey to Palestine in 1898, helped associate Herzl with the Jewish national landscape of *eretz Israel*.[66]

Theodor Herzl's image helped bridge the gap between secular-national aspirations and Jewish messianism. A joke among Zionists, told in several variations, claimed that the success of the Movement was directly related to Herzl's beard – because it recalled traditional Judaism and Jews' image of the prophets. This messianic or prophetic perception of Herzl, especially in the Congress postcards, was often merged with the twin images of the old, pious Eastern-type Jews and the muscular pioneer-farmers, in a Europeanized Palestine landscape [Figure 24].[67] It is not sufficient to dismiss such images as marginal; they should be examined in the light of the attitudes they elicited at the time. Berthold Feiwel, Stefan Zweig, Robert Weltsch, and Gershom Scholem, among others, have written on the tremendous impact the figure of Herzl held for them in their youth – when they were especially impressionable. "In our earliest youth," Feiwel wrote, Herzl signified "the embodiment of all beauty and greatness. We, the young, had been yearning for a prophet, for a leader. We created him with our longing." A common element in their stories is that Herzl's picture was an essential part – if not the essence – of the total world they saw encompassed by Zionism.[68]

The reception of Herzl's image was also influenced by his standing as a member of the German-speaking cultural establishment, as a playwright, and a correspondent and feuilletonist of the *Neue Freie Presse* of Vienna.[69] Some of the settings of postcards and portraits highlight this dimension of Herzl as a culture hero.[70] Nordau, the second most recognized leader of the Zionist Movement, was among the best-known celebrities of *fin-de-siècle* Europe. Nordau's was the next most frequently employed portrait in Zionist representations [Figure 6]; it was common for Nordau and Herzl to appear in the same medium.[71] The idealization of Herzl and Nordau's friendship, the focus of the First Congress portrayal of Okin, was consistent with the notion of men coming together as friends in the framework of the nation.[72]

Nordau too, because of his prophetic countenance, was also able to

23. Promotion for a Jewish National Fund "Herzl stamp."

24. Postcard from the Seventh Zionist Congress (1905) by Carl Pollak.

serve as a symbolic mediator between the world of secular European culture and traditional Judaism. His immense popularity was reflected in the variety of postcards and portraits that appeared before the First World War.[73] This was true even after he sharply curtailed his Zionist activities, and felt himself to be alienated from major portions of the movement – the foretaste of which occurred while Herzl was alive.[74] The perception of Nordau as a "culture hero" was underscored in the numerous depictions of Nordau writing at his desk, intently reading a book, or amidst scientific instruments.[75] One postcard uses a Hebrew translation of the introduction of *Conventional Lies of Our Civilization* for a traditional micrographic portrayal of Nordau [Figure 21].[76] The diffusion of iconography of Theodor Herzl and Max Nordau intensified under the auspices of the Jewish National Fund (JNF), often in conjunction with the *Juedischer Verlag*; the JNF was the means by which the greatest number of Western Jews came into contact with Jewish art, in a national context.[77]

The next most significant institution that combined Zionism and Jewish art on the level of popular culture was the Bezalel Art Institute in Jerusalem.[78] Bezalel was a critical creator and conduit of Zionist media for European Jewry; the institute spawned picture books and pictures for Zionist meeting and reading rooms, with pictures of the works produced in its workrooms. It also opened a floodgate of postcards, but its most effective means of disseminating its spiritual and material fare was through European exhibitions. These were usually held concurrently with the Zionist Congresses, but many more shows were put on between Congresses in a number of medium to large European cities; the goals were to spread information about Bezalel's existence and achievements, to sell its goods, and to solicit contributions.[79]

Bezalel, too, took part in spreading icons of Theodor Herzl; second to Herzl was not Nordau, however, but the Institute's mentor, Boris Schatz. This made Schatz an extremely accessible target for his critics to lampoon through caricature.[80] A main subject of paintings was the Jerusalem landscape and Palestinian flora, and there were also numerous reliefs, paintings and sculptures on biblical themes. Most plentiful, though, were the Jewish ceremonial objects created by the Institute, such as menorahs, kiddush cups, spice boxes, lamps, Holy Arks and bible bindings. The style and quality of these pieces varied greatly.

The context, that these represented fruits of the national Jewish regeneration, must be considered. It may seem paradoxical that there was nothing new about these objects in themselves. Similar to the pictures of orthodox Jews, though, the Bezalel items served to transform the Jewish religious symbols into national symbols. It was part of the larger effort to alter the Jews' allegiance to Judaism into Jewish nationalism. Pictures of Bezalal objects were scattered in the pages of the Zionist press, adorning articles about Palestine or the institute, or sometimes randomly placed within the text.[81] These were meant to be taken as evidence that the creation of things Jewish and beautiful was already underway in Palestine, through the Zionist Movement.

Visitors to the Bezalel exhibitions and viewers of its media were exposed almost as much to the processes of creating the Bezalel products as the products themselves. Scenes of filigree, damascene, and textile workrooms, and studios filled with art students were among the most prevalent picture and postcard subjects [Figure 25].[82] Bezalel styled itself as an institution actively and publicly training its charges, and building a new national culture. The premise behind Bezalel was that it was a prodigious nucleus for Jewish settlement in Palestine; its place in the Zionist discourse wildly exaggerated its significance. Nonetheless, it provided European Jews with images of Jewish artist-craftsmen as central figures in the incipient Jewish society. It affirmed that there was such a thing as Jewish art, with its nexus in the Holy City of Jerusalem. Representations of Bezalel concretized the notion that Jewish productivity, and the innate

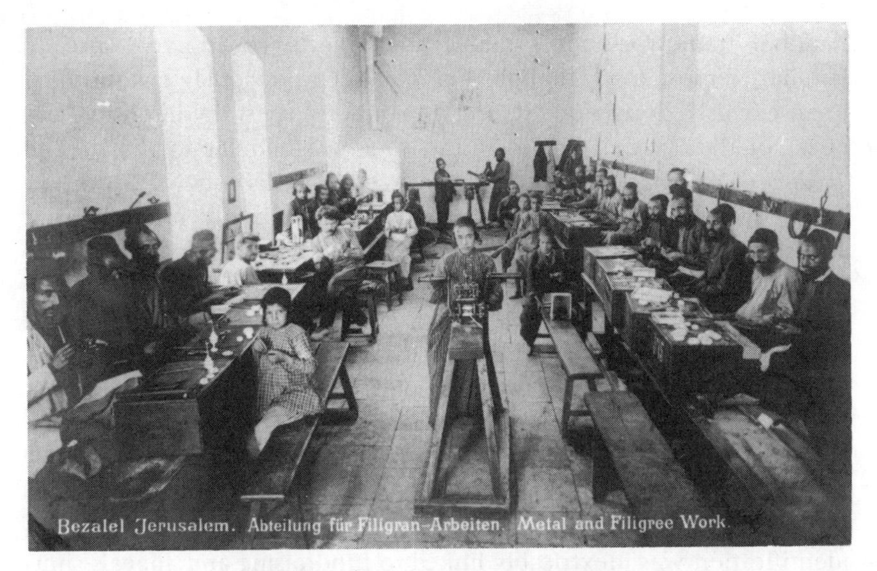

25. Postcard of a Bezalel Institute workroom.

26. The Bezalel Institute.

creativity of Jewish manual laborers was synonymous with Zionism's ideological goals. The building that housed the Institute was shown repeatedly, as a sturdy, oriental structure of Jerusalem stone, symbolizing its permanence [Figure 26].[83] Furthermore, it supplied a secular-national framework for symbols and objects which were already familiar to most Jews, though they had been previously encountered in an exclusively religious setting. In some respects, the intention and effect of the Bezalel pictures and shows was similar to that of the *Juedischer Almanach*: to rattle the alleged complacency of European Jewry by a confrontation with manifestations of a forceful and proud Jewish national consciousness, and to strengthen the commitment of those who were already sympathetic to Zionism.

Similar to the efforts of the Jewish National Fund, the reception of Bezalel as a dignified progenitor of Zionist ideals was undermined by its incessant demands to purchase goods and donate to the Institute, beginning with the inauguration of the institution.[84] This never really abated until the institution's demise in 1929. "The main purpose" of the scores of Bezalel Associations and Societies in Central and Western Europe "was to raise money."[85] Bezalel's attempt to foster national identification was inextricably linked to fundraising and appeals similar to charities. It no doubt partially obstructed the achievement of Bezalel's aim to be perceived as the heart of the Jewish national revival in Palestine. This was one of the central dilemmas of the JNF, which partially supported Bezalel, and was the main agency connecting European Zionists to Jewish life in the Holy Land.

Still, Jewish art in Zionist popular culture was a consequential force in the effort to concretize and personalize a Jewish-national ideology for European Jewry. It is extremely difficult to assess the degree that Zionism was successful in inculcating a sense of belonging to a Jewish nation by such means. This variant of Zionist culture underscored the attempt to reevaluate the Jewish past and present, in hopes of restructuring a radically different future course for the Jews. In these visions, Jews were manly and heroic, and women quietly stood by their sides; here Jews were able to fulfill every traditional, productive function in society, especially agricultural work and craft industries – as delineated in the Zionist program. It was a world in which secular and religious Jews shared a common space in the Holy Land, where there was an ongoing transformation from the old to the new, while retaining Jewish particularity. This was unique to any Jewish utopia up to this point – and it was a utopia which would emerge from more or less conventional politics. It allowed for previously disparaged "Jewish characteristics" to be celebrated as an aspect of national liberation.[86] The Jewish people constituted, according to Zionist popular culture, a coherent cultural order – including all of the Jewish people – and this helped sustain the myth of a like-minded Jewry which would eventually fulfil the Zionist mission. These images were crucial as an expression and preparation for a specifically Jewish nationalism that was beginning to take form, if only in the mind's eye.

CHAPTER SIX

REALISTIC PROJECTIONS OF PALESTINE

One of the most significant, concrete achievements of the early Zionist Movement was to fix specific images of the landscape and the Jewish settlement of Palestine (*Yishuv*) as a part of the Western Jewish consciousness.[1] It provided a common visual stock for the assimilated Jews of Europe – whether or not they chose to identify with Zionism. Before the Zionist Movement, it is likely that the recognizable scenes of Palestine, to most Jews, would have been the Wailing Wall, Rachel's Tomb, and the Tower of David.[2] They were familiar with such places largely through the promotions of *Yeshivot* and charitable societies. Probably their sense of the Palestinian environment was vague, and virtually inseparable from mental pictures of the rest of the dusty Orient.[3] Assimilated Jews would have been called on to activate their connection to Jewish Palestine only occasionally, by giving annual donations to Jerusalem orphanages or *Yeshivot*. For middle-class European Jews of the *fin-de-siècle*, pre-Zionist images of Palestine were marginal religious or philanthropic trappings, with little relevance to the central forces of their lives.[4]

One may assume that most Central and West European Jews neither knew, nor were they especially concerned with how Jews lived in Palestine before 1897. Furthermore, Jewish life in the biblical homeland had no bearing whatsoever on their views of patriotism or nationalism. By 1914, the Zionist Movement was able to effect a change in Jewish consciousness. Many Jews now perceived Palestine as a Jewish country, or an incipient Jewish sovereignty, because it appeared to them a microcosm of the long-term goal of the mainstream of the movement – a Jewish State.[5] The seedlings of a Jewish national life apparently had taken root, were flourishing, and the ground was prepared for the inevitable establishment of a permanent, bountiful, and cultural society.[6]

Artistic representations of Palestine displayed it as a land where the new Zionist Jew and traditional, religious Jews could live harmoniously in a common, sanctified space.[7] In addition to Zionist art, a more authoritative, complex, and nuanced view of Palestine was espoused through photographs, and travelogue-type accounts. This was, of course, abetted by the realities of Jewish life in Palestine. But the meticulous selection and shaping of Jewry's experience in Palestine by the Zionist Movement, for projection to the Jews of Europe, was critical.[8] These less-stylized images became an essential component of Zionist nationalism.

Palestine, from the Zionist point of view, comprised a totality, which was inherently beholden to the Zionist program; the store of images of Palestine was glorified by all shades of Zionists.[9] Despite the realities of the Jews' inconsistent subservience to Ottoman authorities, Palestine was depicted as the only place in the world where Jews were in power to control every aspect of their lives; combined with the fact that this was the Jews' ancestral homeland, promised to them through the covenant, it was the center of the collective Jewish soul.[10] This totality was often characterized as culture. It was a natural landscape, which included the material manifestations of human existence, such as public institutions, private dwellings, and the society's inhabitants.[11] It referred, as well, to the general level of modernization achieved in the *Yishuv*.[12] Culture was also used in a narrower sense, to designate expressions of the Jews' creative impulses, and the means by which these were refined, fortified, and transmitted. Most of the cultural yield was seen as emanating from Jewish sources, in large part because the main language of the *Yishuv* was Hebrew.[13] All of this testified to the development of a specifically Jewish national-cultural life.

Similar to nationalist and "new life" movements of the late nineteenth and early twentieth centuries, Zionism purported to bring into existence an entirely new man: a New Jew or a New Zionist, as has been discussed in relation to the Congresses.[14] Consistent with his depiction in Zionist art and polemics, in photographs and narratives, as well, he was usually shown as a bronzed farmer, working with hand implements in the field.[15] This New Jew, the pictures told, was building a completely new world, on his own, through his own manual and intellectual labor. It was critical that this Jewish society

27. "Young Colonists in Rishon le Zion."

was being built by Jewish hands; in total, it seems that the wielding of implements was more important than the flaunting of muscle, at least before 1914.[16]

This was to accentuate the idea that the fashioning of the environment, which was not owing to the direct hand of God, resided in the hand of a Jew. The slogan of "Hebrew labor" [*avodah Ivrit*] originated in this period. Pictures of Jews tending fields or baling hay were among the most prevalent in the early Zionist archive. Men and women were often shown close up, so that one might view them as individuals, with looks of determination, or smiles on their faces [Figure 27].[17] Insofar as these pictures usually recalled a pre-industrial world, they mirrored the anti-modern imagery employed by the mainstream European nationalisms.[18]

The narratives accompanying the pictures, though, offered a counterpoint to the peasant-type scenes. They asserted that the Jewish colonists were already showing great prowess and innovation in agriculture.[19] It is reasonable to assume that this was proclaimed far earlier than there could have been a factual basis for it – given the failure, and climate of despair of many of the Zionist enterprises.[20] The Jews' agricultural projects, specifically, were said to exemplify modern scientific farming.[21] This was one of the means by which the application of science was exalted in the presentation of the *Yishuv*.[22]

But Zionism, in this regard, did more than proffer a Jewish pioneer-farmer that was intended to be "an ideal for his comrades in civilized Europe" – albeit, this was an essential part of the discourse.[23] As opposed to Zionist art, the more dispassionate treatments of Palestine were compelled to consider the Arab population, which comprised the vast majority of the land's inhabitants.[24] Similar to the means by which the orthodox Jews of Palestine were tamed in art – through the portraiture of elderly men, detached from the landscape – Arabs were, by and large, made to appear as less than vital elements of the Palestinian society.[25] This was achieved through photography and narratives that relegated them to marginality in a Jewish native landscape. The Zionist view of Palestine showed Jews to be operating in a cultural void, that is, in a space where the indigenous population had not created a society with a unique character, discernible to European eyes. Predictably it was often reported the Jews of Palestine were at a higher stage of morality, culture, and education than the Arabs.[26]

This was not, however, a completely impermeable edifice. Either consciously or unconsciously, Zionists did not expurgate accounts which were more sympathetic, or less-Zionist centered about Palestinian Arabs.[27] At the Eighth Zionist Congress, for example, Moses Gaster declared that the Mohammedans of the Orient had "a magnificent culture" which the Zionists would be wise to assimilate with Western civilization as they build up Palestine.[28] There were non-Zionist texts in Zionist reading rooms, such as those published by secular or Christian archaeological societies, and even some popular Zionist accounts that saw an incipient conflict between the Arabs residing in Palestine with Zionist interests.[29] "For the Arab population of the country," stated one such text, a non-Jewish German description of Palestine, "the Jewish invasion is the greatest misfortune," and "every advance for the Jews is a loss for the Arabs of Palestine." This book even went so far as to detect the seeds of a Palestinian nationalist awakening in the responses to Zionism. Perhaps the most significant role this genre might have played was to put the Jewish presence in Palestine into a more empirical perspective – recognizing its relatively small size.[30]

More important were the works by Zionist authors. In a 1911

"Special Palestine Issue" of *Die Welt*, Elias Auerbach expressed "the simple truth" about Palestine, which flew in the face of prevailing Zionist imagery: "Palestine is not an empty land," and "the land takes its character from the predominant element in the population . . . The Arabic language is absolutely supreme. Anyone who lives here must learn Arabic." Auerbach stressed that rather than being inherently "Jewish," it would take "heavy Jewish emigration and land purchase" to begin the Zionist project in earnest. Furthermore, Arab nationalism appeared to be imminent.[31] The standard for impartial, rigorous analysis was set by Leo Motzkin's report on Palestine to the Second Zionist Congress (Basel, 1898); indeed, Zionism hoped to elevate scientific research about Palestine into a sacred devotion.[32] The realistic assessments of Motzkin, Auerbach and others that "Palestine is an Arabic land," however, were consistently overwhelmed by claims that the country could be distinguished, above all, through the legacy of its Judaic origins. This was best summarized in the title of a work by J. H. Kann of 1909: *Erez Israel: Das juedische Land* [*The Land of Israel: The Jewish Country*].[33]

Overall, the message that Arabs in Palestine presented an obstacle to mass Jewish settlement was rarely articulated. On the contrary, most reports claimed that "the Arabs will certainly not be opposed to gradual Jewish settlement."[34] One reporter asserted that "anti-Semitism was simply not to be found in Palestine;" seven years later, a similar account joked that traces of anti-Semitism among the Arabs was a sign of their progress towards modern civilization.[35] Jews and Moslems were said to be naturally suited to coexist, due to their common "Semitic" bonds.[36] Strange as it sounds in retrospect, the prevalent attitude in these accounts was that Zionism had improved the lot of the native Arabs. After all, Arabs were "not degenerate, but poverty was their natural state" – and Zionism portended increased prosperity for all of Palestine.[37] It appeared that the Arabs appreciated, or at least acquiesced in the face of Zionism. This had been Herzl's naive prediction in his utopian novel, *Altneuland* (1902).

Most troubling, from the Zionist point of view, was the notion that Arabs were employed as laborers in the Jewish colonies, whereas the Zionist program asserted that Jews would become the working class of Palestine – the bedrock of the new Jewish civilization. The simple fact of the preponderance of Arabs was not considered as immediate a problem as was their presence in the world of work.

It was especially disturbing to Zionists that the notion of Jews profiteering from the labor of others shadowed them in Palestine. One of the accusations against the Rothschild colonies before the advent of Herzl was that the Jews became indigent and *schnorrers* while Arabs performed most of the physical labor.[38] It was hoped, and supposed, that as Palestine was settled by Jews imbued with Zionist ideology, this problem would gradually disappear. Despite the influx of Jews from Africa and parts of the Ottoman Empire who often took on the role of the underclass, the fact remained that Arab labor was used, in varying degrees, by many Jewish colonies and agricultural settlements from 1881 to 1914, and beyond.[39]

In a widely distributed pamphlet of 1905, Menahem Ussischkin bluntly stated that "anyone who has spent even a short time traveling through the Jewish colonies would be able to see great numbers of Arabs, male and female, working in Jewish fields, gardens, vineyards, and even in Jewish stables and houses. Many thousands of Arabs obtain work from Jews, while many Jews are idle from lack of work."[40] Predictably, though, one is hard pressed to find a picture of an Arab laborer, before 1914, in Zionist photography or art. Arabs were not completely written out of the presentation of Palestine to European Jewry, but they were accessory, at best, to the grand project of the Jews rebuilding their land. Specifically, their labor was excluded from that which constituted the prideful building of a nation.

The issue of employing the indigenous population, versus Hebrew labor, was mostly taken up in the narratives of travelogue-type reports. "The Jewish workman is accustomed to the means of civilization," Zionists read from the Eleventh Congress report, "therefore he desires higher wages and better working conditions than his Arab counterparts. The higher wages are more than aptly compensated because the quality of his work is better."[41] It was claimed that some colonies were at the mercy of Arab laborers, because there simply were not enough Jews to perform the necessary tasks. This was the Jews' only source of livelihood, but it represented a way for the Arabs to get extra money. The result was that Arabs were inclined not to tend to their duties for the Jews, if their own fields demanded attention – and there was nothing the Jews could do about it. The same author expressed frustration that the money Arabs received as wages was never circulated among Jews. One notices a tone of resentment at the Jews' exclusion from their neighbors' and laborers' world.[42]

The labor of Arabs, when it was not relevant to "the labor problem," was usually described as part of a world which belonged more to centuries past, than to the present, and it was not particularly productive.[43] In one of the few instances where Arabs were given credit for any special skill in the realm of labor, they were still set in a simple and pastoral setting: Arab women were acclaimed for their ability to carry large baskets on their heads.[44] Of course, exceptions exist, such as Davis Trietsch's description of Arab farmers making butter with an electric milk-separator from Germany, and of Arab women using Singer sewing machines in the cities – but he qualifies that these exist alongside scenes such as those depicted in *1001 Nights* – to show Palestine as a land of the old and new.[45]

What was to be made of the manifestations of the Arab civilization which were prevalent throughout Palestine? One way Arab society was appropriated by Zionist imagery was through combining Arab structures with Jewish people or symbols. A frequently reproduced woodcut of Jacob Stark shows a pious Jew praying, imposed over a picture of the Dome of the Rock mosque and the Temple Mount.[46] Perhaps the implication is that the Jew calls for the restoration of the Temple, while he waits outside of Zion. An etching by Hermann Struck, that was used for the offical postcard of the Ninth Zionist Congress, and appeared in the *Juedischer Almanach* and other publications, is entitled "Brunnen bei Jaffa" [Well near Jaffa]; a mosque stands next to a tree.[47] Indeed, the mosque is consigned as an aspect of the antiquated landscape of Palestine, along with gnarled olive trees.[48] There is no indication that this comprised a crucial element of a living culture for the vast majority of the population.

As often as possible, Arab towns and dwellings were shown unpopulated, or with very few inhabitants.[49] Pictures of bustling Arab life in Jaffa or Haifa were virtually nonexistent in Zionist photographs. Furthermore, one is hard pressed to find a picture in which an Arab's face could be distinguished. Stories of markets and ports, with dazzling colours and rich aromas, were reserved for the stopover points before Palestine, such as Cairo and Beirut. These were portrayed as wild, colorful and chaotic, as opposed to the quiet and majestic severity of Palestine.[50]

When attention was focused on the Jewish colonies, they were shown to be clean, orderly, prosperous, and calm – notions of bourgeois normalcy were of paramount significance. In a work typical of this genre, the reporter, Jesaias Press, noted that "no Jewish colony lacked a synagogue, school, and pharmacy." He described the colonies as exhibiting "simple, but very tasteful houses, and well-ordered streets; they are joyful to behold due to their pleasant design." Overall, the colonies comprised "outposts of culture" [*Kulturstationen*] in the country.[51] This was demonstrated in a number of ways.

In stark contrast to the reputation of the non-Zionist Rothschild colonies for inept management, which led to waste and encouraged slothfulness, it was related that public affairs in the Zionist-influenced communities were handled systematically, by a wise and sympathetic committee. This was concretized by descriptions of the meeting hall, which could be found in nearly every colony. "There were also post offices, conveniently located, which delivered and sent out mail regularly – locally and abroad – in speedy wagons." These images assured readers that the colonies remained in contact with the outside world; it was also a sign of modern civilization. "Only two institutions of modern communal life were missing in the Jewish colonies" – which here, the author insisted, would have been totally superfluous – "police, and prisons."[52]

Indeed, it is hard to imagine a portrait of a community that could be more antithetical to the anti-Semitic visage of ghettoized Jewish life. There is no hint of restlessness, or any modern social ills – although nearly every beneficent aspect of modernity seems to have been thoroughly assimilated. Such a portrayal of the colonies was juxtaposed to the reality of poverty and hopelessness in the Pale of Settlement, which was the realm to which most European Jews were subject. It was also set against the stereotypes of *Juedischewirtschaft*, the notion of a frenzied pace, irrationality, pettiness, and bungling in Jewish affairs. Civic-mindedness was emphasized as a determinant characteristic of communal life in the Jewish colonies.

A bourgeois Jewish audience would have been familiar with the general features of Jewish community affairs in Central and Western Europe, in which most important decisions were made by rabbis or wealthy patrons of the community.[53] The administration of the colonies, on the contrary, seemed to be fair, democratic, and efficient. The notion of a sound and wise infrastructure of these communities was difficult to render visually, but the claim of pervading quietude was supported by the presence of the meeting hall, as the space in which differences were quelled, and numerous photographs of clean, wide streets with no trace of commotion.[54]

Armand Kaminka in *Meine Reise nach Jerusalem* reported that "there were neat, small houses with gardens, and a little, charming synagogue," when he visited Rishon l'Zion.[55] It was common for the garden, alonside the house, to be included in the descriptions of the colonies.[56] This was largely a reflection of the enthusiasm for home gardens among the middle classes in Central and Western Europe. Furthermore, at home and school horticulture went along with collective agriculture in affirming that Jews could live "in close intimacy with nature, which had brought out their innate sense to care for flowers."[57] Scenes of Jewish gardening in Palestine allowed the colonists to be seen as solidly bourgeois, in touch with nature, and partaking in a truly settled lifestyle.

Rootedness and calmness were part and parcel of the world of good health, which the colonies were said to exemplify. "Eight of the colonies have their own doctors," asserted one reporter. "They serve the colonists in the area and the neighboring Arab villages."[58] Besides demonstrating that health care was available at most of the colonies, medicine was shown as a way that Western culture promulgated by Zionism could serve as a bridge to the greater community of Arabs and the Near East.[59] Boris Schatz, speaking on behalf of his artist-workmen at the Bezalel Institute, claimed that "we are all robust in health and keen in thought, with ambitious designs filling our minds."[60]

Good health, strength, vigor, and happiness characterized the lot of the Jewish colonists, who were continually shown engaged in wholesome pursuits, such as sports, music and dance, when they were not working in fields or craft shops. As Martin Buber had prophesized, the soil of Palestine seemed to be nurturing a complete Jewish folk culture.[61] The songs which were composed and sung by Jews in Palestine were so suited to the authentic Jewish nature, that a Jew would spontaneously move to the rhythm, and their folk dances were more attuned to the Jewish spirit, than, say, the fox-trot.[62]

A counter image, or modification of the largely Europeanized Jewish peasant was the portrayal of orientalized Jews, that is, Jews who had successful adopted some of the ways of the Arabs in fulfilling their new lives. This aspect of the Zionist projection may be seen as a sort of positive orientalism [Figure 28].[63] It was paradoxical that the Jews who most closely resembled Arabs were those entrusted to guard the settlements against attacks and robberies by Arabs. Usually they were pictured on horseback, with rifles, and in Arab head-dresses.[64] It was only in the years immediately preceding the First World War, however, that images of Jewish armed guards appeared to be a significant force in the colonies.[65]

28. Cover of *Bar-Kochba Almanach* by Jacob Stark.

In 1913, Shmarya Levin announced that "in certain circumstances, a group of Jewish pioneers were forced to risk their lives." "These are our new sentries, the *Shomerim,* who defend Jewish property and at times sacrifice their life and health. Quite a new type has arisen among the colonists: the Jew, dauntless and fearless, where the Jewish settlement and honor are concerned." Levin continued that most

Zionists were not yet aware of this "new Jewish type" which had been forged by the Palestinian environment – indeed, the legend would grow to far more significant proportions during the war years and after.[66] What is most striking about the image of Jews in arms, before 1914, is that they assume a relatively inconsequential place in the archive of Palestinian Jewry presented to Jewry west of the Pale of Settlement – compared to farms, schools, pharmacies, and libraries.[67] "As we have neither the desire nor the power to suppress any portion of the population, we must strive to attain the first place through peaceful competition" – was clearly the early Zionist consensus.[68] The notion that Palestine might have to be won through force or militarism played virtually no role in these representations of the *Yishuv*, and when it was brought up, the context was invariably self-defense.[69]

Overall, to the Jews of Central and Western Europe before the First World War, the crux of the Zionist vision, *vis-à-vis* Palestine, was not the individual, new Jew – but Jewish culture in Palestine, centered on noteworthy accomplishments in education, which were the fruits of a thriving, secularized Jewish life.[70] Jesaias Press boasted that "ten colonies possessed good schools with more than ten grades, and kindergartens in which the pupils learned Hebrew as their second mother tongue, and as the language of tuition. The larger colonies have public meeting halls which often sponsor local literary and popular-scientific lectures. These halls also have small public libraries. In each colony there are daily newspapers and technical journals in comparatively large number, that many subscribe to and read."[71] "What is new and original in Palestine," Nahum Goldmann wrote, "finds its purest expression in the schools."[72]

Serious problems and deficiencies were, however, prevalent in discussions regarding education in Palestine. The pictures and literature amplified and elaborated the Congress rhetoric. The chief complaint was that there was not a coherent system, and there were a number of schools which were not serving the ends of Zionism.[73] "But in a brief span of thirty years, there was no element of Jewish life as impressive and complete as the Jewish Palestinian schools."[74] Rather than the typical pattern of communities developing around an economic center, the leading settlements in Jewish Palestine were described as emanating from cultural institutions, especially schools.[75]

The Zionist educational institution, *par excellence*, which was shown repeatedly on postcards and pictures and exalted in texts, was the Herzliya Gymnasium, from around 1907 to 1914 [Figure 29].[76] The

29. "Hebrew Gymnasium (Higher Grade School) in Jaffa."

Herzliya Gymnasium was consciously integrated into the world of European Zionism in its presentation to Western Jewry, to show the harmony of interests between the *Yishuv* and Zionists in the Diaspora.[77] The German-dominated faculty was usually shown with a picture of Herzl in the background, and postcards and pictures of European-based Zionist leaders among the students and teachers at the school were common in the store of images.[78]

The gymnasium epitomized the new national life that Zionism hoped to engender. One of the most cryptic pictures shows the school's brass band, with eucalyptus trees and a mural of Moses receiving the Ten Commandments in the background [Figure 30].[79] The group faculty portraits interwove traditional Jewish images and scenes of biblical Israel around the teachers' pictures [Figure 31].[80] Students, wearing tidy uniforms, were featured in the laboratories, at drafting tables, and diligently working in the wood shop.[81] Upon reading the text one discovers that they also learned the Bible, in modern Hebrew, by way of the most advanced pedagogical theories.[82] In these texts as well, the adoption and development of Hebrew in Palestine was seen

30. Herzliya Gymnasium brass band.

31. Herzliya Gymnasium faculty.

as an integral element in the forging of a new identity: it was an element of the Jewish settlement which marked the society as uniquely Jewish.[83] The Gymnasium was the gem of Tel-Aviv, perhaps the crowning achievement of the Zionist project before 1914.

The naming of the Jaffa quarter "Tel Aviv" was one of the means by which the community was identified with the European-originated Zionist Movement. The Gymnasium was located in an urban center that was incorporated into Zionist imagery by the midpoint of the movement's second decade; it was shown as the original "Zionist city." Tel-Aviv was the Hebrew title given to Herzl's novel *Altneuland* by its translator into Hebrew, Nahum Sokolow. "Tel Aviv," Sokolow informed Herzl, "was a biblical place name, expressing a connection between the old and the new. *Tel* means ruins, and *Aviv* means spring, hence a ruin which lives to experience a new spring – *Altneuland*!"[84] Nearly every Zionist text about Palestine related the connection between Herzl and the naming of Tel Aviv; it was one of the ways that Herzl, and other European Zionist leaders, were integrated into the world of Jewish Palestine.

In the text of *Altneuland*, however, Herzl predicted that the first Jewish metropolis would likely develop from the town of Haifa. He told of the urbanization of Mount Carmel, and the expansion of the port of Haifa into a leading trade center of the world. This spawned descriptions of that city sprinkled, or framed, by Herzl's vision.[85] Towards the end of the prewar period, the leader's premonition about Haifa as an avant-garde Zionist city seemed to be borne out with the founding of the *Technikum* [later *Technion*]. Shortly before the First World War, it was thought that the *Technikum* would, in the near future, become a magnet of culture, science, and modern settlement for the Jews, following the example of the Herzliya Gymnasium. The quarter around the school, "*Atid*" ["future"], was projected as an incipient "second Tel Aviv," but with greater "scenic beauty." Although it might have been clean and orderly, the natural setting of Tel Aviv was less than spectacular as rendered in photographs.[86]

Beyond being simply pleasing to the eye, "*Atid* was situated magnificently," reported Nahum Goldmann, "dominating the slope of Mount Carmel, over the great, beautiful bay. The *Technikum* would be in the center, proudly reigning over the human dimension of the landscape." Goldmann expressed the hope that the institution's splendid setting and fine structure would be symbolic of its championing of Hebrew as the language of tuition for higher education and scientific training in Palestine.[87]

In 1913–14, the reportage on Palestinian Jewry was overwhelmed by what became known as "the language war." A controversy ensued over the use of Hebrew, versus German, for the language of instruction in the functioning lower school, which thrust the *Technikum* into the forefront of Zionist discussion; the polemics were deeply embittered and emotional.[88] The event started as essentially a pedagogical disagreement between the main sponsor of the *Technikum*, the *Hilfsverein fuer deutsche Juden*, and some of the members of the school's governing board and faculty. The *Hilfsverein* contended that for the purpose of assuring the greatest clarity and utilization of the best texts, German should be used for the technical course. This was not, in itself, an unreasonable directive, given the nascent state of modern Hebrew. Nonetheless, it was seized by some Zionists as an attempt to counter the revival of Hebrew culture with *Deutschtum*, as a means of exerting extra-territorial, German control over the school. Most Zionists believed that it was in their best interests to use Hebrew, in order to help socialize the students coming from different linguistic backgrounds, and because it would help Zionism remain neutral *vis-à-vis* the European powers.[89] Furthermore, the conflict was exacerbated with the *Hilfsverein*'s claim that the push for Hebrew was more a product of national chauvinism, than sound pedagogical practice.[90]

Perhaps the greatest consequence of the affair, from the perspective of the projection of Zionism to European Jewry was that the *Technikum* appeared to have crystalized a defiant nationalistic spirit, set against the dominant language of technology, German, to pursue the advancement of science in a Hebraic form.[91] This is evidenced by the sympathetic demonstrations and meetings of European Zionist groups.[92] From the wave of strikes of Jewish teachers in Palestine, the *Technikum* was shown as setting the standard in providing a total Hebrew world for its students to explore.[93] While attempting to nurture an avant-garde institution of scientific learning, the language war seemed to prove that the *Yishuv* had indeed taken on a life and national character of its own.

Before the language war, there was no special ire reserved for the *Hilfsverein* as a possible progenitor of an anti-Zionist spirit in the *Yishuv*.[94] The schools of the *Alliance Israélite Universelle* and the Evelina Rothschild school, however, had long been castigated for not acculturating their students to the realities of existence in Palestine.[95] As the orthodox Jews of Jerusalem were symbolic of talmudic Judaism as a reactionary force in Jewry, these schools were seen as remnants of the *Galut* in the sea of the Jewish renaissance. Most Zionist tracts denounced the *Alliance* institutions for turning out little French men and woman who would be inclined to continue their studies in France and remain there.[96] The Evelina de Rothschild school for girls in Jerusalem, though shown as a model of domesticity, was often reproached for fashioning a sort of gentlewoman who had no place in Palestine.[97]

Consistent with the image of Jewry in the Old City of Jerusalem, the schools of the "old *Yishuv*," that is, the *Chadarim* and *Yeshivot*, were not positively influenced because they existed in the Holy Land. In fact, they were considered inferior to their East European counterparts in producing great scholars, rabbis, and *halachic* literature. Many of these religious schools seemed to be corrupt and preoccupied with collecting money from abroad, rather than concentrating on serving their students.[98] Furthermore, for some of the same reasons that many *Maskilim* had scorned the "excesses" of talmudic education, with its emphasis on arcane points and rote learning, the Zionists criticized the religious education that ruled in Palestine.[99] It was against this world that the Herzliya Gymnasium, Haifa *Technikum*, and Bezalel Art Institute stood as portending a distinctly Jewish, secular order, which prized the finest fruits of *Bildung*, or the complete, independent cultivation of the mind.

The Bezalel Institute vied with the Herzliya Gymnasium for a central place in the visualization of the *Yishuv*. Typically, more text and pictures would be devoted to these two institutions than any other aspect of the Jewish settlement. Few reports, however, claimed that Bezalel was indicative of a larger Zionist enclave in Jerusalem. As a predominantly Jewish urban center in Palestine, Jerusalem was juxtaposed to Tel Aviv. Despite occasional romanticized praise and pictures of the Old City walls, the Dome of the Rock mosque, or the Tower of David – the overwhelming sense from accounts of Jerusalem was one of misery and despair. Paradoxically, Jerusalem exemplified the worst of the *Galut* – it was poor, crowded, disease-infested, and filthy – and peopled by intolerant chauvinists.[100] There was also a sense that it attracted bizarre types and lunatics: "as a resident expressed the situation, at a time when there was a talk of erecting an asylum for imbeciles, we should not be altogether in the wrong if we took down the walls of Jerusalem, and built them up again, so as to include the suburbs."[101] Upon witnessing the Jews in the Old City, Nahum Goldmann wrote that for the first time in his life, he felt ashamed to be a Jew.[102] It provided a sort of pre-Zionist picture, in contrast to the actualized Zionist vision of Tel Aviv. The Zionists hoped that these *Chalukah Judentum*, or Jews living primarily from charity, could be secularized, morally reformed, and literally cleaned up.[103]

Most of the reports misrepresented the approximate population of the *Chalukah Judentum*. In proportion to the remainder of the Jewish population, they made up at least 60 per cent of Palestinian Jewry; they also obstructed the Zionist attempt to reconstruct perceptions of Jewish labor. By living off of donations, and supposedly engaging in a life of study detached from a greater community, they did not engage in "productive labor." As part of the Zionist program, the younger generation of the *Chalukah Judentum* would have to be trained in "productive occupations."[104] At least one author thought that the best means for turning the youth into good Zionists would be through establishing a network of national-religious schools.[105] More common, though, was the implicit or explicit hope that they would be weaned from orthodoxy.

Jerusalem's symbolic significance, however, was not simply downplayed due to the presence of the *Chalukah Judentum*. It was the home of the Jewish National Museum and the National Library, which were quite conscious components of the Zionist appropriation of Palestine. The national museum, which was part of the Bezalel Art Institute, primarily exhibited the natural history of Palestine and the work of Jewish artists in Palestine.[106] The library aspired to comprise the breadth of Jewish intellectual activity. Both of these were essential components, for European Jewry, of the national expression, collective memory, and means to disseminate an aesthetic sensibility and scientific information requisite to a modern state.[107] Simultaneously, these were shown to be living centers of culture for the local Jews, while they functioned as vital organs of the collective consciousness of Jewry.[108] They were not simply embellishments to most Zionists; they were facts which displayed the peoplehood of the Jews, which were organically tied to Jerusalem.

Jerusalem was also home to a large proportion of the non-European Jews who inhabited Palestine. The Sephardim, and other Jews from the Arab world or Ottoman Empire, were made into a romantic sideshow to the featured, European-Jewish scheme. This was similar to the treatment of Arabs and orthodox Jews, who seriously threat-

32. Caucasian mountain Jews.

ened the implementation of the Zionist program, and thus were relegated to marginal elements of Palestine. Non-European Jews were seen mostly among themselves, in pictures of the Bezalel workrooms, and from portraits of "Mountain Jews from the Caucasus," replete with long daggers, tunics, and bullet-belts across their chests [Figure 32].[109] Only rarely would one gain a sense of the wide gulf separating the Russian and Polish Jews from their Oriental counterparts.

Uncharacteristic of most accounts, Ussischkin wrote that "in their habits and ideas," they were closer to the Arabs, not the Jewish Palestinians. Their immigration patterns were different from those of the European Jews, and "they looked on the new Jewish immigrants with deep mistrust, and were not at all ready to associate with them. Only on rare occasions did the Sephardim feel a Jewish solidarity with the Ashkenazim, and it was believed that many years would pass before a younger generation is won for the idea of [Zionist] Jewish activity."[110]

Predictably, these Jews, especially the Yemenites, were called on to fulfil the lowest rung of service in the colonies, to alleviate the persistent problem of Arab labor while pursuing "a quiet, contented, and humane existence." They were shown as the solution for making the Jewish colonies "gradually independent of the surrounding Arab population."[111] In contrast to this lower-class status, however, pictures typically displayed them working in a skilled craft at Bezalel, such as jewelry making.[112] Nevertheless, the visualization of non-European Jews does not suggest, even remotely, that Palestine comprised "the most divided community in the world."[113] On the contrary, as part of the mosaic of Jewish Palestine, they were given bourgeois attributes, such as industriousness and skill in gardening, while they were shown to be welcomed as brothers by the Ashkenazi of the *Yishuv*.[114]

Superseding the peopling of the land, Zionism necessitated an appropriation of the Palestinian landscape, so that it might, at some time, be accepted as a legitimate native land in the mind's eye of European Jewry. To be sure, beautiful, panoramic vistas could be found in Palestine, but these were less than successfully rendered in photographs, or in the lone cinemagraphic attempt to capture the landscape. Lack of clarity made it difficult to distinguish the scenes.[115] Predictably, there were those who waxed enthusiastic upon seeing *erez Israel* for the first time. "The joy moved me to tears," recounted one visitor's tale of 1907, savoring the view from Mount Carmel. "My land! My beloved country! My beloved mountains, my blue sky, my blue sea!"[116] The Jewish fraternities' Commers and "Hatikvah" also sang of a resplendent Jewish Fatherland.[117] A claim of witnessing profound beauty, however, was not seconded by many other Zionist writers.[118] The mountains, for instance, were infinitely less majestic than the Alps, and the sea-side appeared no more enticing than other southern Mediterranean shorelines.[119] Indeed, the artistic representations were much better suited to extol Palestine's natural beauty.[120]

The land of Palestine was only occasionally referred to as unlovely; it was much more common to hear it described as sparse, or severe.[121] Repeatedly, in the Zionist literature, one was informed that the land was predominantly empty.[122] One "Account of a Tour in Palestine," that was not written by a Zionist, bears the title *The Land That Is Desolate* (1912).[123] Much of Palestine was desert, or what is referred to now as chaparral – a patchy, sparsely vegetated area – which was not then recognized as arable topography.[124] The notion of barrenness – a lack of distinguishing natural characteristics, of trees, of cities, of people – was presented as a divinely ordained precondition for the Jewish national regeneration.[125] The land was seen as a metaphor for the national aspirations of the Jews, which had lain dormant for centuries. "The land offers an abundance of natural beauty," asserted Jean Fische in *Das heutige Palaestina* (1907). "The picturesque landscapes, with numerous ravines, hills, valleys and mountains can – once rebuilt – be comparable with the most beautiful countries."[126]

The subtext was clearly that in order to be amenable to mass Jewish settlement, the land would have to be thoroughly rejuvenated. The Jewish National Fund (JNF) was the component of the Zionist Movement empowered to enact this process, which also served to personalize European Jewish integration into the regenerated landscape.[127]

Indeed, the Zionist accounts of the Jewish colonies bear witness to the seemingly miraculous permutation, beginning with the initiation of the JNF in 1901. A response from a non-Zionist observer, which was more subdued than the typical chronicle from within the movement, observed that "they have added considerably to the varieties of fruits under cultivation, and even to the chance traveller there is a continuous change perceptible in the landscape. Year after year, the hillsides are increasingly covered with vineyards, oliveyards, orange-gardens and orchards, where but lately all was desolate and bare."[128] The landscape was not yet restored to its ancient grandeur by the First World War, and less than completely suitable to accept the Jewish State, but the supposedly irreversible process of reclaiming Zion seemed to be well underway.[129]

Whatever the reality, according to a classic formulation of the movement, the Palestine imagined for the Jews of Europe was to be the only earthly place that could engender "a natural Jewish life."[130] It was said that the new leadership of Jewry would not arise from "the spiritual ghetto of the lands of exile, but out of the free spirit of the mountains of Judea and Galilee, to plant the blue and white banner of liberated Israel upon Mount Zion."[131] Zionism proposed that "without the strains of living between worlds, and as a minority, Jews could be free to develop their own inner and communal selves." Further, "the national-cultural aspect of the problem of Jewish consciousness had not yet been completely overcome in Palestine – but the base of a solution had been soundly laid, and the contemporary trends and continuing development pointed to the ultimate resolution of the *Judenfrage*." Jews could create a complete life and culture for themselves as Jews in Palestine.[132]

Early Zionism asserted, through its visual sensibility, that Jews would attain sovereignty in Palestine by being the bearers of a progressive, Western culture.[133] If the Zionist project was actualized, the Arabs and the remainder of the Near East would be compelled to hail the Zionists as their friends and champions. Certainly, one may label the Zionists' pretension of being a "guide" for the Arab population as a variety of imperialism; as Europeans, the early Zionists saw themselves as culturally superior to the Arabs.[134] Nevertheless, such condescension was tempered in part by a sincere desire to live in friendship with the Arabs, and win over their hearts to acceptance of a Jewish national regeneration in Palestine.[135] Interestingly, most early Zionists saw little if any hope of becoming friends or living together with the orthodox Jews of Palestine, unless the latter were radically transformed.[136] Cultural work was seen as "one of the most essential means of attaining the territorial goal."[137] Indeed, it is a strange nationalism of the twentieth century – in the face of more aggressive and exclusive ideologies – which proclaims that the community producing the finest books, the most sublime poetry, a comprehensive research university, and an advanced agricultural-experiment station would "win" a country.[138] Many currents of Zionist culture in Palestine are summed up in an image related by Herzl, of "a great medical facility, which the whole of Asia will pour into, and it will prepare the way for the elimination of disease in the Orient. At its entrance will be a monumental fountain – Moses, by the rock that he has struck, with water pouring out of it."[139] Herzl's vision prefigured the totality of Palestine projected by Zionism, from his own time to a decade after his death. He attempted to capture the strains of beauty, modernity, science, health, the memory of biblical Israel, and the attainment of honor in the eyes of the world, which were woven into the mental tapestry of Zionist Palestine.

CHAPTER SEVEN

CULTURE AND CHARITY: THE JEWISH NATIONAL FUND

With the significant exception of material intended for self-promotion, the Jewish National Fund (JNF) has been undervalued as a source and transmitter of Zionist national culture. Furthermore, it has been underestimated by scholars as an important component of the history of the Zionist Movement and modern Jewish history. Founded in 1901, the JNF or KKL (for the Hebrew translation, *Keren Kayemet l'Israel*), is the part of the Zionist Movement that reached the greatest number of Jews living west of the Pale of Settlement by 1914.[1] Proposed at the First Zionist Congress (1897) by Professor Hermann Schapira, the JNF began operating under Johann Kremenezky prior to the Fifth Zionist Congress (1901).[2] The fundraising activities of the JNF, for the purchase of land for collective Jewish settlement, agriculture, and cultural endeavours in Palestine, developed a bureaucratic apparatus and even myths and symbols of its own. No other segment of Zionist material culture was as pervasive a force in Western Jewish life as the multifaceted efforts of the JNF to nationalize the Jews.

Anecdotal evidence and self-generated, jingoistic promotions far outweigh the contemporary and retrospective comment on the JNF that one might regard as more or less detached from the enterprise.[3] But if as sensitive and critical a participant in the movement as Gershom Scholem never paused to question the assumptions and functions of the JNF, it is likely that his positive reminiscences of the institution were widely held in Central and West European Zionist ranks. It seems that its images were seen by the larger Jewish public as representing an admirable, altruistic, and highly efficacious enterprise. Many elements of the vanguard of the new Jewish culture, created through Zionism, appeared to be products of the JNF.

In his memoir *From Berlin to Jerusalem*, Scholem wrote that "I am describing the life of a young Jew whose path took him from the Berlin of his childhood and youth to Jerusalem and Israel. This path appeared to me to be singularly direct and illuminated by clear signposts . . ." Scholem, who places his family in the ultra-assimilated bourgeoisie, had an uncle, Theobald Scholem, who was one of the founders of the Berlin Jewish gymnastic society. He had "performed for Theodor Herzl at the Basel Congress of 1903. A photo of the squad of gymnasts with Herzl in the middle hung in the parlor of his home." Also in Uncle Theobald's home, "the collection box of the Jewish National Fund for the acquisition of land in Palestine hung in a prominent place. When he won a bet he had made with his brothers, it usually was paid by throwing a one-mark piece into this box."[4]

Nahum Goldmann had similar recollections about the role of the Jewish National Fund during his childhood in Frankfurt. The JNF box was the most worthy receptacle for spare change and money won from friendly wagers.[5] In England as well, Leon Simon proclaimed in 1908 that "the box and stamp of the JNF had become part of the environment of Jewish life."[6] Certainly, Gershom Scholem, Nahum Goldmann, and Leon Simon were extraordinary individuals, and their routes to Zion were not well-travelled by other members of their class. Yet among the most clear "signposts," they would affirm, were the blue and white box on the parlor shelf and the JNF stamps on their letters, postcards, and envelopes.

The JNF produced the greatest share of promotional materials for the movement, the most common of which were JNF stamps. These were distributed to recognize even the smallest donations to the JNF and to help spread the message of Zionism. Originally issued by the Head Office, and later also from the regional organizations, some thirty million JNF stamps were sold between 1902 and 1914.[7] The biggest selling stamp before the First World War was the "Zion" design, which seemed to confirm Herzl's intuition that people are most profoundly moved by uncomplicated symbols.[8] Over twenty million "Zion" stamps were purchased between 1902 and 1914; most of that issue were blue and white, with the word "Zion" (in Hebrew) inscribed within a Star of David [Figure 33]. Each sold for five Pfennig in Germany and one half-penny in England (the equivalent of one 1902 US cent), and were usually bought in strips of ten or in sheets of three hundred.[9] This

33. "Zion" stamps.

accompanied the Zionists' appropriation of the Star of David on their flags, banners, and numerous insignias.

The next most popular version was the so-called "Herzl" stamp, issued from 1909 to 1914, which showed Herzl gazing at a group of workers in Palestine. It superimposed the famous Rhine Bridge picture of Herzl from the First Zionist Congress onto a balcony, outside the Old City of Jerusalem.[10] There the leader overlooked a joyful team of men with farm implements marching to their task, alongside the city walls; around four million of these were sold. Stamps with pictures of Max Nordau, David Wolffsohn, the Wailing Wall, a map of Palestine, Palestine historical scenes, and the Palestine landscape sold around a million each.[11] It is doubtful that any more than a handful of Western Jews, by 1914, would not have recognized many of the JNF stamps; in addition, they probably would have been able to relate the general features of the movement to which they belonged. In the onslaught of images in which Zionism was engaged, JNF stamps – even though they were small in size – played a significant role.[12]

All of the visual motifs of Jewish culture discussed above found expression in JNF stamps, as well as in postcards, pamphlets, certificates for specific donations, and medals. Cultural institutions in Palestine that were in some way related to the JNF were featured incessantly in their materials, through photographs and narratives. Most popular were likenesses of the Hebrew *Gymnasium*, followed by the Bezalel Art Institute, the Jewish national museum, and library; these gained currency in the Zionist discourse after 1907. Even in the promotions of the Tree Fund, the cornerstone of the JNF, the relationship of afforestation to "the renaissance of our language and culture" was emphasized. Directly borrowing the symbolism of the forest and tree from German nationalism, the existence of trees somehow "accelerated" the flourishing of culture in a purely Jewish atmosphere, with its own "spiritual ideals and intellectual strivings."[13] Another announcement metaphorically claimed that forests would "enable us to educate the children of our people in our land, in a Jewish spirit, and to develop Jewish culture upon congenial soil, so that it shall blossom anew."[14] The JNF was portrayed as playing a leading role in the operations of the Hebrew Gymnasium, workmen's educational organizations, the founding of the Jewish university, and the Jewish technical institute. It was even seen as having a hand in the development of a uniquely Jewish aesthetic, through its subvention of the Bezalel Institute; "the advent of a new Hebrew style" was at least partially indebted to the JNF. Especially through the great success of the Hebrew Gymnasium, which the JNF implied would not have come about without its gift of a building site, there had been a "large influx of new settlers" engaged in the task of building a national culture.[15]

The JNF supplied land and funding to make Palestine amenable to mass Jewish settlement in order to create a "centre of attraction for Jewish emigration." Its "fundamental principle" was to engender "Jewish labour upon Jewish soil" through the purchase of land which would become the permanent, collective possession of the Jewish people. "The wanderings and distress of the Jews would come to an end," an official publication asserted, "only if the Jews could settle upon a particular territory and establish a self-contained economic life of their own upon the basis of a peasant class." The notion that the JNF was the vehicle of the Zionist Movement that was literally providing soil under Jewish feet, in a Jewish land, was of paramount significance. It implied that the foundation of a normal national existence, a Jewish "peasant class," was being brought to life.[16] It conjured all of the imagery of the complete Jewish civilization that was cultivated by the movement, and allowed the donors to the JNF to share in the endeavour. The imagery of Jews baling hay, milking cows, and harvesting crops was more often than not set in the context of the activities of the JNF [Figure 34].[17]

The JNF was the institutionalized connection to the native landscape that the Zionists wished to impress on European Jews. The movement intended Jews to identify the territory and incipient Jewish society of Palestine as their true homeland and the focus of their national consciousness. One of the main functions of the JNF which served this goal was afforestation.[18] In addition to its role as a cultural backdrop,

34. "Ernte-Arbeiten auf einem der nationalfonds-Guter in Galilea."

the planting of forests was not simply a means of agricultural reclamation or aesthetics. It epitomized the idea of Jewish integration into the imagined Jewish landscape and nation. The certificate one received as a donor of a tree included a romanticized, pastoral scene with a portrait of Herzl in the center [Figure 35].[19] The Tree Fund, originally the Olive Tree Fund (*Oelbaumspende*) was perhaps the single most ingenious means devised by Zionism to foster Western Jewish connections to Palestine.

Symbolizing the harmony of Jewry and nature, as opposed to the anti-Semitic stereotype, the Tree Fund was shown as brilliantly commanding the renewal of the Jewish landscape. It was the ideal complement to the myth that Palestine was an empty land, which was to be re-created by the Jews themselves.[20] Actualizing one's relationship to this central aspect of the Zionist project simply meant giving money to the JNF. In 1912, it cost approximately the equivalent of one US dollar to "plant a tree" in Palestine. Donors of five trees or more received "an artistically designed diploma." Jews were also urged to donate "gardens" of one hundred, and "groves"of one thousand trees; they were assured that this was not an uncommon practice among their coreligionists.[21]

By receiving a certificate, the donor was recognized by the "nation" for his efforts. From the suggestion of JNF promotions it became very popular to honor the memory of loved ones by planting a tree or trees in that person's name. The movement also encouraged leaving money

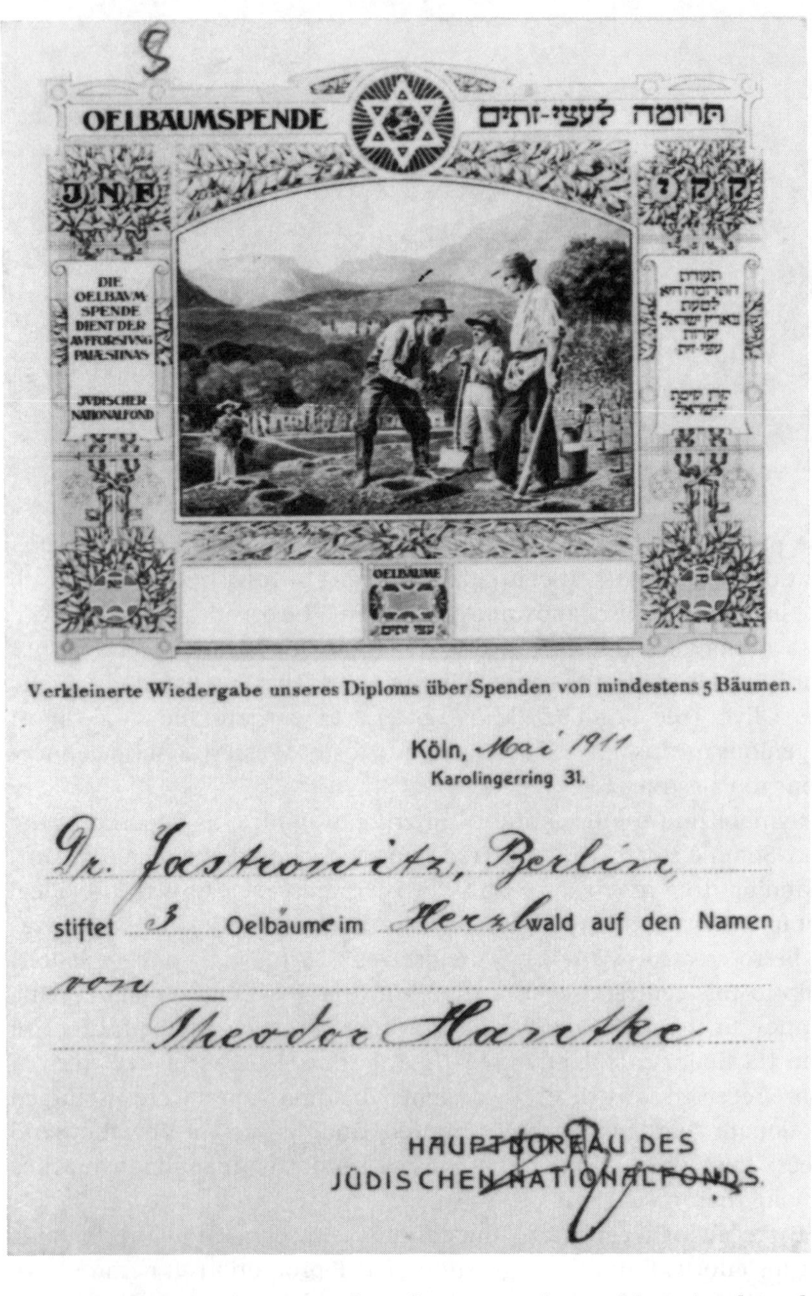

OELBAUMSPENDE תרומה לעצי-זתים

JNF קקי

DIE OELBAVM-SPENDE DIENT DER AVFFORSTVNG PALÄSTINAS

JÜDISCHER NATIONALFOND

OELBÄUME

Verkleinerte Wiedergabe unseres Diploms über Spenden von mindestens 5 Bäumen.

Köln, Mai 1911
Karolingerring 31.

Dr. Jastrowitz, Berlin,

stiftet 3 Oelbäume im Herzlwald auf den Namen

von

Theodor Hantke

HAUPTBUREAU DES
JÜDISCHEN NATIONALFONDS.

35. Certificate for donating at least five trees to the Jewish National Fund.

for trees in one's will, to create "an eternal memorial." Having trees planted in Palestine after one died was tantamount to fulfilling the *Mitzvah* of being buried in the Holy Land, the JNF proclaimed. Moreover, the JNF promised that "measures were being taken" "so that in the near future it will be possible actually to point to a particular tree for every one that has been contributed." Despite the fact that such exact record keeping and markings supposedly initiated more than a decade after the fund began, the general assumption was that the tree literally had the name of the donor or honoree on it – and could be located in Palestine.[22]

For those who had been more than marginally committed to Zionism, the Tree Fund of the JNF comprised another aspect of integration which had potential for great significance. After the death of Theodor Herzl in 1904, the JNF implored Zionists to donate to the Tree Fund in honor of the deceased founder. These trees would be consecrated in "an historically important and prominent site in Palestine" toward the creation of the "Herzl Forest," which was located on the outskirts of Jerusalem.[23] This campaign was phenomenally successful; it tapped into the immense outpouring of grief for the leader. The founding announcement of the Herzl Forest proclaimed that "the sentiments of eternal gratitude for this great man seek a form of expression," bestowing a life of its own on Herzl's memorial. "There is a necessity to create a memorial that is worthy to carry the name of the dead leader, and equally, to advance his life's work – as a source of good fortune and well-being for the people for which he sacrificed his life, and for the country, to which all of his efforts led." A forest was also fitting, because "[Herzl's] modesty forbade the erection of gorgeous monuments and marble columns."[24] A quiet forest, where it would be possible to take a tranquil walk, was thought to reflect the humility and character of the leader.

Even though Herzl originally had opposed what he regarded as "infiltration," that is, small-scale efforts at colonization that might or might not have had the sanction of Ottoman authorities, the JNF appropriated him as their leading symbol. Herzl had, the institution maintained, "created the instruments that were necessary for the continuous advancement of the colonizing work." He was said to have determined "the essential character of the JNF." The main legacy of Herzl that was embodied by the JNF, the organization touted, was his slogan that the goals of Zionism, and the betterment of the Jews could be accomplished "solely through the organized self-help of the people."[25] The JNF was repeatedly described as the Jewish instrument of self-help *par excellence*.

During the Fifth Zionist Congress (1901), in which the JNF was officially commenced, Herzl reportedly made the first pledge to the fund when he was called to the Torah at the *Shabbat* service.[26] It was typical on special occasions in middle-class congregations, when one was given the honor of an *aliya* [to recite one of the blessings before the Torah portion read on a special occasion], to make a public declaration of a donation. It seems, then, that Herzl initiated the process of integrating the JNF into synagogue life, so it would replace or supplement donations to traditional Jewish charities. In one of the first circulars sent to leaders of regional Zionist organizations about the JNF, the Head Office stated that "no joyous or sorrowful event, no closing of a business deal, no private or business letter, no holiday or get-together, and no synagogue service should forget the Jewish National Fund." To stress the participation of the masses of Jewry, and therefore, the ostensibly populist base of the movement, it proclaimed that "[t]he rich and the poor are equal here, when they give the same portion for the same cause." The circular also made it clear that a "good Jew" was to be equated with one who sacrificed his fair share for this purpose; this was continued by similar directives given at the Zionist Congresses, and by special materials designed for the Purim, Chanukah, and T'sha b'Av holidays. The Purim and Chanukah leaflets included an enlarged reproduction of E. M. Lilien's drawing from the Fifth Zionist Congress postcard.[27] There was to be no mistaking the JNF as a central institution of the Zionist Movement.

Promotions for the Herzl Forest also encouraged Jews to contribute "to commemorate births, Bar Mitzvahs, engagements, weddings, completion of studying a Talmud tractate, and house-warmings." Donations should also serve, they were told, "as an expression of thanks for a favor, for honoring presidents of Zionist organizations and other functionaries, to celebrate the passing of an important exam, and to show one's gratitude for being saved from a dangerous situation."[28] Western Jews responded in kind; this was probably one of the most successful manifestations of Herzl's plan for "the conquest of the Jewish communities."[29]

"Special acitivites for collection should take place," the movement advised, "for Herzl's *Jahrzeit* [the annual commemoration of a loved one's death in Jewish tradition] on the 20 of *Tamuz* of the Jewish year." Every Jewish home, where "a gleam of Herzl's spirit existed" should make the occasion in conjunction with the JNF.[30] This was a significant attempted addition to Jewish ceremony; it was not common practice among (non-Hasidic) Jews to observe the *Jahrzeit*, in one's home, of a person other than a relative. No major Jewish holidays were principally in recognition of the birth or death of an individual, biblical or historical. On the whole, Jewish tradition eschewed the sanctification of individuals as deities or even near deities. Martyrs for the faith, on the other hand, were recalled on Yom Kippur, the Day of Atonement. To be sure, Herzl was depicted by the movement as a modern Jewish martyr, whose re-creation of a new nationalism required an institutionalization of new liturgical forms.[31]

The movement also advanced the idea of transforming a little known festival into a major JNF holiday. "The 15 of *Shvat*," or *Tu b'Shvat* was publicized as "the most appropriate day for collecting for the Herzl Forest, because it signified the beginning of the spring in Palestine, and it is the 'New Year's Day of the Trees' according to Jewish tradition." It was described as an important holiday in Palestine, "when school children hike in the open, observing the mountains with their teachers where young trees have been planted, and they greet the coming of spring with Hebrew songs." In the typical Zionist fashion, the scene of children and their teachers completely at home in nature, in Palestine, was juxtaposed to their coreligionists in "the cold countries of the *Golus*," where on that holiday they were said to experience "a doubly strong attraction to the [Jewish] Fatherland."[32]

Parents were implored to use the occasion as a lesson for their children not only "to remember the bygone days, but to fill the future with hope, with help from the Tree Fund, to replenish the neglected soil of Palestine, and to raise a happy, younger generation in Palestine, fulfilled in their work and optimistic of their future."[33] Middle-class Jewish children were one of the main groups targeted for promotions by the JNF. In the mass mailings that children received, they too automatically detached from the process of directly taking part in settling Palestine. The Jewish youth of Palestine, described or pictured, are clearly separate from diaspora children. To be sure, European Jews were disparaged for living in the *Golus*. But they were rarely, if ever, challenged to make the pioneering life in Palestine their own fate. They were to be educated about Palestine, but not socialized to actually live in *eretz Israel*. Jewish children in Central and Western Europe were specifically instructed that fundraising was the preeminent way to express their identification with Zionism.

In *Der Traum von der Nationalfondsbuechse: Ein Maerchen fuer Kinder* [*The Dream of the National Fund Box: A Fairy Tale for Children*] (around 1910), German and Austrian children were shown that "being good children and Jews" meant urging their parents, uncles, aunts, and grandparents to give to the JNF. The playmates of little Josef Loewenstein in the story trifle away their money at the candy store; Josef, instead, puts his change into the JNF box, to help build the Jewish nation. The reproduction on the first page is of Samuel Hirszenberg's "Golus," which shows sick, cold, old, stooped Jews treading across snow-covered ground. These are easily recognizable as East European *Shtetl*-Jews, from the Pale of Settlement, probably fleeing a *pogrom*.[34] When Josef asks his mother where the money from the JNF goes, she replies:

> Do you remember our trip last year, when we saw a group of pale, weary people, with men in long coats, and women in ragged clothes with small children in their arms? They were Jews from Russia, Jews like us, who were driven out from where they lived into the wide world. It has been many, many centuries since we Jews lost our beautiful homeland, the Land of Israel. Now we collect money, lots of money, so we can send our persecuted brothers back to our home.[35]

Although little Josef is told that the Russian Jews are "Jews like us," the lesson he is being taught objectifies the contrary. Regarding Palestine, Josef's vocation is to gather money; for the poor Russian Jews, it is to work the land. Throughout the book, there are idyllic scenes of farming in Palestine, which envision the new life of the Russian Jews, and a reproduction of a certificate, to recognize a donation to the fund to build a worker's house, which Josef would receive if he gives a large enough donation. Palestine, except in pictures, is not in the immediate future for German and Austrian children like Josef. "When you get big," the book preaches, "you can then visit the Holy Land, and there you will see rolling fields and blooming gardens, and the joyful, upright people. You can take pleasure in having helped create so much good fortune with your collection."[36] "Visiting" and "helping" *eretz Israel* would remain dominant aspects of Western Zionist culture, made into essential forms of participation by the JNF.

The message of the primacy of collecting money is reinforced by the image on the front of the booklet, which is a photograph of a medal. It displays a child, next to a map of Palestine labeled in Hebrew. The child is dropping a coin into a JNF box. If the child is successful in fundraising, he is promised a handsome medallion of his own, given out on Chanukah or Purim, which he can "proudly wear on his chest." The medallion is supposedly representative of Josef's counterparts in Palestine, fully integrated in their natural setting. One side has a child sitting under an apple tree, playing a flute, and the other shows a girl with two small lambs at her feet, carrying a bundle above her head.[37]

A JNF leaflet, which begins "Dear Children," includes the same image of the child dropping the coin in the box, and the assertion is repeated that the Jews "in Russia, Rumania and in some barbarous lands of Africa" are of the same "flesh and blood" as the children. This promotion, however, includes the Western Jewish children as future beneficiaries of the "beautiful and glorious country," Palestine. To demonstrate that they were "good and noble Jews," like the "noble men, good Jews, who were trying to collect this great sum of money, so that the land may soon be bought" – the task of the children remained collecting money. The priority, clearly, was to relieve the distress of their persecuted brethren.[38] The land was possibly bought "for them," in this instance, but no directive was given to the children concerning that land, besides giving money. Another common image, used on postcards and leaflets, shows an old, white bearded, black-clad Jew, with his arm around a modern child in a cap, dropping a coin into a JNF box.[39] This was probably intended to signify the continuity between the religious tradition of giving money for *zedakah*, or charity, and giving to the JNF. They had most likely been taught the virtue of charity in their homes and in school as a part of religious instruction. In these ways, children were locked into place in the Zionist cultural scheme, as mediators beween the old and new, and the guarantors of Jewish survival. Furthermore, the reality of the revolt of middle-class youth was mitigated by imagining children as miniatures of their fund-raising parents, and by posing the supreme ideal of calm and restful children, happy in play and work, in Palestine.

Such materials aimed at children were probably among the more effective devices of the JNF and the Zionist Movement overall. But in garnering the interest and concern of children, Zionism risked making its mission seem trivial or banal. In some sense, the process of collecting money had become a game, with the prize being the medal which might be won, or perhaps for the reward of praise from parents and "noble men" for their Zionist activity. It is true that Zionism was a totality that showed and offered a complete world in which they might take part. But the JNF was a well-marked route by which they were to participate in the movement and was an element of the Zionist culture to which they were repeatedly exposed. Zionism, to children, might, or might not have consisted of nothing more than JNF stamp collecting and the gathering of money. But the potential, at some point, for their being seized with the sense that this was part of a larger mission, or even their awareness that Zionist work was being done, was infinitely beneficial to Zionism. It outweighed the possible detrimental effects from the trivialization of the project and Zionist culture.

Middle-class women were also assigned the role of givers to the JNF through distinct promotions. In "An Appeal to Jewish Women," the recipients were praised for the "charity that they had traditionally displayed towards the poor." Similar to the children, they would play a special part in the linkage between the Jewish past and future. "The need for the extension of the sympathies of Jewish women were never greater than at the present day," the JNF declared. "The loving aid that she has always given so freely to those around her in distress must now be invoked for millions of the House of Israel who walk in darkness." Again, it was not for the women themselves, but for the masses that this money was principally intended. What was said to be their traditional calling to help the poor was enlisted, as was their ability to persuade their families to support the cause. Predictably, the leaflet for women displayed a more sophisticated expression of Jewish culture than the promotions for children. On the top was a reproduction of Eduard Bendemann's "By the Waters of Babylon," considered one of the finer examples of early nineteenth-century Jewish art, showing women yearning for Zion [Figure 36].[40] Women were also encouraged to support the JNF, because the Jewish possession of a "place of refuge" would help to give their children a moral means to resist the pangs of social humiliation and temptations of assimilation.[41]

The charitable instinct of Jewish men was indisputably the main focus of most JNF materials. "How Can I Do Something for My Poor Brethren?" was the heading of one of their principal mass mailings. "What effort," it asked, directly under the masthead, "stands closest to us Jews, as we prepare to bring to life a home for our poor, persecuted brethren?" The "preeminent idea" of the JNF was "not alms, but education leading to productive labor, and the creation of possibilities for earning one's living!" Self-help again emerges as the key. Accord-

Leaflet Nr. 8.

An Appeal to Jewish Women.

Women of Israel!

We wish to invite your earnest attention to the appeal which we herewith address to you. The Jewish woman has always been distinguished for the love and devotion she has lavished upon her home, and for the charity she has displayed towards the poor. These sterling qualities have contributed in no small degree to the spirit of solidarity in Israel, even though they have been exercised for the most part within the somewhat limited sphere of the domestic circle. But those same virtues can and should be exercised in the interests of a larger circle — for the welfare of Jewry at large. The need for the extension of her sympathies was never greater than at the present day: the loving aid that she has always given so freely to those around her in distress must now be invoked for millions of the House Israel who walk in darkness.

Ever and again we hear the heartrending cries of our fellow-Jews in Russia who are exposed to deadly peril. They are denied all rights and wage a desperate struggle for mere existence. Hundreds of thousands forsake Russia, Roumania and Galicia, to seek a new and

36. "By the Waters of Babylon" by Eduard Bendemann; Jewish National Fund leaflet "An Appeal to Jewish Women."

ing to this leaflet, contributions filtered to the JNF through a variety of schemes, including the purchase of JNF "telegram-forms" – actually telegram-style letters, sent through the regular mail – which were "artfully designed," for special occasions. It also requested male Jews to give a sizeable donation to the JNF "Golden Book." This was

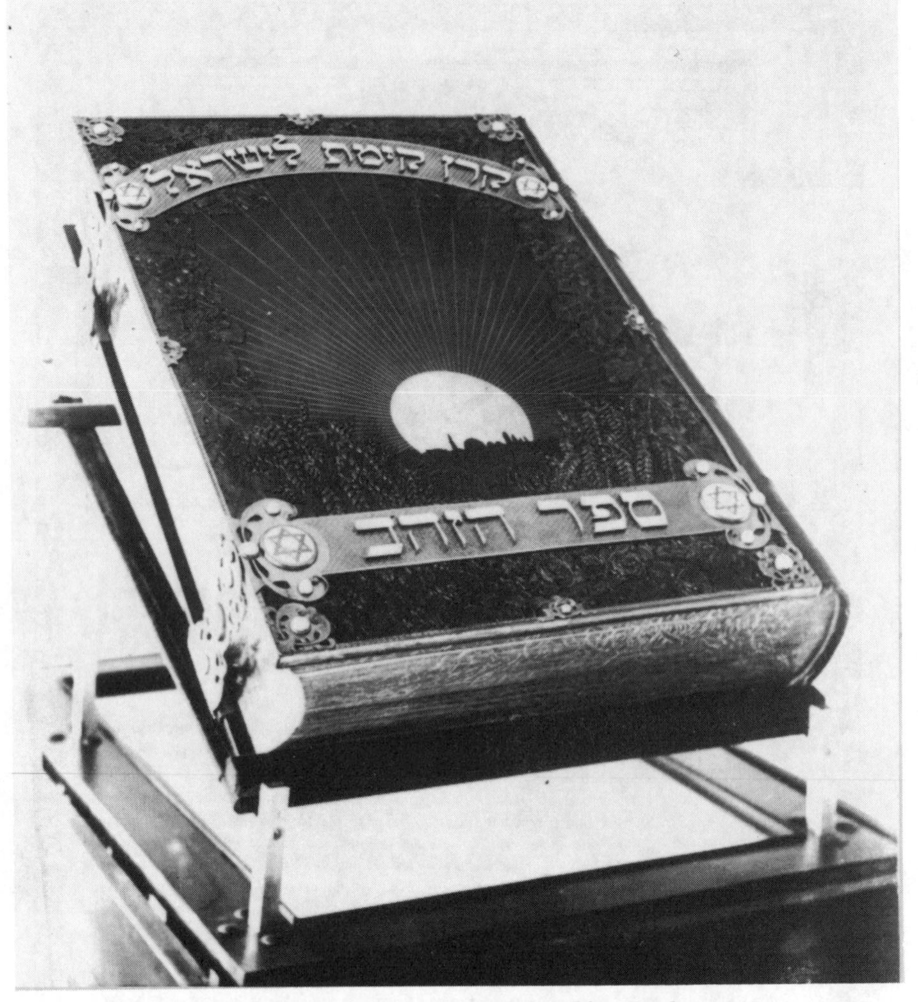

37. First Jewish National Fund Golden Book.

originally "a massive volume," swelling to at least six volumes by 1914, "of magnificent design, kept in the rooms of the Head Office of the JNF" in Central Europe. Pictures of the "Golden Books" were displayed during Zionist Congresses, in travelling JNF exhibitions, and in the Zionist press [Figure 37].[42] "The names of all persons and organizations, on whose behalf the sum of ten pounds (50 dollars) was paid either at once or in installments within three years," was entered into the log. One also received an "aesthetically pleasing

38. "Im Golus" by S. Rovkhomovsky; postcard issued by the Jewish National Fund.

diploma," and *"Most appropriate for this purpose, the certificate is done in your Hebrew name."*[43] Therefore, by making a donation, one received a distinct sign of having entered the realm of Hebrew culture. The names of contributors to the "Golden Book" were also recorded in the pages of the Zionist press.

A number of other schemes for collection and donation were listed in such pamphlets, with which one could also order picture postcards, such as "*Im Golus*" ["In Exile"], by S. Rovkhomovsky, showing an old religious man holding a dying boy [Figure 38], and the "Remember the Jewish National Fund" design, of the old man and modern boy dropping the coin, along with the ubiquitous portraits of Herzl. JNF announcements and pamphlets typically used Jewish subjects, Hebrew characters, and art nouveau motifs in their graphic design.[44] Although the message was in great part somber, the format was bright, and the object of the fund was always somewhat removed – albeit related – from the recipients of the promotion.

In almost every instance where there is text concerning the JNF, the "JNF Box" or the "Blue and White Box," it is usually in a tone of warmth, respect, and sometimes awe – for the power it seems to have wielded, and its potential for being a chief instrument to uplift the

Jewish nation. In the children's fable, the box comes to life, grows wings, and whisks little Josef off to Palestine to show him the new life there.[45] The small, tin boxes deployed around the world were not completely uniform, but there were elements common to all: they were mostly blue, had a Jewish Star, proclaimed that their proceeds went to the JNF, and that this would help establish a Jewish country for the Jewish people [Figure 39]. For adult males, there were at least five versions of small lapel pins depicting the JNF box.[46]

A number of myths circulated about how the box came into use; one of them posed that the original Zionist advocate of the JNF, Hermann Schapira, had a dream in which the box appeared to him.[47] Most Jews, though, recognized the similarity between the JNF box and *pushkes*, or charity boxes that they had seen all of their lives. These were for *Yeshivot*, orphanages, and the like; most Jews must have assumed that the Zionists simply appropriated the established method. Before, during, and after this time, *Yeshivot* and Jewish charities continued to use their own boxes to support their institutions.

The exaltation of the many fundraising devices seemed, to some in the movement, to be detrimental to Zionism's quest for respectability. There were others who intimated that it depleted the energies of the movement that might be better exerted for more lofty cultural endeavours.[48] Such arguments carried little weight; most Zionists took for granted the notion that the "elevation of the Jews involved a question of money."[49] Yet the JNF provoked responses within Zionism to counter the materialistic fundraising operation that sometimes seemed to dominate the movement. This sentiment critical of the JNF was most creatively and brilliantly expressed in a short-lived humor magazine, *Shlemiel*, which was actually sponsored by the movement from May 1903 to December 1905. Later, it appeared as an occasional annual Purim-edition from 1906 to 1911. Edited in Berlin by Max Jungmann, it was distributed mainly to coffee houses and Zionist reading rooms in cities such as Berlin, Cologne, Vienna, and their environs.

Sammy Gronemann, at the Seventh Congress, offered high praise for *Shlemiel* and expressed the hope that it could be revived. It was a first-rate vehicle for the popularization of Zionism, he said, and the value of satire should not be underestimated.[50] He had been one of the main contributors. In *Shlemiel*, caricature and other forms of humor served to extend the discussion about Zionism as a viable political alternative, and worked as a tool of self-criticism for the

ſchien ins Zimmer, ſo daß es ganz hell war. Joſef ſchaute ſich um, und da ſah er: ſeine blaue Nationalfondsbüchſe war es. Die hing an ihrer Stelle,

Büchſe des Jüdiſchen Nationalfonds.

6

39. "Buechse des Juedischen Nationalfonds."

movement. Mirroring the movement as a whole, much of the material in *Shlemiel* lampooned the JNF.

Shlemiel was one of the first Zionist publications to address the possible affinities or tensions between traditional concepts of charity, commonly referred to by the Hebrew *zedakah*, and fundraising for Zionism. The back cover of a 1904 issue shows "The Future Hall of Victory in Jerusalem." One of two figures in the forefront, to the left, is Johann Kremenezky, founder of the JNF. Inscribed on the pedestal of Kremenezky's statue is "Johann der Schnorrer" [Yiddish for "beggar"]. He points to a can strapped to his stomach labeled "Give;" and there are two "Collection Boxes" at the base of the statue.[51] The irony of a statue of a beggar at the front of a nation's "Hall of Victory" is intensified, because Kremenezky wears the cap of a worker. In fact, he was a wealthy owner of a light bulb and electronic supply factory; for his nation, though, he was the lead beggar.

A long poem, entitled "The Perfect Zionist," parodied the numerous inducements of the JNF. *Shlemiel* was bold in asserting that there might be connections between enthusiasm for this component of the movement and hucksterism: "The Perfect Zionist" tries to get you officially enrolled into the movement, insisting he won't be obstructive; but beware: "He holds you – doesn't let you pass 'til he's taken one mark from you." After trying to sell shares of the Jewish Colonial Trust and the National Bank, the narrator claims that he "tried to run away" from "The Perfect Zionist."[52]

"No, then he starts talking about the stamps [Jewish National Fund stamps], because you just have to buy twenty stamps from the fund. Then he's putting them on your letters with great skill. And spit. But mostly they're crooked, and he puts them on all the letters. And suddenly he pulls out his collection box and shakes it to make a noise. Nothing will help you. If you can anticipate this, pull a button off your trousers and put that in. Now you think it's over, but just imagine it – he has a tree which he takes out from behind his back. Immediately he's pushing a full olive tree before your eyes. And you have to take it, because this is the latest thing from the Zionists. He insists that you must get one for your wife as well." The final plea is reserved for the Golden Book. "And if you've saved diligently, and donate enough money, they'll inscribe you in the Golden Book, and your name will appear on the last page of the *Rundschau*," the German Zionist Federation organ. "If you're really clever, you'll send this to Vienna, then you are 'in' – before the eyes of Christian and Jew, a perfect Zionist."[53]

Certainly, this piece indicates that Zionism had partly assumed the character of an aggressive charitable society. Some of its trappings, at any rate, were petit bourgeois inducements, with which some middle-class Jews would not care to enjoin. But this was truly an essential part of Zionist culture – and it could be parodied with only slight twists and exaggeration. Overall, though, *Shlemiel* highlighted a fledgling political movement faced with seemingly insurmountable obstacles, while it exuded tremendous confidence and political maturity.[54] Only six years after the movement was launched, Zionism inspired and sustained a journal which brusquely pointed to the severe flaws and contradictions in its program and leadership. It also implied that some of what the movement passed off as national culture was nothing more than kitsch. The founders of the movement believed that self-parody was possible, and even desirable; they realized that internal criticism would be a lasting and prominent feature of a revived Jewish polity, and laughed along with *Shlemiel*.[55] The stress on fundraising was inevitable; possibly, the leadership felt that they might as well use humor to acknowledge the contradictions, and harness the wittiest parody so that it might serve the ultimate aims of the movement.

Even though the demise of *Shlemiel* was due to factors beyond its acrid criticism of the JNF, it did occasionally receive some harsh words from the leadership. Kremenezky feared that the journal might actually discourage Jews from giving to the JNF.[56] The reprimand of *Shlemiel* was representative of a trend in Zionism to deny that the JNF was a form of charity. The movement seemed compelled to combat the perception of Zionism as a charitable society, similar to those which could be found in any Jewish community. From a Zionist perspective, these were engaged in trifling, innocuous, and possibly self-serving projects. After the First Zionist Congress, Herzl chided a letter writer to the London *Times* for alleging that "the Congress was not a real national assembly because certain charity organizations and community bodies were not represented." "They were not there?" Herzl mocked. "Parbleu! We had not invited them. What have we got to do with the charity organizations, the community boards, the Jewish Pickwick clubs?" Obviously, to the reader, and many others, a great deal. They were competing for the sympathies and money of the Jews; and they both claimed to be ameliorating the degraded state of the Jews. "The dear gentleman," Herzl concluded, "simply has not understood our movement. He does not know what the rebirth of a nation is."[57]

In a similar vein, professing to clarify one of the major "misunderstandings" about Zionism at the Eighth Zionist Congress (1907), Nordau emphasized that they had not embarked on "a great philanthropic movement." Rather, Zionism was "a beneficent movement;" it was not "a benevolent movement. You cannot give alms to a whole people."[58] Many of the tracts of the JNF seemed to be sparring with that question. As opposed to most charitable enterprises, which allegedly offered "merely temporary relief," Zionism and the JNF claimed to have attacked "the evil at its root . . . to place the existence of the entire Jewish people upon a thoroughly sound basis."[59] Furthermore, Zionists differentiated themselves from philanthropists, because they styled themselves as advocating "the organized self-help of the people," borrowing Herzl's phrase from the First Congress.[60] Also, in theory and in practice, the JNF was to be "a people's treasure," a national treasury whose work benefited all of Jewry and whose bounty accrued from the rich and poor. Indeed, echoing the insight of many critically minded Western Jews, the JNF maintained that the non-Zionist charities implied heavy-handed control and maintenance of the status quo; these were spread out to so many different institutions that no single one could make much of an impact.[61] Traditional charities, distributed unsystematically if not arbitrarily, merely allowed for survival and subsistence. Zionism's purpose, as presented to the Western Jews and championed by the JNF, was to foster *Bildung* – limitless cultivation, toward the perfection of the individual and the social order – as the reality for the most downtrodden of the Jews. Above all, the goal of creating a new, eternal, national culture, which would make it possible "in Palestine for Judaism and Jewry to develop with the utmost of freedom" removed it from the province of charity.[62]

An exhibition adjacent to the Bezalel show at the Tenth Zionist Congress (1911) displayed JNF stamps, pamphlets, diplomas for the Tree Fund, models of houses, pictures of schools, a diarama of a workers' quarter in Jaffa, and charts detailing the fund's development. "The prosperity and growth of the JNF," reported *Die Welt*, "is the new blood of Jewry and Palestine."[63] Also at the Tenth Congress, Otto Warburg proclaimed that "it is clear that the Olive Tree Fund would not have had such an auspicious expansion, if its goals did not simultaneously serve various intentions. Its success is without a doubt owing to the comprehensive concerns of the members of the Zionist Organization. It is to re-afforest Palestine, while creating a fund for an everlasting culture; but it is especially to immortalize the memory of our great leader, in the land of his ardent desire, for eternity."[64] Warburg's analysis, from the movement's public perspective, could not have been more cogent. Zionism had encouraged Western Jews to avail themselves of a nation of their own – and there was little risk involved. It was a means by which they were able to transcend the local, national, and even Jewish communities of which they were a part, and to join a resplendent Jewish community – possible, for Central and West European Jews, just from giving money. In short, it offered them a piece of eternity.

A critical evaluation of the JNF shows that fundamental tensions between state-building and charity emerged in early Zionism that were far from being resolved by 1914. Unfortunately, from the perspective of the leadership, Zionism never possessed the authority to force a compulsory taxation on all of the world's Jews, whom they claimed as their citizenry. Therefore, the financial basis of the movement had to be erected voluntarily, which helped bind the JNF to the cultural renewal promised by Zionism. This led to the expressions of Zionist culture in unfortunate and self-defeating forms, and the legitimation of an ever-increasing fundraising apparatus.

In the first few years Zionism had been in danger of becoming ever more marginal; instead it grew, and moved toward the mainstream of European Jewish life. While Zionism spread, it generated myths and symbols that were originally intended to discredit anti-Jewish stereotypes and promote a positive self-image among Jews. There was some success at this. Yet these symbols also carried the potential of being turned into stereotypes and of locking in patterns of perception for Central and West European Jews. One of the paradigms was to see themselves as Zionists removed from Zion – except for the possibility of visiting or studying in the Holy Land for a given period.[65]

An antidote for this tendency of inner-Zionist alienation was the persistence of Zionist self-criticism within its national culture, which was in force from the very beginning. Besides being the legacy of Ahad Ha-Am, it might also have been an outgrowth of *Bildung*, in which the process of self-cultivation meant examining the myths which governed one's life and society, even as a Jew and Zionist.[66] Furthermore, primarily philanthropic Zionism was called into question by those who asserted that the most legitimate way to speed the redemption of Zion was to get behind the plow in Palestine; obviously, this was the most personally threatening and least tried route for Central and West European Jews before 1914.[67]

After it established a relatively solid basis, Zionism was increasingly threatened by the prospect that the movement could become trivialized among those having sympathy with its aims. True, Zionism desperately needed the material support of non-Zionists to realize its program. The price, though, for the movement, was cultivating a polity whose main connection to the movement was giving money. Moreover, the encouragement of an attitude that Western Zionists were patrons of Zionism, not just participants, reflected the alleged character of the leadership of the Jewish colonies in the 1880s, and the Jews who presided over diaspora communities, primarily by virtue of their personal wealth. The leaders in Palestine had especially been maligned by the early Zionists as detached, uncreative, myopic, unprosperous, and unpopular. Indeed, Zionism was partly built on the scorn that Ahad Ha-Am and Herzl had heaped on those endeavours.

The Jewish National Fund professed to correct this misdirection of the magnates who had preceded Herzl. In the end, the JNF gave Western and Central European Jews the opportunity to participate in Zionism through the most miniscule donation, and to be considered a good or great Zionist for delivering a significant sum. By 1913, it was admitted in a party organ that even "the so-called 'assimilates' could subscribe to present-day Zionism. They could find it quite in accordance with their principles to help in building schools and universities in Palestine."[68] The writer might have added that one did not have to be an enthusiastic Zionist to plant trees in Palestine, an activity which was certainly popular among Jews not officially affiliated with the movement. After all, who could object to planting a tree? Indeed, with the JNF's support of forests, libraries, agricultural research, and the revival of the ancient tongue, a mere gift of money was an entry ticket to Jewish culture, which Zionism was making ever more visible and dignified.

Fundraising necessarily became part of the movement's matrix of culture and Jewish nationalism. The diaspora was in principle denigrated, but Western Jews were treated gingerly because they helped bankroll the movement. Albeit somewhere, in the recesses of the movement's mythology, they too might someday emigrate to Palestine – but most materials targeted to Western Jews assumed that it would never be the case. In this sense the JNF abetted the reduction of

Zionism to what David Vital has termed "a pious cause," and bears witness to the emergence of the movement as a "special interest" – but perhaps not a vital interest – for most assimilated Jews.[69] Zionist culture, in some part intentionally, made a tremendous impression on Western Jewry due to the affinities between the complex Jewish tradition of *zedakah* and giving to the JNF.[70]

The JNF emerged as a secularization and nationalization of *zedakah*. In the same way that Zionism took on selected symbols and elements of the Jewish religious traditions, the JNF sanctified the political, social, and economic existence of the Jews – toward the fueling of an ongoing cultural process.[71] The JNF was the greatest success of the early Zionist movement in Central and Western Europe, because it offered transcendence of one's self and the present-day world of the Jews. This had always been part of the spiritual core of *zedakah*. It simultaneously objectified and sanctified a Western Jew's solidarity with the wretched Jewish masses.[72] Indeed, the prophetic tradition held that "Zion shall be redeemed with justice, and they that return to her through *zedakah*" (Isa. 1:27). One recent commentator has written that "this reflects the optimism that characterizes the individual who, having heard the cry of the weak and helpless, believes that he can rally the forces of his own redemption for the redemption of the other."[73] The Zionists made *zedakah* more centralized, pragmatic, and nationalistic through the JNF; it was accompanied by a clear vision of a gloriously normal sovereignty. Thereby Zionism inaugurated a formidable secular institution, at the center of which was "a redemptive cultural process."[74]

CONCLUSION

A SUPPLEMENTAL NATIONALITY

"At times, a self-satisfied Jewish bourgeoisie, especially in the Europe of the nineteenth century, has succumbed to the temptation to identify Judaism with an uncritical faith in the possibility of human salvation through cultural enlightenment and progress." This synopsis, expounded by Samuel Hugo Bergman many decades after his journey from Prague to Jerusalem, assumed that the dominant "faith" of his former milieu was "superficial and inadequate."[1] Such criticism was central to Zionism's challenge to Central and West European Jews, and informed the content of Zionist culture. In *Der Judenstaat*, Herzl warned that to wait for all men to see the world like Lessing's character of Nathan would be to no avail for the Jews; progress toward the further emancipation of European Jewry "was neither automatic nor inevitable."[2] Furthermore, on a level which would have been unthinkable a generation earlier, Zionist culture aspired to rouse the Jews to take responsibility for their lives, as Jews. A principal way that this was attempted, which was historically unparalleled, was to build a nation in the mind's eye of the Jews, apprehending a complete Jewish life in Palestine as the ideal – while there were, in fact, shockingly few prerequisites for the establishment of a Jewish nation-state.

Nevertheless, modern history shows that Zionism failed to divert the flow of emigrants from the New World to Palestine, or to save the masses of European Jewry from ultimate destruction. Concurrently, traditional patterns of Jewish authority proved themselves unable to address the problems posed by the social, economic, political, and ideological consequences of emancipation. Zionist culture revealed the structures of real and imagined inequality within the Jewish world, and the disparate attitudes, habits, dreams, and cultural predilections of Jews. Moreover, Zionist culture was marked by its members' wishes to be happy, healthy, normal, and to remain Jewish, while being full-fledged members of the modern world.

Zionist national culture emerged as a relatively late product of European nationalism. Several means of national self-creation, which Jews had been exposed to as members of the European states, were employed to nationalize the Jews. Yet because of their deep and complex fragmentation – and especially the lack of common ground under their feet – original, highly imaginative means also had to be fashioned to accomplish their aims. The degree to which the early Zionists were able to adapt and spread their nationalist ideology, while their constituents were far removed from the "nation," or loyal to other nations, was indeed remarkable. Part of the basis of their nationalization efforts was the ideological content of Zionist culture, which reflected a reaction to the political and social atmospheres in which Western Jews lived, as well as their educational backgrounds and general disposition toward culture. Zionist culture materialized as an expression of the Jews' urge toward national "normalcy," and was molded on the one hand by severe material constraints and promises by the movement that it could surmount such obstacles in a spectacular manner. On the other hand, it was forced to conform to the unrelinquished hopes of the vast majority of Western Jews for full emancipation in Europe. Indeed, even most Western Zionists, before the war, were unwilling to give up their lives in Europe. Zionist culture was partially successful in giving middle class, assimilated Jews a means to support and celebrate their Jewish identity; simultaneously, it supplied a way for Jews to criticize themselves and the world constructively – and offered the conceivability of recreating themselves as individuals, and as greater autonomous Jewish communities.

Whereas Zionist culture fostered new opportunities for Western Jews' engagement with themselves as Jews, individually and communally, it also offered – primarily through the manifestations of the movement as a charity – a detachment from the Zionist project. The movement had little choice but to accept this as a risk. At any rate, ideas and conceptions that had been only dimly perceived before 1897 were transformed and developed into an accessible symbolic language and set of prominent images by 1914. For Western Jews, Zionist culture could be a reservoir for a secular faith and confidence in Jewish self-will, which could be called on when their material conditions and non-Jewish attitudes toward the *Judenfrage* changed beyond recognition. Western Jewry, from the turn of the century to the First World War, was given a fresh Archimedean point – Zionist myths and symbols – that engendered new ideas of social responsibility, power relations, and possibilities of personal and collective renewal. In part, for the Zionists of the *fin-de-siècle* this was accomplished through the linkage of Zionism and culture, envisioning a nationalism which was rooted in the greatest hopes of their grandfathers' emancipatory ecstasy.

NOTES

INTRODUCTION

1 The framework of this discussion is the history of Zionist politics and institutions; see David Vital's three volumes, *The Origins of Zionism* (Oxford: Oxford University Press, 1975), *Zionism: The Formative Years* (Oxford: Oxford University Press, 1982), and *Zionism: The Crucial Phase* (Oxford: Oxford University Press, 1987); Stephen Poppel, *Zionism in Germany, 1897–1933* (Philadelphia: Jewish Publication Society of America, 1977); Stuart A. Cohen, *English Zionists and British Jews: The Communal Politics of Anglo-Jewry, 1895–1920* (Princeton: Princeton University Press, 1982); Jehuda Reinharz, *Fatherland or Promised Land* (Ann Arbor: University of Michigan Press, 1975), and Reinharz, ed. *Dokumente zur Geschichte des Deutschen Zionismus 1882–1933* (Tuebingen: J.C.B. Mohr, 1981); Yehuda Eloni, *Zionismus in Deutschland: Von den Anfaengen bis 1914* (Gerlingen: Bleicher, 1987). The most enlightening interpretation of several of the themes to be treated here, until the death of Herzl (1904), is Ehud Luz, *Parallels Meet: Religion and Nationalism in the Early Zionist Movement, 1882–1904*, trans. Lenn J. Schramm (Philadelphia: Jewish Publication Society of America, 1988); useful essays also appear in Yosef Salmon, ed., *Religion and Zionism: First Encounters* [Hebrew] (Jerusalem: Hasiffriya ha-Tsioniot, 1990), and Gideon Shimoni and Hayim Avni, eds., *Zionism and its Jewish Opponents* [Hebrew] (Jerusalem: Hassifriya ha-Tsioniot, 1990). Very little attention will be paid to France, due to the early Zionists' resigned attitude towards enlisting French support; France also constitutes a special case because the *Alliance Israélite Universelle* played a leading role in shaping perceptions of Zionism and Palestine; "[w]hile Zionist societies were established in Paris as early as the 1890s, it was not until the 1930s ... that Zionism began to overcome its association with immigrants and leave its imprint on French Jewry[;]" Paula Hyman, *From Dreyfus to Vichy: The Remaking of French Jewry, 1906–1939* (New York: Columbia University Press, 1979), 194; see also

Michael Marrus, *The Politics of Assimilation: A Study of the French Jewish Community at the Time of the Dreyfus Affair* (London: Oxford University Press, 1971), 281, 241.

2 Theodor Herzl, "Eroeffnungsrede zum ersten Kongress," *Theodor Herzls Zionistische Schriften* (Berlin–Charlottenburg: Juedischer Verlag, 1908), 223. The Basel Program, the Zionists' objectives as drafted at the First Congress (1897) read: "Zionism aims at the creation of a home for the Jewish people in Palestine to be secured by public law./ To that end, the Congress envisages the following: I. The purposeful advancement of the settlement of Palestine with Jewish farmers, artisans and tradesmen. II. The organizing and unifying of all Jewry by means of appropriate local and general arrangements subject to the laws of each country. III. The strengthening of Jewish national feeling and consciousness. IV. Preparatory moves towards obtaining such governmental consent as will be necessary to the achievement of the aims of Zionism. Printed material file, Central Zionist Archives, Jerusalem [hereafter cited as CZA].

3 See Karl Kraus, "Eine Krone fuer Zion [1898]," in *Karl Kraus fruehe Schriften 1892–1900*, II, ed. Joh. J. Braakenburg (Munich: Liesel, 1979), 298–314.

4 David Vital, *The Origins of Zionism*, vi.

5 See Arthur A. Cohen, *The Natural and the Supernatural Jew* (London: Valentine, Mitchell, 1962), 306ff.

6 See *Festschrift der Juedische Turnverein "Makkabi" Graz 1904–1914 im Verbande der Juedischen Turnerschaft* (Graz: "Lykam," 1914); *Festschrift zur Feier des 100. Semesters der akademischen Verbindung Kadimah*, ed. Ludwig Rosenhek (Vienna: 1933), 50ff., 81ff.; *Zionistisches A–B–C* (Berlin–Charlottenburg: Zionistisches Zentralbureau, 1908). 150–1.

7 See David Sorkin, *The Transformation of German Jewry* (New York: Oxford University Press, 1985), 15, 19.

8 See Arthur Hertzberg, introduction to *The Zionist Idea: A Historical Analysis and Reader* (New York: Atheneum, 1977).

9 George Mosse, *German Jews Beyond Judaism* (Bloomington: Indiana University Press, 1983), 3ff.

10 See Moses Gaster in *Stenographisches Protokoll der Verhandlungen des II. Zionisten-Kongresses gehalten zu Basel vom 28. bis 31. August 1898* (Vienna: "Erez Israel," 1898) [hereinafter cited as SP II.], 204; *Stenographisches Protokoll der Verhandlungen des V. Zionisten-Congress in Basel 26.27.28.29, und 30. Dezember 1901* (Vienna: "Erez Israel," 1901) [hereinafter cited as SP V.], 396–7; see Sorkin, 5ff, 15–8, 86–104, 172–7, and Mosse, *German Jews Beyond Judaism*, on the centrality of the concept of *Bildung* as a secular ideology for German Jewry.

11 Theodor Herzl, *Theodor Herzl Briefe und Tagebuecher, II. Band: Zionistisches Tagebuch 1895–1899*, eds. Alex Bein, Hermann Greive, Moshe Schaerf, Julius H. Schoeps (Berlin, Frankfurt a.M., Vienna: Propylaeen, 1984), 86.

12 Jacob Alexander, "Centrifugal and Centripetal Forces," in *Zionism and the Western Jew: A Symposium Read Before the London Zionist League on 24th*

December 1908 (London: H. Ginzburg, 1909), 10; Georg Hecht, *Der Neue Jude* (Leipzig: Gustav Engel, 1911), 9.

13 Leon Simon, *Ahad Ha-Am* (Philadelphia: The Jewish Publication Society of America, 1960), 240.

14 See Adolf Boehm, *Die Zionistische Bewegung, I. Band* (Berlin: Juedischer Verlag, 1935), 47ff.

15 Michael Meyer, *The Origins of the Modern Jew: Jewish Identity and European Culture in Germany 1749–1824* (Detroit: Wayne State University Press, 1980), 43.

16 Quoted in Alfred Werner, "The Story of Jewish Art," in *Jewish Affairs* 14 (December 15 1946): 27.

17 Theodor Herzl, "Eroeffnunungsrede," 223.

18 See Moses Gaster, SP V., 396–7; Marcus Ehrenpreis, "Moralische Zionismus," *Die Welt* (December 17, 1897): 44; Hans Kohn, "Geleitwort," and Hugo Hermann, "Erziehung im Judentum," im *Vom Judentum: Ein Sammelbuch Herausgegeben vom Verein juedischer Hochschuler Bar Kochba in Prag* (Leipzig: Kurt Wolff, 1913), vii–xi, 186–91; Martin Buber, "Das juedische Kulturproblem und der Zionismus" in *Die Stimme der Wahrheit: Jahrbuch fuer wissenschaftlichen Zionismus*, ed. Lazar Schoen (Wuerzburg: N. Philippi, 1905), 209–10; Buber, "Theodor Herzl and History", in *Theodor Herzl and We*, trans. Chaim Arlosoroff (New York: Zionist Labor Party, 1929), 51; "Moderne Kultur und ihr Einfluss die Juden," in *Zionistisches A–B–C*, 150–1; Max Besser, "Der russische Zionistentag in Minsk," *Juedische Turnzeitung* 10 (October 1902): 167 ; Shmarya Levin, in *Stenographisches Protokoll der Verhandlungen des X.–Zionisten–Kongresses in Basel vom 9 bis inklusive 15 August 1911* (Berlin: Juedischer Verlag, 1911) [hereafter cited as SP X.], 151; see also Israel Kolatt, "Zionism and Political Messianism," in *Totalitarian Democracy and After: An International Colloquium in Memorial of Jacob Talmon* (Jerusalem: Magnes, 1984), 346–7; Arthur A. Cohen, *The Natural and the Supernatural Jew*, 306ff.

19 Hugo Bergman, in "Die Grundlagen nationales Erziehung," *Die Welt* (August 22, 1913), 1090; see also Martin Buber, "Das juedische Kulturprobleme und der Zionismus," in *Die Stimme der Wahrheit*, 209, 216; Nahum Syrkin in SP X., 212; Simon Bernfeld, "Zwei juedische Kongresse" in *Ost und West* (February 2, 1910): 72.

20 David Yellin, "The Renaissance of the Hebrew Language in Palestine" in *Zionist Work in Palestine*, ed. Israel Cohen (Leipzig and London: T. Fischer Unwin, 1911), 143.

21 See Michel Foucault, *The Archaeology of Knowledge and the Discourse on Language*, trans. A. M. Sheridan Smith (New York: Pantheon, 1972), 37–8, 49, 107, 136–7; see also Edward Said, *Orientalism* (New York: Vintage, 1977), 94; George Mosse, *The nationalization of the Masses: Political Symbolism and Mass Movements in Germany from the Napoleonic Wars through the Third Reich* (New York: Meridian, 1977); Murray Edelman, *Politics as Symbolic Action: Mass Arousal and Quiescence* (Chicago: Markham, 1972), 6–7, 14–15, 31, 54, *passim*; Vernon L. Lidtke, *The Alternative Culture:*

Socialist Labor in Imperial Germany (New York: Oxford University Press, 1985).

22 See Paula Hyman, in "The History of European Jewry: Recent Trends in the Literature," *Journal of Modern History* 54, 2 (June 1982): 304ff., and David Vital, "The History of the Zionists and the History of the Jews," *Studies in Zionism* 6 (Autumn 1982): 159. Among the small number of works concerning the visual dimension of Zionism are *Bezalel 1906–1923*, ed. Nurit Shilo-Cohen (Jerusalem: Israel Museum, 1983); *Herzl in Profile: Herzl's Image in the Applied Arts*, ed. David Tartakover (Tel Aviv: Tel Aviv Museum, 1978–9); Mark H. Gelber, in "The *jungjuedische Bewegung*," *Leo Baeck Institute Year Book 31* (1986): 105–19; Milly Heyd, in "Lilien and Beardsley: 'to the pure all things are pure,'" *Journal of Jewish Art*, 7 (1980): 58–69.

23 See Paula Hyman, "The History of European Jewry," 304ff.

24 See Schlomo Aveneri, *The Making of Modern Zionism* (New York: Basic, 1982), 31; Rupert Emerson, *From Empire to Nation: The Rise to Self-Assertion of the Asian and African Peoples* (Boston: Beacon, 1969), 106, 156.

25 Vital, "The History of the Zionists and the History of the Jews."

26 Quoted in Schmuel Almog, *Zionism and History: The Rise of a New Jewish Consciousness* (Jerusalem: Magnes Press and St. Martins, 1987), 39.

27 See Elias Auerbach, in "Theodor Herzl," *Juedische Turnzeitung* 7 (July 1904): 114.

28 See M. Ussischkin, "Palestine and Other Countries," in *Zionist Work in Palestine*, 22.

29 This model is borrowed extensively from Ezra Mendelsohn, *The Jews of East Central Europe Between the World Wars* (Bloomington: Indiana University Press, 1987); "The West European type of Jewish community obviously closely corresponds to the Jewries of such Central and West European countries as Germany, France, and England. In East Central Europe it was found in Bohemia and Moravia (the so-called Czech lands), in Hungary, in certain parts of Latvia, and in Romanian Wallachia . . ." 7. To a certain extent, these perceptions were shared by many Russian Zionists, especially before Labor-Zionism gained a significant following, because they would have received the Zionist message from the perspective of the middle class; "[u]nexpectedly perhaps, [the] primary following [of the Zionist Movement in Russia until 1904] was drawn from the middle classes;" Joseph Goldstein, "The Zionist Movement in Russia, 1897–1904," (Ph.D. dissertation, the Hebrew University of Jerusalem, 1982), d.

30 See, i.e., Maurice Friedman, *Martin Buber's Life and Work: The Early Years 1878–1923* (New York: Dutton, 1981), 58.

31 See Richard Lichtheim, *Die Geschichte des Deutschen Zionismus* (Jerusalem: Rubin Mass, 1954), 142; Dennis B. Klein, *Jewish Origins of the Psychoanalytic Movement* (Chicago and London: University of Chicago Press, 1985), 21.

32 *Jewish Chronicle*, September 12, 1913, 19.

CHAPTER ONE: CONGRESS–ZIONISM IN MOTION

1 Jehuda Reinharz, *Chaim Weizmann: The Making of a Zionist Leader* (New York: Oxford University Press, 1985), 53–4.
2 Schmarya Levin, *Forward from Exile*, ed. and trans. Maurice Samuel (Philadelphia: Jewish Publication Society of America, 1967), 372.
3 See, i.e., *Jewish Chronicle*, August 23, 1907, 5; *Die Welt*, 18 August 1911, 873, 876.
4 Alex Bein, *Theodor Herzl*, trans. Maurice Samuel (Philadelphia: Jewish Publication Society of America, 1940), 215.
5 Theodor Herzl, *Der Judenstaat* (Leipzig and Vienna: M. Breitensten's Verlags-Buchhandlung, 1896), 68–71.
6 After the First Congress, Herzl "asked his friend, Oscar Marmorek, the architect, to design a proper Congress building in Basel . . ." After the exodus, the building would remain one of the landmarks of Switzerland. Marmorek's preliminary sketch displeased him; it fell short of evoking what Herzl called a "neo-Jewish style;" Amos Elon, *Herzl* (New York: Holt, Rinehart, and Winston, 1975), 257. That was apparently the only instance Herzl used such a term.
7 Nordau to Herzl, March 25, 1897, HVIII 614/15, No. 42; Herzl to Nordau, April 20, 1896, HN 41, CZA.
8 Ernst Pawel, *The Labyrinth of Exile: A Life of Theodor Herzl* (New York: Farrar, Straus, and Giroux, 1989), 256.
9 Bein, 217–19; see Herzl quote in *Theodor Herzl: A Memorial*, ed. Meyer Weisgal (New York: New Palestine, 1929), 190.
10 *Jewish Chronicle*, July 9, 1897, 13.
11 Joseph Wenkert, "Herzl and Sokolow" in *Herzl Year Book*, II, ed. Raphael Patai (New York: Herzl Press, 1959), 187.
12 David Farbstein to Herzl, June 11, 1897, HVIII/226, CZA; see *The Complete Diaries of Theodor Herzl*, ed. Raphael Patai, trans. Harry Zohn (New York: Herzl Press, 1960) [hereafter cited as THD], 171.
13 Marcus Cohn, in "Erinnerungen eines Baslers an den ersten Zionistenkongress," *Sonderdruck aus der Festschrift des Schweizerischen Israelitischen Gemeindebundes* (Basel: Brin, 1954), 4.
14 Theodor Herzl, *Theodor Herzl Briefe und Tagebuecher, II. Band*, 223.
15 See, i.e., *The Letters and Papers of Chaim Weizmann*, II, Series A, gen. ed. Meyer Weisgal (London and Jerusalem: Oxford University Press and Israel University Press, 1974) [hereafter cited as WP, with corresponding volume number], 15, n.1.; SP X., 154–5.
16 Farbstein to Herzl, June 11, 1897, HVIII/226, CZA.
17 Farbstein to Herzl, June 11, and July 2, 1897, HVIII/226, CZA; see Herzl, *Judenstaat*, 25ff.
18 Farbstein to Herzl, June 13, 1897, HVIII/226, CZA.
19 THD, 165, 27.
20 Farbstein to Herzl, July 2, 1897, HVIII/226, CZA.
21 Farbstein to Herzl, July 2, 1897, HVIII/226, CZA.

22 Adolf Boehm, 282, 286; see, e.g., Heinrich Gurenau-Gruenzweig, "Was Herzl Uns War," in *Zeitgenossen ueber Herzl*, ed. T. Nussenblatt (Bruenn: Juedischer Buch- und Kunstverlag, 1929), 86; Adolf Friedemann, *Das Leben Theodor Herzls* (Berlin: Juedischer Verlag, 1914), 10; the earlier versions of Herzl's plan were framed as a letter to the Rothschilds, and as directives to a "Family Council", which included Jews such as Baron Hirsch, and the Rothshilds; THD, 102, 64, 66, 148.

23 *Jewish Chronicle*, September 3, 1897, 10.

24 Marcus Cohn, 13, 7.

25 Farbstein to Herzl, July 2, 1897, HVIII/226, CZA; see *Die Welt*, September 3, 1987, 14; see also Leon Simon, *Ahad Ha-Am*, 171–72; it is not known exactly how this "honor guard" was identified; they did not wear uniforms. *Theodor Herzl Briefe und Tagebuecher, II. Band* 65.

26 Herzl, *Old-New Land*, trans. Lotta Levensohn (New York: Bloch and Herzl Press, 1960), 4.

27 Erwin Rosenberger, *Herzl as I Remember Him*, trans. Louis Jay Hermann (New York: Herzl Press, 1959), *passim*; Elias Auerbach, *Pionier der Verwirklichung* (Stuttgart: Deutsche Verlags-Anstalt, 1969), 70ff.

28 Farbstein to Herzl, July 26, 1897, HVIII/226, CZA.

29 Berthold Feiwel, *Die Welt*, September 3, 1897, 7.

30 George L. Mosse, *Nationalism and Sexuality: Respectability and Abnormal Sexuality in Modern Europe* (New York: Howard Fertig, 1985), 67–70.

31 See THD, 585, 602, 613–17, 779, 785, 1156.

32 See below, Chapter 5.

33 Martin Buber, "Theodor Herzl and History" in Martin Buber and Welsch, *Theodor Herzl and We*, 12; "Maennerlied" in *Juedische Turnzeitung*, 7/8 (1901): 101.

34 *Theodore Herzl Briefe und Tagebuecher*, vol. II, 57.

35 See Hans Kohn, in *Von Judentum*, v; Elias Auerbach, *Pionier der Verwirklichung*, 131.

36 "Of course, the women are very honored guests, but they cannot take part in the voting," Herzl, *Zionisten-Congress in Basel Officielles Protocoll* (Vienna: "Erez Israel," 1898) [hereafter cited as SP I.], 115; *Jewish Chronicle*, September 3, 1897, 10; see Vital, *The Origins of Zionism*, 357; see Nordau, in SP X., 20; *Jewish Chronicle*, September 12, 1913, 18; Martin Buber, "Theodor Herzl and History" in Martin Buber and Weltsch, *Theodor Herzl and We*, 12; "Maennerlied" in *Juedische Turnzeitung*, 7/8 (1901): 101.

37 *Die Welt*, September 3, 1897, 2; see Stanley Nash, *In Search of Hebraism: Shai Hurwitz and His Polemics in the Hebrew Press* (Leiden, Netherlands: E. J. Brill, 1980); Shmuel Amog, *Zionism and History*.

38 *Jewish Chronicle*, September 2, 1903, iii; see also *Jewish Chronicle*, September 12, 1913, 29; *Jewish Chronicle*, September 19, 1913, 19.

39 "The First Zionist Meeting," [Hebrew song sheet], in the Printed Material File for the First Zionist Congress [hereafter cited as PMF I; succeeding Congress number II.–XI.], CZA.

40 *Jewish Chronicle*, September 3, 1897, 14; *Hermann Schapira: Founder of the*

J.N.F. (New York: Youth and Education Department, Jewish National Fund, 1962), 24; see, e.g., "Dialog zum Commers des X. Zion.-Congress," PMF X; "Festcommers zu ehren des IX. Zionisten-Kongresses zu Hamburg am 28 Dezember 1909," PMF IX, CZA.

41 Amos Elon, 245.

42 "Concert Program," PMF IV., "Konzert-Programm," PMF XI.; PMF I–XI.

43 A song on the same sheet as "Hatikvah" was "Nes Ziona," about one of the earliest Jewish colonies in Palestine, PMF I., CZA.

44 Theodor Herzl, "Dr Guedemann's *National-Judentum*" in *Theodor Herzl Zionist Writings*, I, 67; *Die Welt*, September 3, 1897, 14.

45 "Hatikvah" in "The First Zionist Meeting," PMF I., CZA; translation assistance by Israel Romano and Andrew N. Bachman.

46 Max Jungmann, *Erinnerungen eines Zionist* (Jerusalem: Rubin Mass, 1959), 36.

47 Louis Lipsky, *A Gallery of Zionist Profiles* (New York: Farrar, Straus, and Cudahy, 1956), 133–6.

48 "Preisausschreiben Nationalhymne" file, HN VB9, CZA; *Zion*, April 30, 1897; between the Fourth and Fifth Congress another ultimately unsuccessful contest was held; no one even bothered preserving the applicants (as opposed to the standard practice of saving nearly all correspondence).

49 *Jewish Chronicle*, September 12, 1913, 20; see below. "Hatikvah" has remained an unofficial national anthem of the State of Israel.

50 Emil Berhard Cohn, *David Wolffsohn: Herzl's Successor* (New York: Zionist Organization of America, 1944), 38; some believe it was simply appropriated from a Jewish student society, the V.J. St. (Vereine juedische Studenten) of Berlin; Max Jungmann, *Erinerrungen*, 36.

51 Gershom Scholem, *The Messianic Idea in Judaism* (New York: Schocken, 1971), 280–1.

52 *Prelude to Israel: The Memoirs of M. I. Bodenheimer*, trans. Israel Cohen, ed. Henriette Hannah Bodenheimer (New York: Thomas Yoseloff, 1963), 97–8; THD, 165, 236, 63.

53 PMF I., CZA; Herzl, *Der Judenstaat*, 76–7.

54 Bodenheimer, 110.

55 Herzl, *Der Judenstaat*, 76–7.

56 *Stenographisches Protokoll der Verhandlungen des VII. Zionisten–Kongresses und des ausserordentlichen Kongresses in Basel vom 27. 28. 29. 31. Juli 1. und 2 August 1905 (Berlin: Juedischer Verlag, 1905) [hereafter cited as SP VII.], 314–15.*

57 *Die Welt*, September 3, 1897, 12; Shmarya Levin, 375, 384ff.

58 CZA, PMF.I; "In der feierlichen Eroeffnungssitzung ist das schwarze Festkleid und weisse Halsbinde vorgeschrieben;" *feierlich* also connotes that it was a solemn occasion.

59 Alex Bein, *Theodor Herzl*, 230; see Ahad Ha-Am, "The Jewish State and the Jewish Problem" in *Nationalism and the Jewish Ethic: Basic Writings of Ahad Ha-Am*, ed. Hans Kohn (New York: Schocken, 1962), 70–1, 81–2, 76–9; Karl Kraus, in "Eine Krone fuer Zion," 298ff.

60 "Karpel Lippe (1830–1915)," entry in *Encyclopaedia Judaica*, X, 285; in

fact, there was at least one delegate ten years older than Lippe, Professor Hermann Schapira (1820–98); possibly Schapira was passed over because he was scheduled to deliver a major address.

61 SP I., 1.
62 Ben-'Ami, quoted in David Vital, *The Origins of Zionism*, 356; Bein, 230; cf. *Theodor Herzl Briefe und Tagebuecher, I. Band*, 540; Herzl was perturbed that Lippe "droned on" past his allotted time.
63 *Jewish Chronicle*, September 3, 1897, 11.
64 Bein, 231–2.
65 Z. Bychowski, in "Die Intuition Herzls," in *Zeitgenossen ueber Herzl*, 47.
66 Bein, 232.
67 THD, 68, 104, 57, 21, 3, 13, 27, 19, 236, 165.
68 THD, 3, 54, 157–9, 166, 61, 43, 21; quoted in Foreword to *Theodor Herzl Zionist Writings*, 13.
69 Herzl, "Opening Address at the First Zionist Congress," in *Theodor Herzl Zionist Writings*, I, 132–8; emphasis mine.
70 *Jewish Chronicle*, September 19, 1913; Robert Weltsch, "Theodore Herzl and We", in Martin Buber and Weltsch, *Theodor Herzl and We*, 23–4.
71 Georg Hecht, *Der Neue Jude*, 7; "German Jewry of To-day," in *Jewish Chronicle*, September 19, 1913; Sigmund Freud to Theodor Herzl, September 28, 1902, HVIII/247, CZA; Harry Zohn, *Karl Kraus* (New York: Twayne, 1971), 38–41.
72 Herzl, *Zionist Writings*, I, 132–8.
73 *Jewish Chronicle*, September 3, 1897, 12.
74 Max Bodenheimer, 101.
75 *Theodor Herzl Briefe und Tagebuecher, I. Band*, 538; postcards of "Herzl at the Opening Session of the First Congress," Herzl personality file, CZA.
76 For the latter, Nordau wrote the annual political review for several years.
77 In the few instances when he did, Nordau was less than sympathetic to traditional views of Judaism, and this was used against him in the controversy over Herzl's utopian novel, *Altneuland* (1902); see "Die Juden von Gestern" (Eine Erwiderung), *Ost und West*, 4 (April 1903): 225–6.
78 Milton P. Foster, *The Reception of Max Nordau's "Degeneration" in England and America* (Ph.D. dissertation, University of Michigan, 1954), 2, 40; *Jewish Chronicle*, February 9, 1923, 10; *Palestine Weekly* (Jerusalem) January 26, 1923, 53; the latter points out that this was sometimes due to anti-Semitism.
79 Nordau, *Degeneration* [1893] (New York: Howard Fertig, 1968), 560.
80 Israel Zangwill, "Nordau and Abarbanel" (1923) *Speeches, Articles, and Letters of Israel Zangwill*, ed. Maurice Simon (London: Soncino, 1937), 146; Meir Ben-Horin, *Max Nordau: Philosopher of Human Solidarity* (London: London Jewish Society, 1956).
81 "First Congress Address," in *Max Nordau to His People: A Summons and a Challenge*, ed. B. Netanyahu (New York: Scopus, 1941), 63.
82 *Jewish Chronicle*, September 3, 1897, 13; Chaim Weizmann, *Trial and Error* (New York: Schocken, 1966), 47; Ahad Ha-Am, "The First Zionist

Congress," in *The Jew in the Modern World* eds. Paul R. Mendes-Flohr and Jehuda Reinharz (New York: Oxford University Press, 1980), 431–2.

83 Ahad Ha-Am, "The First Zionist Congress," 431–2.

84 Leon Simon, *Ahad Ha-Am*, 73, 78.

85 See the debate over the telegram that was to be sent to Nordau, in response to his cable to the Eleventh Congress, the first Zionist Congress which he did not attend, *Stenographisches Protokoll der Verhandlungen des XI. Zionisten-Kongresses in Wien vom 2. bis 9. September 1913* (Berlin and Leipzig: Juedischer Verlag, 1914) [hereafter cited as SP XI.], 54–59.

86 Max Bodenheimer, *Prelude to Israel*, 106; cf. *Hermann Schapira: Founder of the J.N.F.* (New York: Youth and Education Department, Jewish National Fund, 1962), 2, 24.

87 *Jewish Chronicle*, September 3, 1897, 15; Bodenheimer, 107; PMF I., CZA.

88 Chaim Weizmann, *Trial and Error*, 46–8; *The Times* [London], August 17, 1897; "I'm in favor of the Jewish State as long as I can be the ambassador to Paris," ran a common joke; see Max Nordau, "Zionism," in *Zionism and Anti-Semitism* (New York: Scott Thaw, 1903), 12.

89 *Jewish Chronicle*, September 3, 1897, 15.

CHAPTER TWO: THE EMERGENCE OF HEBREW AND DISSENT

1 See Adolf Boehm, *Die Zionistische Bewegung, I. Band*, 116–34, 297–300, 504–20; Shlomo Aveneri, *The Making of Modern Zionism*, 112–24, 83–7.

2 Jacques Kornberg, preface to *At the Crossroads: Essays on Ahad Ha-am* (Albany: State University of New York Press, 1983), viiff.

3 Israel Friedlander, in "Achad Ha-am" (delivered at the Jewish Theological Seminary, New York, February 8, 1906), *The Jewish Exponent* (February 16 and 23, 1906), no pagination.

4 Theodor Herzl, in "The Menorah" in *Theodor Herzl Zionist Writings*, I, 203–6; *Theodor Herzl Briefe und Tagebuecher, II. Band*, 81, 128–9; cf. Amos Elon, *Herzl*, 178, *passim*.

5 Herzl, in "The Menorah," 206.

6 THD, 56, 133, 102.

7 THD, 151.

8 THD, 22; Shmuel Almog, *Zionism and History*.

9 *Jewish Chronicle*, September 12, 1913, 28.

10 Reinharz, *Chaim Weizmann*, 72–3, *passim*; *Zionistisches A-B-C Buch*, 43–5.

11 Israel Kalusner, *Oppozitizia l'Herzl*[*Opposition to Herzl*] [Hebrew] (Jerusalem: Achiavar, 1960), 51–4, *passim*; cf. Josef Fraenkel, *Dr. Sigmung Werner: Ein Mitarbeiter Herzls* (Prague: Zionistische Propagandastelle Prague, no date), 16–18.

12 David Vital, *Zionism: The Formative Years*, 195; Herzl "personality" file, CZA.

13 *Stenographisches Protokoll der Verhandlungen des IV. Zionisten-Kongresses in London* (Vienna: "Erez Israel," 1900) [hereinafter cited as SP IV.], 110–11.

14 Alex Bein, *Theodor Herzl*; Nash, 203.

15 Maurice Friedman, *Martin Buber's Life and Work: The Early Years,* 39; Chaim Weizmann to Catherine Dorfman, September 12, 1901, no. 128 and August 27, 1902, no. 300 in WP I., 180, 384; Leon Simon, *Ahad Ha-Am,* 83, 112.
16 Moses Gaster to Richard Gottheil, October 30, 1898, A203/113, 39 CZA.
17 Joseph Goldstein, "The Zionist Movement in Russia," g; Almog, 175.
18 M. Ehrenpreis, in "Herzl und der 'Kultur-Zionismus' in *Zeitgenossen ueber Herzl,* 54.
19 See Berthold Feiwel, "Stroemungen im Zionismus" in *Ost und West* (October 1902): 687; cf. Israel Friedlander, "Achad Ha-Am" (delivered at the Jewish Theological Seminary, New York, February 8, 1906; reprinted from *The Jewish Exponent,* February 16 and 23, 1906), no pagination.
20 See David Vital, *Zionism: The Formative Years,* 41–3.
21 Marcus Ehrenpreis, in SP I., 183.
22 The centrality of history is the main theme of Almog in *Zionism and History.*
23 Quoted in Carlton J. H. Hayes, *Essays on Nationalism* (New York: Macmillan, 1933), 53–4.
24 The reporting in the London *Jewish Chronicle,* which was originally opposed to Zionism, but taken over by a group of Zionists in 1907, indicates a strong identification with the German language and culture on the part of British Zionists which rivalled that of the Central Europeans.
25 SP I., 184.
26 See, i.e., Chaim Weizmann to Catherine Dorfman, August 27, 1902, no. 300, in WP I., 384.
27 SP I., 184.
28 SP I., 184–7, 189.
29 This view is reflected in much of the historiography of the *Kulturdebatte,* see, i.e., Jacques Kornberg, "Theodor Herzl: A Revaluation," *Journal of Modern History* 52 (June 1980): 226–52, *passim.*
30 SP I., 184.
31 Most of the comment on this issue has been written from the perspective of the fiercest participants in the *Kulturdebatte;* in *Zionism and History* Shmuel Almog provides an excellent an essential exposition of the debate from this viewpoint, up to 1906, 85–176, *passim.*
32 Leon Simon, *Ahad Ha-Am,* 73, 78, 171ff.
33 Ahad Ha-Am, "Jewish State and Jewish Problem" in *Nationalism and the Jewish Ethic: Basic Writings of Ahad Ha-Am,* ed. Hans Kohn (New York: Schocken, 1962), 72.
34 Osais Thon, "Achad Haam," in *Die Welt,* March 13, 1914, 254.
35 Shmaryau Levin, quoted in *The Uganda Controversy, I,* ed. Michael Heymann (Jerusalem: Israel Universities Press, 1970), 20.
36 Ahad Ha-Am, "Jewish State and Jewish Problem."
37 Marcus Ehrenpreis, "Moralische Zionismus," *Die Welt,* December 17, 1897, 44.

38 Leon Simon, *Ahad Ha-Am*, 172, 194, 213; M. Gluecksohn, "Die Streitfrage" (Herzl und Achad-Haam), *Die Welt*, July 10, 1914.
39 Jacques Kornberg, "Theodor Herzl," 236ff.
40 Leon Simon, *Ahad Ha-am*, 173–4.
41 Michael Berkowicz, "Herzl and Hebrew" in *Theodor Herzl: A Memorial*, 74; M. Ehrenpreis, "Herzl und der Kultur-Zionismus," 54–7.
42 Ehrenpreis, "Herzl und der Kultur-Zionismus," 54–5.
43 Ben-Ami, "Erinnerungen an Theodor Herzl," *Die Welt*, July 3, 1914: 691.
44 THD, 56; Herzl, *Der Judenstaat: Versuch einer Modernen Loesung der Judenfrage* (Leipzig and Vienna: M. Breitenstein's Verlag-Buchhandlung, 1896), 75.
45 Berkowicz, 74.
46 Moshe Schaerf provided this insight; Herzl, "The Solution to the Jewish Question" in *Theodor Herzl: Zionist Writings*, I, 24.
47 Martin Buber, introduction to *Juedische Kuenstler* (Berlin and Leipzig: Juedischer Verlag, 1902), no pagination.
48 Joseph Wenkert, "Herzl and Sokolow" in *Herzl Year Book*, II, ed. Raphael Patai (New York: Herzl Press, 1959), 189.
49 Shai Hurwitz, quoted in Nash, 154; Hugo Hermann, "Erziehung im Judentum" in *Vom Judentum*, 186–91; David Yellin, "The Renaissance of the Hebrew Language in Palestine" in *Zionist Work in Palestine*, 143.
50 David Vital, *The Origins of Zionism*, 222–3.
51 *Theodor Herzl Briefe und Tagebuecher, II. Band*, 541.
52 See Norbert Elias, *The Civilizing Process: The Development of Manners*, trans. Edmund Jephcott (New York: Urizen Books, 1978), 3–40.
53 Nathan Birnbaum, in SP I., 84.
54 See Samuel Hugo Bergman, *Faith and Reason*, trans. and ed. Alfred Jospe (New York: Schocken, 1972), 135; Birnbaum, in SP I., 88, 92.
55 Birnbaum, SP I., 94.
56 Erwin Rosenberger, *Herzl as I Remembered Him*, 11ff.
57 A delegate to the First and Second Zionist Congresses, Davidson then turned to the Bund and Russian Social Democracy, eventually becoming a history professor in Kiev.
58 Untitled announcement to the members of the First Zionist Congress, August 30, 1897, signed "Das Comite." PMF I, CZA. The Congress announcements also included a publicity notice for the Hebrew publishing company, "TECHIJA," sponsored by Ehrenpreis and Michael Berdyczewski, Z 1/280, CZA.
59 See, i.e., Nash, 3.
60 Ehrenpreis, "Theodor Herzl und der Kultur-Zionismus" in *Zeitgenossen ueber Herzl*, 57.
61 See, e.g., Maurice Friedman, *Martin Buber's Life and Work: The Early Years*, 58.
62 Markus Cohn, "Erinnerungen eines Basler an den ersten Zionistenkongress," in *Sonderausdruck aus der Festschrift des Schweizerischen Israelitischen Gemeindebundes* (Basel: Brin, 1954), 4.

63 Richard Gottheil (New York) to *Erez Israel* [Zionist Office] Vienna, February 19, 1902, A138/5, CZA.
64 SP II., 200–2.
65 SP II., 197; 202.
66 SP II., 199–201.
67 Rabbi Rabbinowitsch, SP II.; the text of his speech does not appear in the protocol; the text just states that he spoke "in Jargon" [Yiddish], and no German translation followed. It might have been omitted because the German stenographers did not know Yiddish well enough. Nonetheless, from the later statements of Rabbinowitsch, it is possible to reconstruct the main lines of his argument, 213; see Vital, *Zionism: The Formative Years*, 218–19.
68 See Gaster to Gottheil, October 30, 1898, A203/113, 39,30, CZA.
69 See Gaster to Gottheil, October 30, 1898, A203/113, 39,30, CZA.
70 SP III., 206–7.
71 *Stenographisches Protokoll der Verhandlungen des IV. Zionisten-Kongresses in London 1900* (Vienna: "Erez Israel," 1900) [hereafter cited as SP IV.], 223–6.
72 SP V., 393–4.
73 SP V., 320–31.
74 SP V., 395.
75 SP V., 395–6.
76 SP VIII., 64–5ff.
77 See David Vital, *Zionism: The Crucial Phase*, 4.
78 There was also a current argument that Jews would simply fare no better under socialism than they had under liberalism, because eventually "the masses would dictate an anti-Semitic policy;" another Zionist argument held that for Jews, "socialism can only be realized in Zionism;" Max Nordau, quoted in Walter Laqueur, *A History of Zionism* (New York: Schocken, 1972), 388–9; see "Max Nordau on Socialism," in *Jewish Chronicle*, February 10, 1899, 15; Nordau, "Socialism in Europe," *Cosmopolitan* 36 (March 1904): 519ff.
79 See Ehrenpreis, "'Moralischer' Zionismus," in *Die Welt*, December 17, 1897, 4–5. I am indebted to Moshe Haleavy of the Tel Aviv University for bringing this article to my attention.
80 *Stenographisches Protokoll der Verhandlungen des VIII. Zionisten-Kongresses im Haag vom 14. bis inklusive 21. August 1907* (Cologne: Juedischer Verlag, 1907) [hereafter cited as SP VIII.], 64–6.
81 SP VIII., 87–90.
82 SP VIII., 305–6.
83 "Masel" means "luck" in Hebrew and Yiddish; it is not clear which intonation Sokolow used.
84 SP VIII., 338.
85 "Bericht des Aktionskomitees, Allgemeine Uebersicht der zionistische Bewegung (1907–1909), (Kulturell-politischer Teil)" in *Stenographisches Protokoll der Verhandlungen des IX. Zionisten-Kongresses im Hamburg vom 26. bis inklusive 30. Dezember 1909* (Cologne: Juedischer Verlag, 1909) [hereafter cited as SP IX.], 360.

86 See "Die zionistische Kongresse im Lichte der Kultur," *Die Welt*, December 17, 1909, 1121–3

87 Gaster to Gottheil, October 30, 1898, A203/113, 39, 30, CZA.

88 See, e.g., Mascha Hoff, *Johann Kremenezky und der Grundung des KKL* (Frankfurt a.M.: Peter Lang, 1986), *passim*; Lipsky, 26ff.

89 A 203/107/40, CZA. The circular continues that "the coordinator will decide whether suggestions by third parties will be sent to committee members to be voted on. If suggestions by third parties are handed in by a member of the committee they will be regarded as coming from the committee member himself . . . Documents, proposals, and other materials sent to the coordinator by the committee members have to bear the heading J.C. (Jew. Culture). The coordinator arranges and duplicates them and distributes them to the members of the committee . . . The *original* documents as well as the votes have to be registered and filed and should be available for perusal by all committee members. From the quarterly report the coordinator will prepare a general report which he will send to all committee members. These reports as well as resolutions adopted should be published by the coordinator in newspapers friendly to the Zionist idea if publication seems appropriate."

90 Protokoll der Konferenz der Kultur-Kommission, abgehalten am 20.u.21 November 1902 in Odessa," 6, Z1/380, n. 2456, CZA; Circulars to the "Vertrauensmaenner" in Russia, nos. 10, 11, 24, 27, 30, Z1/380, CZA.

91 SP III., 199–200.

92 SP V., 169.

93 SP V., 390–3.

94 SP V., 390–3.

95 SP V., 426–7; see Josef Fraenkel, *Dubnow, Herzl, and Ahad Ha-Am* (New York: Ararat, 1946); Fraenkel attributes the myth of Herzl's strong antipathy to the Faction to the historian Simon Dubnow, 21.

96 Lipsky, 27, 76.

97 SP. V., 70.

98 Herzl and Kokesch to the culture commission, January 27, 1902, HE 1 153/HB 443; August 7, 1902, Z1/211, CZA.

99 Reportedly, Ahad Ha-Am was also a "totally unconstructive" participant in the Hebraists' Conference of 1909; Nash, 289.

100 Protocoll der Sitzung der russischen Kultur-Kommission vom 28 Februar bis 13 Maerz, n. 663, Z1/223, CZA. In attendance were I. Bernstein-Kohan, J. Rawnitzky, and Ahad Ha-Am.

101 Protokoll der Konferenz der Kultur-Kommission, abgehalten am 20 u. 21 November 1902 in Odessa, Z1/380, n. 2456, CZA; cf. Weizmann to Vera Khatzman, August 11, 1902, n. 279 in WP 1., 362; bridgenote, 395.

102 "Bericht des Aktionskomitees, Allgemeine Uebersicht der zionistische Bewegung (1907–1909), (Kulturell-politischer Teil)" in SP IX., 376; "Die Bedeutung der Palaestinaarbeit," in *Festschrift des zionistischen Vereines "Jeshrun," 1901–1911* (Troppau) [Moravia].

103 "*Ha-Sifrut ha Illemet*" ("The Silent Literature"), *Hashiloach* 17 (1908), quoted in "Marcus Ehrenpreis," in *Encyclopaedia Judaica, VI*, 510.

104 *Stenographisches Protokoll der Verhandlungen des X. Zionisten-Kongresses in Basel vom 9 bis inklusive 15 August 1911* (Berlin and Leipzig: Juedischer Verlag, 1911) [hereafter cited as SP X.], 14, 16.
105 SP X., 194ff.
106 Quoted in Nash, 299ff; see also Meyer Waxman, *A History of Jewish Literature*, IV, Pt. 1 (New York: Thomas Yoseloff, 1960), 92–105.
107 SP X., 209.
108 SP X., 210–12, 294.
109 "Leon Chasanowich," in *Encyclopaedia Judaica*, IV 362–3.
110 SP X., 209.
111 See, i.e., Berthold Feiwel, ed. *Jung Harfen* (Berlin: Juedischer Verlag, 1903).
112 SP X., 215.
113 SP X., 215.
114 SP X., 215–6.
115 *Juedische Statistik* was seen as a scientific means to greater self- and group knowledge through an objective analysis of material conditions; similarly, scientific research on Palestine was perceived as a way to gain access to the Jewish essence; see Bertold Feuchtwang, "Juedische Statistik als Kulturarbeit des Zionismus," in *Die Stimme der Wahrheit*, 218; Alfred Nossig, *Juedische Statistik* (Berlin: Juedischer Verlag, 1903), *passim*; Nossig, *Das juedische Kolonisationsprogramm* (Berlin: Juedischer Verlag, 1904), passim; *Aus dem Protokoll der Kommission der Demokratisch-zionistischen Fraktion* (Berlin: 1902), CZA; *Altneuland* 1, 1 (1904): 1–2; see also Herzl, *Der Judenstaat*, 4ff., 10ff., *passim*.
116 SP X., 216.
117 SP X., 210.
118 See *Zionistisches A-B-C Buch*, 43–5.
119 For instance, the Congress did not permit Davis Trietsch to make a disparaging speech about Herzl; he was shouted down; SP X., 177ff.
120 SP X., 216.
121 A similar, less publicized meeting was held in Manchester, June 1909 with identical results; see Stuart A. Cohen, *English Zionists and British Jews: The Communal Politics of Anglo-Jewry, 1895–1920* (Princeton: Princeton University Press, 1982), 108–9.
122 SP X., 216.
123 SP X., 330ff.
124 SP X., 152.
125 SP XI., 74ff.
126 SP XI., 156ff.
127 SP XI., 156ff.
128 SP XI., 75; see also 85ff.
129 See *Vom Judentum*, *passim*; see SP VIII., 109–10, 282, 285, 289–90; SP IX., 53, 212ff., 218, 267 ff., 277–8.
130 See, i.e., Hugo Bergmann, "Die Grundlagen nationales Erziehung," in *Die Welt*, 22 August 1913, 1089–91; *Jewish Chronicle*, September 12, 1913, 28–9.

131 SP XI., 193ff., 257ff.
132 SP XI., 311ff.
133 *Jewish Chronicle*, September 19, 1913, 18–19.
134 *Jewish Chronicle*, September 12, 1913, 28–9.

CHAPTER THREE: CARRYING OUT THE CULTURAL PROGRAM

1 Martin Buber, "Theodor Herzl and History," 14.
2 See Shmarya Levin, *Forward from Exile*, 373; Stuart A. Cohen, *English Zionists and British Jews: The Communal Politics of Anglo-Jewry, 1895–1920* (Princeton: Princeton University Press, 1982), 112–13ff.
3 Moses Gaster, in SP II., 204; emphasis mine.
4 Theodor Herzl, "The Menorah," 206.
5 SP II., 205–6.
6 Moses Gaster, in SP II., 204–7.
7 See, i.e., SP X., 334–5.
8 Moses Gaster, in SP II., 204–7.
9 Moses Gaster, in SP III., 160–4.
10 See below, Ch. 6.
11 Osaias Thon, "The First Big Visions: When Herzl Taught the Zionists to Think in Millions," in *Theodor Herzl: A Memorial*, 54.
12 Osaias Thon, SP II., 213–14.
13 Fabius Schach, SP II., 214–15.
14 See "Preface" to the *The Jewish Encyclopaedia*, I (New York: Funk and Wagnalls, 1901), which was a non-Zionist project, but the leading American Zionist, Richard Gottheil, was a principal editor. The chief editor was Isidore Singer; twelve volumes appeared between 1901 and 1906.
15 Gaster to Gottheil, October 30, 1898, A203/113, 39, 30, CZA.
16 Ibid.
17 See Richard Lichtheim, *Die Geschichte des deutschen Zionismus*, 142; Dennis B. Klein, *Jewish Origins of the Psychoanalytic Movement*, 21.
18 Martin Buber, in SP III., 191–3; *Beschluesse und Resolutionen der Zionisten-Kongresse I–VII.*, ed. Hugo Schactel (Vienna: Zionistischer Zentralverein, 1906), 15–18.
19 Lieb Jaffe, in SP III., 214–15; SP VIII., 343ff.; "Protocoll der Sitzung der russischen Kultur-Kommission vom 28 Februar bis 13 Maerz," no. 663, Z1/223, CZA; "Protokoll der Konferenz der Kultur-Kommission, abgehalten am 20 und 21 November 1902 in Odessa," n. 2456, Z1/350, CZA.
20 SP III., 191–3.
21 Leopold Kahn, in SP III., 199–200.
22 Nahum Sokolow, SP III., 208–10.
23 Chaim Weizmann, SP IV., 95; emphasis mine.
24 See "The Mizrahi Manifesto" [1902], in *The Jew in the Modern World: A Documentary History*, 436.
25 Motzkin, SP. IV., 100.

26 See George Mosse, *The Crisis of German Ideology: Intellectual Origins of the Third Reich* (New York: Grosset and Dunlap, 1964), 188.
27 Chaim Weizmann to Theodor Herzl, 6 May 1903, in *The Letters and Papers of Chaim Weizmann*, II, gen. ed. Meyer Weisgal (London: Oxford University Press, 1971) [hereafter cited as WP II.], 312–13.
28 Maurice Friedman, *The Life and Work of Martin Buber: The Early Years*; Reinharz, *Chaim Weizmann*, 65–91.
29 See Maurice Friedman, 34–73.
30 Shmarya Levin, *Forward from Exile*, 375.
31 Weizmann to Herzl, 306.
32 See footnote 6, WP I., 345–6.
33 Weizmann to Herzl, 307.
34 WP II., 308–13, emphasis added.
35 See, e.g., Theodor Herzl, *Old-New Land*, 4; Herzl, *Der Judenstaat*, 4, 10ff., 16, *passim*; there are references to the leading role of youth throughout his first and second *Tagebuecher*; see *Theodor Herzl Briefe und Tagebuecher, II. Band, passim*.
36 WP II., 308–13.
37 WP II., 313.
38 A long paper on "Hebrew Language and Literature" by Ehrenpreis was distributed to the delegates; PMF V., CZA; SP V., 30–1, 35–6.
39 See note 115, Ch. 2.
40 SP V., 11ff., 17–18, 100, 111, 122–7, 182–4, 7, 27–32, 99–115.
41 SP V., 44–5, 18.
42 See Yosef Yerushalmi, *Zakhor: Jewish History and Memory* (Seattle and London: University of Washington Press, 1983), 86ff.
43 SP V., 140ff.
44 SP V., 114–15.
45 SP V., 152ff., 157, 167.
46 SP V., 157.
47 SP V., 168.
48 Moshe Schaerf provided this insight.
49 See Buber, in "Theodor Herzl and History," 11ff.; cf. Herzl to Buber, September 28, 1901, HB 35, CZA.
50 SP V., 390–3.
51 SP V., 397–402; Buber was actually jeered and heckled, 400.
52 Reinharz, *Chaim Weizmann*, 90.
53 SP V., 424–5.
54 Introduction to WP I., 25–6.
55 Reinharz, *Chaim Weizmann*, 65–166.
56 "Fabius Schach," in *Encyclopaedia Judaica*, XIV, 936; there is no separate entry for Miriam.
57 Emma Gottheil, SP IV., 276, 181; see also Gottheil, "The Early Days of Zionism", in *Theodor Herzl Jahrbuch*, ed. Tulo Nussenblatt (Vienna: Henrich Glanz, 1937), 255ff.; R. Ellman, in *Stenographisches Protokoll der Verhandlungen des II. Zionisten-Kongresses gehalten zu Basel vom 28. bis 31. August 1898* (Vienna: "Erez Israel," 1898), 239ff.; 48; Rosalie Gassman-

Sherr, *The Story of the Federation of Women Zionists of Great Britain and Ireland* (London: Federation of Women Zionists, 1968); Maurice Friedman, *Martin Buber's Life and Work: The Early Years*, 51; Marsha Rozenblit, *The Jews of Vienna, 1867–1914*: Assimilation and Identity (Albany: State University of New York Press, 1983), 163, 165; Harriet P. Freidenreich, *Jewish Politics in Vienna* (Bloomington: Indiana University Press, 1991), 59, 236; Yehuda Eloni, in *Zionismus in Deutschland: Von den Anfaengen bis 1914* (Gerlingen: Bleicher, 1987), 144–8, and Michael Berkowitz, "Organized European Women Zionists, 1897–1933," in *Women in Jewish Culture*, ed. Maurie Sacks (Urbana: University of Illinois Press, 1992), forthcoming. Women Zionists are mentioned in passing in the leading works of German-Jewish women, Marion A. Kaplan, *The Making of the Jewish Middle Class: Women, Family, and Identity in Imperial Germany* (New York and Oxford: Oxford University Press, 1991), xi, and *Jewish Feminist Movement in Germany: The Campaigns of the Juedischer Frauenbund, 1904–1938* (Westport, Connecticut: Greenwood Press, 1979); see also Edward J. Bristow, *Prostitution and Prejudice: The Jewish Fight Against White Slavery*, 1870–1933 (New York: Schocken, 1983) and Linda Gordon Kuzmack, *Women's Cause: The Jewish Women's Movement in England and the United States 1881–1938* (Columbus: Ohio State University Press, 1990), pp. 5–6; on women in Palestine see Margalit Shilo, "The Women's Farm at Kinneret, 1911–1917: A Solution to the Problem of the Working Woman in the Second Aliya," in *Jerusalem Cathedre* (1981): 246–83; and Deborah Bernstein, *The Struggle for Equality: Urban Women Workers in Prestate Israel* (New York: Praeger, 1987).

58 See Ch. 5.
59 SP. X., 219ff.
60 Theodor Herzl, *Theodor Herzl Briefe und Tagebuecher, II Band*, 140.
61 SP IX., Weyl, 208.
62 SP IX., Lebowitsch, 209.
63 See Sammy Gronemann, *Memoirs of a Yekke* [Hebrew] (Tel Aviv: Lador, 1946); SP VII., 163–4.
64 See also SP VIII., 109–10.
65 SP VII ., 166–72.
66 SP VII., 177.
67 See Ch. 6.
68 SP VII., 176.

CHAPTER FOUR: ZIONIST HEROES AND NEW MEN

1 See Meyer Weisgal, ed. *Theodor Herzl: A Memorial, passim*; T. Nussenblatt, ed. *Zeitgenossen ueber Herzl.*
2 See Ch. 7.
3 No. 9144, photography collection [hereafter cited as PC]. CZA; PMF VII., CZA.
4 SP VII., 5ff.
5 SP X., 177ff.

6 SP VII., 316–17.
7 Lionel S. Reiss, "Through Artists' Eyes: The Portraits of Herzl as Revelations of the Man," in *Theodor Herzl: A Memorial*, 113.
8 Cf. *Prelude to Israel: The Memoirs of M.I. Bodenheimer*, ed. Henriette Hannah Bodenheimer, trans. Israel Cohen (New York: Thomas Yoseloff, 1963), 117–18.
9 SP VII., 387–8.
10 SP VIII., 118.
11 Reiss, 113–14.
12 Cf. Alex Bein, introduction to *Arthur Ruppin: Memoirs, Diaries, Letters*, ed. Alex Bein, trans. Karen Gershon (London and Jerusalem: Weidenfeld and Nicolson, 1971), xiv.
13 See SP X., 212, 178ff.; SP IX., 208ff.; SP XI., 46, 94, 110.
14 *Jewish Chronicle*, September 5, 1913, 7–8; *Jewish Chronicle*, September 12, 1913, 18.
15 "Besuch des Herzl-Grabes," PMF XI., CZA.
16 Herzl "personality" file, CZA.
17 *Jewish Chronicle*, September 12, 1913, 27, 18; *Jewish Chronicle*, September 5, 1913, 7; see inscription on Figure 24, quote from Joseph on burial in Palestine.
18 Medals collection, Herzl "personality" file, CZA.
19 David Vital, *Zionism: The Formative Years*, 423–4; see Zangwill, in SP VII., 134.
20 Vital, *Zionism: The Formative Years*, 422–3.
21 *Jewish Chronicle*, September 12, 1913, 26.
22 David Wolffsohn "personality" file, CZA.
23 *Jewish Chronicle*, September 12, 1913, 18, 26; *Jewish Chronicle*, August 18, 1911, 22.
24 SP XI., 55ff., 72.
25 Lipsky, 15.
26 See George Mosse, introduction to *Degeneration* by Max Nordau (New York: Howard Fertig, 1968), xvii–xv.
27 Max Nordau, "Muskeljudentum," in *Juedische Turnzeitung* (June 1900): 10–11.
28 Nordau, "Muskeljudentum."
29 Nordau, "Muskeljudentum;" see also Nordau, "Was bedeutet Turnen fuer uns Juden?," *Juedische Turnzeitung* (July 1902): 109–12.
30 SP II., 212.
31 See Gershom Scholem, *From Berlin to Jerusalem: Memories of My Youth*, trans. Harry Zohn (New York: Schocken, 1980), 23ff.
32 Elias Auerbach, *Pionier der Verwirklichung*, 70ff.
33 See, i.e., "Georg Arendt's Gedaechtnis," in *Juedischer Turnzeitung* (December 1909): 213–14.
34 See Jerimias Posen, "Turnen und Nervensystem" in *Juedischer Turnzeitung* (September 1904): 154–6; M. Jastrowitz, "Muskeljudentum und Nervensystem," in *Juedische Turnzeitung* (March/April 1909): 53–5.
35 See Nordau, "Muskeljudentum;" Nordau, "Was bedeutet Turnen fuer

uns Juden?," *Juedische Turnzeitung* (July 1902): 109–12; "Geburtstag vom Dr Max Nordau," in *Juedische Turnzeitung* (August 1909): 125–6.

36 See, i.e., *Jewish Chronicle*, August 23, 1907, 19, 37.

37 "Was wir wollen," in *Juedische Turnzeitung* (May 1900): 1.

38 "Nationaljudentum und Patriotismus," in *Juedische Turnzeitung* (November 1903): 185–8.

39 "Heinrich Heine und der deutsche Turnerei" in *Juedische Turnzeitung* (August 1902): 131–3.

40 See, i.e., review of "Juedischer Almanach 5663" in *Juedische Turnzeitung* (December 1902): 202; "Aus Ch. N. Bialik: Gedichte" in *Juedische Turnzeitung* (August/September 1911): 171; "Die Kolonisation Palaestinas" in *Juedische Turnzeitung* (December 1908); "Die russische Zionistentag in Minsk" in *Juedische Turnzeitung* (October 1902); 167–9; Martin Buber, "Neue Jugend" in *Juedische Turnzeitung* (December 1908): 202; "Bialik als Naturdichter" in *Juedische Turnzeitung* (January 1908): 8.

41 *Jewish Chronicle*, September 12, 1913, 27; *Jewish Chronicle*, September 19, 1913, 19.

42 SP XI., 193.

43 SP VIII., 53ff., 255ff.

44 *Jewish Chronicle*, August, 11, 1911, 15.

45 SP II ., 200–2; SP III., 199–200, 208–10; SP IV., 209, 263–4.

46 SP III., 199–200, 208–10; SP IV., 209, 263–4.

47 SP I., 183ff., 84ff., 187ff.

48 SP XI, 341.

49 See *Die Welt*, July 16, 1897, 14; Israel Abrahams, "A Jewish University for Jerusalem" in *Zionist Work in Palestine*, 54–7; Martin Buber, Berthold Feiwel, and Chaim Weizmann, *Eine juedische Hochschule* (Berlin: Juedischer Verlag, 1902).

50 SP I., 187–8.

51 SP V., 390–3; *Die Welt*, October 31, 1902, 2, 5; *Die Welt*, November 7, 1902, 3–4, 11–12.

52 SP XI., 287ff.

53 SP XI., 309.

54 SP XI., 312.

55 SP XI., 341.

56 SP XI., 345; *Jewish Chronicle*, September 19, 1913, 17.

57 See Ch. 7.

58 Lipsky, 82.

59 SP VIII., 214–16.

60 SP VIII., 217–18.

61 SP VIII., 218–19.

62 Elias Auerbach, "The Jewish Outlook in Palestine", in *Zionist Work in Palestine*, 172–3.

63 SP VIII., 255–7.

64 SP VIII., 220–1.

65 SP VIII., 321.

66 SP VIII., 349.

67 SP VII., 198.
68 See Ch. 6
69 Joseph Klausner, introduction to *Boris Schatz: 31 Oil Paintings* (Jerusalem, 1929), 4–5.
70 See SP VII., 62; Leo Motzkin, in SP XI., 156.
71 SP VII., 202–4.
72 SP VII., 70.
73 *Jewish Chronicle*, December 31, 1909, 31.
74 *Jewish Chronicle*, August 23, 1907, 16; *The Letters and Papers of Chaim Weizmann*, V, Series A, general ed. Meyer Weisgal (London and Jerusalem: Oxford University Press and Israel University Press, 1974), 44.
75 SP VIII., 225–6.
76 Heinrich Loewe slides, special collection, CZA; "Nationalfonds Lichtbildervoltrag," in *Die Welt*, 5 May 1911, 405.
77 "Palaestina in Film zu sehen," announcement to the Eleventh Zionist Congress, Printed Material File XI., CZA.
78 "First Film of Palestine," Rad Film Archives, Jerusalem; "Palestine on the Cinematograph: An Interesting Exhibition," in *Jewish Chronicle*, August 11, 1911, 24.
79 "Die zehnte Zionistenkongress," in *Ost und West* (August/September 1911); 714.
80 *Jewish Chronicle*, September 19, 1913, 19.
81 SP IX., 55–7, 108–9, 206–9; SP X., 130.
82 SP XI., 257ff,; cf. 94.
83 SP IX., 212ff., 218, 267ff., 277–8; SP XI., 51, 75 , 85ff.; SP XI., 317ff.
84 SP XI., 193ff., 257ff.

CHAPTER FIVE: ART AND ZIONIST POPULAR CULTURE

1 See George L. Mosse, *Fallen Soldiers: Reshaping the Memory of the World Wars* (New York: Oxford University Press, 1990); Carl E. Schorske, *Fin-de-Siècle Vienna: Politics and Culture* (New York: Vintage, 1980), xx–xxviiff.
2 See the *The Dreyfus Affair, Art, Truth, and Justice* ed. Norman L. Kleeblatt (Berkeley: University of California Press, 1987) (for the Jewish Museum), 11–24ff.
3 See Marsha L. Rozenblit, *The Jews of Vienna*, 99, 113, 4–5.
4 THD, 116.
5 THD, 165, 27.
6 THD, 236, 33.
7 THD, 27.
8 THD, 67.
9 See David Vital, *The Origins of Zionism*, 354–75; PMF I., CZA.
10 Heinrich York-Steiner designed the card; Pollak drew the picture; see *Die Welt*, September 10, 1897, 16.
11 *Jewish Chronicle* (London), September 3, 1897, 10; *Die Welt*, September 10, 1897, 16.
12 Psalms 14:7.

13 See Herzl, "Eroeffnungsrede zum ersten Kongress," 227; Leon Simon, *Ahad Ha-Am*, 105; *Mizrahi* medals collection, box 2, CZA.
14 PMF I.; medals collection, CZA.
15 "Die Congress-Medaille" in *Die Welt*, August 5, 1898, 5.
16 George L. Mosse, *Nationalism and Sexuality*, 90–100; see Maurice Agulhon, *Marianne into Battle: Republican Imagery and Symbolism in France, 1780–1880* trans. Janet Lloyd (Cambridge: Cambridge University Press, 1981), *passim*; Lynn Hunt, *Politics, Culture, and Class in the French Revolution* (Berkeley: University of California Press, 1984), 93–4.
17 PMF VI., CZA; quoted from Psalm 126, the "Song of Ascents" or "Song of Returning Exiles"; the symbol was also used for the certificate given to donors to the Golden Book of the Jewish National Fund, PMF VI; see Plate 189, reproduction of Edouard Debat-Ponsan's painting, "She is Not Drowning" or "Truth Leaving the Well," in *The Dreyfus Affair: Art, Truth, and Justice*, 258.
18 PMF II., CZA.
19 Ezekiel 37:21.
20 Rosenberger, 141–2.
21 THD, 32, and Herzl, *The Jewish State*, trans. Harry Zohn (New York: Herzl Press, 1970), 39.
22 Mosse, *The Crisis of German Ideology*, 126–45.
23 There is very little or no information concerning M. Okin's background, or career after he ceased submitting work to the Zionist Movement; *Die Welt*, 9 September 1898.
24 See Ch. 1 and Figure 2.
25 Reproductions of this picture, for hanging in reading rooms as postcards, were not among Zionists' favorites. Far more popular was a Congress portrait of most of the partipants done in cameos, with an enlarged Herzl in the center, PMF I., CZA.
26 PMF III., CZA.
27 Arthur Hertzberg, *The Zionist Idea: A Historical Analysis and Reader* (New York: Atheneum, 1977), 418; see Israel Kolatt, "The Organization of the Jewish Population of Palestine and the Development of its Political Consciousness Before World War I," in *Studies on Palestine during the Ottoman Period*, ed. M. Ma'oz (Jerusalem: Magnes Press, 1975), 211–43.
28 See Rosenberger, *passim.*; CZA, Adolf Pollak, *Die Welt Index – Zionistische Chronologie* (vom Juni 1897 bis Juli 1914) (Tel Aviv), 1–24.
29 Alfred Werner, "The Tragedy of Ephraim Moses Lilien," *Herzl Year Book*, 2 (1959): 100; cf. Mark H. Gelber, "The *jungjuedische Bewegung*" in *Leo Baeck Institute Year Book 31* (1986): 108ff.
30 Israel Zangwill, introduction to a portfolio of heliogravures by E. M. Lilien, *The Holy Land* (Berlin and Vienna: Benjamin Harz, 1922), no pagination.
31 See, e.g., medals collection; PMF XI; "For the 9th of Ab," Pamphlet No. 3, A 2/6/7/1; "Purim," Flugblatt No. 2.; all in CZA.
32 PMF V., CZA.
33 A2/6/7/1, CZA.

34 Lilien's relationship to Beardsley was consciously antithetical, yet he selectively appropriated many of Beardsley's techniques and motifs; Milly Heyd, "Lilien and Beardsley: to the pure all things are pure" in *Journal of Jewish Art* 7 (1982): 58–69.
35 Israel Zangwill introduction to *The Holy Land*; Almog, *Zionism and History*, 169.
36 Alfred Gold, "E. M. Lilien," in *Juedische Kuenstler*, ed. Martin Buber (Berlin: Juedischer Verlag, 1903), 87.
37 PMF V., CZA.
38 See p. 16; this was part of an effort to make political Zionism seem continuous with proto-Zionist thought; David Farbstein to Theodor Herzl, Zurich 29 July 1897, HVIII/226, CZA.
39 *The Letters and Papers of Chaim Weizmann*, V, Series A, general ed. Meyer Weisgal, (London and Jerusalem: Oxford University Press and Israel University Press, 1974), 44.
40 See above, Ch. 4.
41 The majority of delegates probably had a difficult time following Buber's German; see Shmarya Levin, *Forward from Exile*, 373.
42 SP V., 152–70.
43 SP V., 162.
44 Nordau, "Der Zionismus der Westlichen Juden" in *Max Nordaus Zionistische Schriften* (Cologne and Leipzig: Juedischer Verlag, 1909), originally appeared in *Israelitische Rundschau* (Berlin, 1901), 316–17; see Nordau, *Von Kunst und Kuenstlern* (Leipzig: B. Elischer, no date), *passim*; Nordau was one of Europe's most outspoken opponents of the notion of "art for art's sake."
45 Buber, in SP V., 168; and Berthold Feiwel to Theodor Herzl, April 7, 1902, HVIII, CZA.
46 See Mark Gelber, "The jungjuedische Bewegung," 112ff.
47 Feiwel to Herzl, CZA, HVIII, April 7, 1902; "Juedische Renaissance": Press-Stimmen ueber den *Juedischen Almanach* (Berlin: Juedischer Verlag, 1903), HVIII 124, CZA; see Dennis Klein, 25.
48 *Almanach 1902–1964*, (Berlin: Juedischer Verlag, 1964), 7; Theodor Herzl, founding statement of *Die Welt*, June 4, 1897.
49 Hermann Struck, "Polnischer Jude," *Juedischer Almanach, II*. ed. Berthold Feiwel (Berlin Juedischer Verlag, 1904), 28.
50 *Juedischer Almanach, II.*, 107; CZA, PMF IX, XI; see Nathanja Sahuwi, "Vor Hermann Struck's Herzl-Portrait," *Ost und West* (September 9, 1903), 709–14.
51 Struck, "As an Artist Saw Him" in *Theodore Herzl: A Memorial*, 36; *Radierung von Hermann Struck: Mit einem Essay von Max Osborne* (Berlin: Berliner Verlag, 1904), 2; Karl Schwarz, *Hermann Struck Memorial Exhibition Museum Tel Aviv* (1944), CZA.
52 Cf. Jacques Kornberg, "Theodore Herzl: A Re-evaluation," 227.
53 Martin Buber, "Introduction," Buber, ed. *Juedischer Kuenstler* (Berlin: Juedischer Verlag, 1903), no pagination.
54 Josef Israels, "Thoraschreiber" (Skizze) in *Juedischer Almanach, II*, 94.

55 See Fritz Stahl, "Josef Israels" in *Juedische Kuenstler*, 12, 14.
56 Harold Rosenberg, *Rediscovering the Present* (Chicago: University of Chicago Press, 1973), 223–31; Avram Kampf, *Jewish Experience in the Art of the Twentieth Century* (Hadley, Massachusetts: Bergin & Garvey, 1984), 7–10.
57 SP X., 159.
58 See the advertisements in the back pages of *Die Welt*, January 7, 1910, for example, and the *Juedische Rundschau*, and advertising supplements of the *Juedischer Verlag*, CZA A6/77.
59 David Tartakover, ed. *Herzl's Image in the Applied Arts* (Tel Aviv: Tel Aviv Museum, 1978–9); and M. Narkess, "The Arts Portray Herzl," in *Theodore Herzl: A Memorial*, 119–20.
60 *Prelude to Israel: The Memoirs of M. I. Bodenheimer*, 117–18.
61 Ahad-Ha'am, quoted in Tartakover, 51.
62 See Nathanja Sahuwi, 712–13.
63 See Hecht, 113; 124; Stefan Zweig, *The World of Yesterday*, trans. Harry Zohn (Lincoln and London: University of Nebraska Press, 1964), 105; Dr Ch. Lippe, "Theodor Herzl," Osakar Marmorek, "Herzl als Freund," Emma Nuestadt, "Die Wehklage der Zionisten," Daniel Pasmanik, "Dr Theodor Herzl," in *Die Stimme der Wahrheit*, 129–43; *Festschrift zu Feier des 100. Semesters der akademischen Verbindung Kadimah, 1933*, 82; J. Silberbusch, "Herzl-Eine legendaery Erscheinung," in *Zeitgenossen ueber Herzl*, 185ff.
64 Herzl "Personality" File, PMF, CZA.
65 Alfred Werner, "The Tragedy of Ephraim Moses Lilien," 92.
66 Herzl "Personality" File, PMF; Jewish National Fund Stamp Collection, Photography Collection [hereafter referred to as PC], ZP.17001, CZA.
67 "Tree Fund" certificate, reproduced in *Herzl in Profile*, 24; Herzl "Personality" File; PMF VIII, IX., CZA.
68 Feiwel, memoir of meeting with Richard Beer-Hoffmann, K11/147, CZA; Stefan Zweig, *The World of Yesterday*, 105; Robert Weltsch, "Theodor Herzl and We," 26–7; Scholem, *From Berlin to Jerusalem*, 28; David Biale, *Gershom Scholem*, 53; Leo Motzkin, quoted in Simcha Kling, "Leo Motzkin," in Herzl Year Book, ed. Raphael Patai (New York: Herzl Press, 1959), 238.
69 See *Festschrift zu Feier des 100. Semesters der akademischer Verbindung Kadimah, 1933*, 82; Stefan Zweig, 105.
70 Herzl "Personality" File; PC 17.196, CZA.
71 Herzl "Personality" File; PC 17.196, CZA; *Herzl in Profile*, 27; Nordau "Personality" File, CZA.
72 See Stephen E. Aschheim, *Brothers and Strangers: The East European Jew in German and German Jewish Consciousness, 1800–1923* (Madison: University of Wisconsin Press, 1982), 84; see Ernest Jones, *The Life and Work of Sigmund Freud* (New York: Basic, 1966), 124; Desmond Stewart, *Theodor Herzl* (Garden City, N.Y.: Doubleday, 1974), 322–3; P. M. Baldwin, "Liberalism, Nationalism, and Degeneration: The Case of Max Nordau," *Central European History* 13 (June 1980): 99.

73 Nordau "Personality" File, PMF, CZA.

74 CZA, HVIII 614/15, No. 162, Nordau to Herzl, 28 December 1903, no. 162, Nordau to Herzl, HVIII 614/15, CZA; Chaim Weizmann to Richard Lichtheim, No. 84, December 1, 1920, *The Letters and Papers of Chaim Weizmann*, X, Series A, 107; Weizmann and Lichtheim were perturbed that Nordau was so popular while they considered him a troublesome anachronism.

75 Nash, 170–1, 188; PC 13.792, CZA.

76 Nordau "Personality" File, CZA.

77 *Die Welt*, 31 March 1911, 301; see Ch. 7.

78 See Chs. 4 and 6.

79 For example, between 1910 and 1913, there were two exhibitions in London and Vienna, and major shows were held included Amsterdam, Karlsbad, Zurich, and Berlin; see "Bezalelausstellung in Wien', *Die Welt*, February 11, 1910, 124.

80 *Bezalel 1906–1929*, ed. Nurit Shilo-Cohen (Jerusalem: Israel Museum, 1983), 329, 156–8

81 See "Aus dem Geschaftsberict des 'Bezalel'," *Die Welt*, January 14, 1910, 38–40; October 17, 1910; January 19, 1912, 69–72; March 28, 1913, 406–7; April 25, 1913, for some of the numerous examples.

82 PC. 1635, 415; PMF "Bezalel" File, CZA.

83 Jean Fischer, *Das heutige Palaestina* (Antwerp: "Hatikvah," 1907), 97; CZA, PC. 451, 15.683, 15.600. In fact, the buildings, bought from a Turkish *effendi*, were intended to house an orphanage; Gideon Ofrat-Friedlander, "The Periods of Bezalel," *Bezalel 1906–1929*, 49–51.

84 See Ch. 7.

85 Gideon Ofrat-Friedlander, "Bezalel Sales and Promotion", *Bezalel 1906–1929*, 351.

86 "Zionistisches Gartenfest," *Die Welt*, August 18, 1911, 876.

CHAPTER SIX: REALISTIC PROJECTIONS OF PALESTINE

1 Many of the books used in this chapter are included in the bibliography of Davis Trietsch's *Palaestina Handbuch* (Berlin-Schmargendorf: Orient-Verlag, 1910), which went through several editions.

2 See Tartakover, 61. The remnant of the retaining wall around the Herodian Temple Mount is now referred to as the "Western Wall", and by its Hebrew names, "Kotel" and "Kotel Maaravi." "The Tower of David," located in the Old City of Jerusalem, was neither built nor used by King David, however, it is commonly remembered, by Jews, as a fortress of King David.

3 See Edward Said, *Orientalism*, for an exegesis of European perceptions of the Orient. I have borrowed extensively from Said's methodology. His account is most helpful in assessing the role of imperialism in determining attitudes towards the Arab world; he sees "Orientalism as a Western style for dominating, restructuring, and having authority over the Orient."

Zionism's view of the Orient was far more diverse and complex than he indicates; (New York: Vintage, 1979), 1–3, 95, 286, 307.

4 Osaias Thon, "The Zionist Programme and Practical Work in Palestine;" in *Zionist Work in Palestine*, 13–14; Jean Fischer, *Das heutige Palaestina* (Antwerp: "Hatikvah," 1907), 69; cf. *Palaestina Ansichten von denkwuerdigen Staetten in des heiligen Landes und Doerfen juedischer Bauern*, which includes scenes of Jewish colonies and Holy Places, but lacks a national orientation (Berlin: Hugo Schildberger, 1896).

5 A large share of historiography of Zionism assumes that most Jews' impression of Palestine derives from the Second Aliya, the second wave of settlers of the Jewish colonies who came mostly from Russia and Poland to establish a new socialist life in their ancestral homeland. I believe that the picture the *Western* Jews formed of Palestine, and especially Jewish life in Palestine were determined, and disseminated on a rather wide scale, before the Second Aliya. The images of Jews and Jewish life in Palestine received by Western Jews through Zionism between 1897 and 1914 was more or less continuous. I am indebted to Professor Gabriel Motzkin of the Hebrew University for this insight.

6 Daniel Pasmanik, "Vorrede" in Lazar Felix Pinkus, *Palaestina und Syrien: Untersuchung zur Wirtschaftspolitik* (Geneva: Verlag der Zionistischen Monatshefte, 1903), ix; Otto Warburg, and "Bericht des Aktionskomitees Allgemeine Uebersicht der zionistischen Bewegung" (1907–9) (Kulturell-politischer Teil) in SP IX., 146, 390).

7 See Ch. 5.

8 See letter from the Actions-Committee to Richard Gottheil, October 1, 1900, A138/4/1, CZA. The main sources of this discussion are photographs and first-hand accounts, in the form of travel literature. These are treated separately from the artistic representations of Palestine, because "a text [photographs are considered texts] purporting to contain knowledge about something actual . . . is not easily dismissed. Expertise is attributed to it. The authority of academics, institutions and governments can accrue to it, surrounding it with still greater prestige than its practical success warrants. Most important, such texts can *clear* not only knowledge, but the very reality they appear to describe," Said, 94 (emphasis in original).

9 Martin Buber, in "Die Entdeckung Palaestina" lavishes praise on one of the most typical works in the genre, Adolf Friedemann and Hermann Struck, *Palaestina: Reisebilder* (Berlin: Bruno Cassier, 1904), in *Ost und West* (February 2, 1905): 128–30.

10 Boehm, *Die Zionistische Bewegung, I. Band*, 45; Jesaias Press, *Die juedischen Kolonien Palaestinas* (Leipzig: J. C. Heinris'sche Buchhandlung, 1912), 1.

11 Samuel Daiches, in SP X., 209.

12 Press, 21; Shmarja Levin, "Unsere Kulturaufgaben in Palaestina" in *Ost und West* (September 25, 1912), 1209–11; Adolf Friedemann, "Juedische Kunst in Palaestina" in *Ost und West* (May 5, 1911): 445–52).

13 On the significance of Hebrew in the *Yishuv*, see Itmar Even-Zohar, "The

Emergence of a Native Hebrew Culture in Palestine: 1882–1948" in *Studies in Zionism* 4 (October 1981): 172–5ff.

14 See *Juedische Turnzeitung* (May 1900), 1; (June 1908), 109; Georg Hecht, *Der Neue Jude*, 113ff.; *Jewish Chronicle*, September 12, 1913, 23.

15 Untitled photograph, *Die Welt* (November 26, 1897), 9; "Juedische Feldarbeiter beim Auackern des Bodens" in Davis Trietsch, *Bilder aus Palaestina* (Berlin: Orient-Verlag, no date), 78; "Ernte-Arbeiten auf einem der Nationfonds-Gueter in Galilaea" in *Spenden-Buch des Juedischen Nationalfonds*, A2/6/7/1, CZA.

16 See "Eine Leidensgeschichte," reproduction of a painting by M. Okin with story, in *Die Welt*, 20 August 1897, 6; cf. Franz Oppenheimer, *Co-operative Colonisation in Palestine* (The Hague: Head Office of the Jewish National Fund, no date) [probably around 1915], for a view of the changes in imagery during the war, stressing "strong-armed young men, with adventurers' blood within their veins, who do not shun danger, but love it," 3.

17 Photograph of "Young Colonists in Rishon le Zion" in *Zionist Work in Palestine*, 157.

18 George Mosse, *The Culture of Western Europe: The Nineteenth and Twentieth Centuries* (Chicago: Rand McNally, 1974), 67–9.

19 See, i.e., Adolf Friedmann and Hermann Struck, *Palaestina: Reisebilder* (Berlin: Bruno Cassier, 1904), 31.

20 See Boehm, *Die Zionistische Bewegung, I. Band*, 239–40.

21 Aaron Aaronsohn, "The Jewish Agricultural Experiment Station and its Programme" and Arthur Ruppin, "The Return of the Jews to Agriculture" in *Zionist Work in Palestine*, 114–20, 137–42; Josef Gerstman, *Kultur-und-Bildungsfortschritte unter den Juden Palaestinas* (Munich: Max Steinebach Buch-und Kunstverlag, 1909), 19.

22 J. H. Kann, *Erez Israel: Das juedische Land* (Cologne and Leipzig: Juedischer Verlag, 1909), 153.

23 Boris Schatz, "The Bezalel Institute" in *Zionist Work in Palestine*, 62.

24 Kemal Karpat, *Studies in Ottoman Population 1864–1914* (Madison: University of Wisconsin Press, 1984); Y. Porath, *The Emergence of the Palestinian–Arab National Movement 1918–1929* (London: Frank Cass, 1974), 16–20; Neville Mandel, *The Arabs and Zionism before World War I* (Berkeley: University of California Press, 1976).

25 Cf. Shmuel Almog, ed. *Zionism and the Arabs* (Jerusalem: The Historical Society of Israel and the Zalman Shazer Center, 1983), "Foreword" by Shmuel Ettinger: "All the authors refute the widespread contention according to which the Zionist movement as a whole – save for small and marginal groups within it – did not take into account the Arabs dwelling in *Eretz Israel* and ignored the Arab question altogether," viii.

26 Gerstman, 54–5; cf. Rabinersohn, in SP X., 267.

27 Elias Auerbach, *Palaestina als Judenland* (Berlin and Leipzig: Juedischer Verlag, 1912).

28 SP VII., 257.

29 Hermann Guthe, *Palaestina* (Bielefeld and Leipzig: Velhagen und Klating,

1908); G. Hoelscher, *Die Geschichte der Juden in Palaestina seit dem Jahre 70 nach Chr.* (Leipzig: J. C. Heinrichs'sche Buchhandlung, 1909), 64; Leonhard Bauer, *Volksleben im Lande der Bibel* (Leipzig: H. G. Wallmann, 1903).

30 R. Eckhardt, E. Zickermann, F. Fenner, *Palaestinensische Kulturbilder* (Leipzig: Georg Wigsand, 1907), 242–3; this work, by members of a German archaeological institute, stressed the Christian heritage of Palestine. Only one of forty photographs is of a Jewish subject.

31 Elias Auerbach, "The Jewish Outlook in Palestine" in *Zionist Work in Palestine*, 172–3, 175–80.

32 Motzkin, SP II., 99–127; Daniel Pasmanik, "Vorrede" to *Palaestina und Syrien: Untersuchung zur Wirtschaftspolitik* by Lazar Pinkus (Geneva: Verlag der Zionistischen Monatshefte, 1903), xix.

33 Press, 1; Fischer, 3–7; J. H. Kann, 153.

34 Fischer, 120; cf. A. Goodrich-Freer, *Things Seen in Palestine* (London: Seely & Service, 1913), 195.

35 Fischer, 115; Friedemann and Hermann Struck, 71.

36 Friedemann and Struck, 96.

37 Fischer, 120.

38 Fischer, 121; see Ahad Ha-Am's classic criticism, "The Wrong Way" (1889), in *Ten Essays on Zionism and Judaism*, trans. Leon Simon (London: George Routledge & Sons, 1922), 1–24.

39 See Kemal Karpat, *Studies in Ottoman Population*; see Nahum Goldmann, *Erez-Israel* (Reisebreife aus Palaestina) (Frankfurt a.M.: Voigt & Gleiber, 1914), 10–11.

40 M. Ussischkin, *Our Program: An Essay*, trans. D. S. Blonheim (New York: Federation of American Zionists, 1905), 25.

41 Shmarya Levin, in SP XI., 31ff.

42 Joshua Feldman, *The Yeminite Jews* (published on behalf of the Head Office of the Jewish National Fund) (London: W. Speaight & Sons, 1913), 25–6; Friedemann and Struck, 71.

43 Gerstman, 55; Friedemann and Struck, 35, 5; Trietsch, 76; Jacob Thon, in SP X., 91.

44 Friedmann and Struck, 96.

45 Davis Trietsch, *Bilder*, 10–11.

46 "Book Plate by Jacob Stark (Jerusalem)" in *Zionist Work in Palestine*, 64, and in *Die Welt*, October 17, 1910, 1024.

47 Martin Buber, "Die Entdeckung Palaestinas" in *Ost und West* (February 2, 1905): 130.

48 PMF IX, CZA.

49 See photographs "Typisches groesserres Araberdorf," Saida (Das alte Sidon)," and "Brunnen in einem Araberdorf" in Davis Trietsch, *Bilder*, 38, 30, 37; "View of Tiberias" in *Zionist work in Palestine*, 73.

50 Friedemann and Struck, 6–7, 202, 25–27.

51 Jesaias Press, 21.

52 Jesaias Press, 21–22.

53 See Rosenblit, 148–61.

54 Armand Kaminka, *Meine Reise nach Jerusalem: Skizzen aus Aegypten und*

Palaestina (Frankfurt a.M.: J. Kaufman, 1913), 43; see photographs, "Herzl Street in Tel-Aviv (Jaffa)," "Colony of Zichron Jacob," "A House in Tel-Aviv" in *Zionist Work in Palestine*, 172, 165, 114; "Strasse in Kolonie Petach-Tikwa," "Teilansicht einer juedischen Kolonie,", "Marktplatz in Petach-Tikwa" in Davis Trietsch, *Bilder* 57, 66, 102; "Hauptstrasse des neuen juedischen Stadtviertels Tel-Awiw bei Jaffa" in *Spenden-Buch des Juedischen Nationalfonds*, CZA, A2/6/7/1; "Rothschild-Boulevard in den juedischen Stadtviertel Tel–Awiw in Jaffa" in *Die Welt*, October 1, 1913, 1365.

55 Kaminka, 43.

56 Adolf Friedemann, "Juedische Kultur in Palaestina" in *Ost und West* (May 5, 1911): 451–2.

57 "Ein Blumengarten in den Colonien" in *Die Welt*, August 27, 1897, 9; Jacob Thon, "Jewish Schools in Palestine," in *Zionist Work in Palestine*, 96; Gerstman, 19.

58 Jesaias Press, 21.

59 Entry for April 9, 1896, in *Theodor Herzl Briefe und Tagebuecher, II. Band*, 317.

60 Boris Schatz, "The Bezalel Institute," in *Zionist Work in Palestine*, 60.

61 Buber, introduction to Juedische Kuenstler, no pagination; Buber, SP V., 155; photographs "Von der Chagiagah in Rechoboth," "Schauturnen des 'Makkabi'," and "Pferdrunnen" in *Die Welt*, May 23, 1913, 656–7; Gerstman, 44; photograph, "Von den 'Olympischen Spielen' der juedischen Kolonie Rechoboth" in Trietsch, *Bilder*, 73.

62 CZA, PC. 4913; see Goldmann, 9–10, 19, 46; David Yellin, "The Renaissance of the Hebrew Language in Palestine" in *Zionist Work in Palestine*, 155–6.

63 See photographs in Max Grunwald, "Das neue Palaestina" in *Ost und West* (June 6, 1913): 462–4; cover of *Bar-Kochba Almanach* by Jacob Stark in *Zionist Work in Palestine*, 150. As opposed to Said, I believe that this did not necessarily entail the view of indigenous Arabs as the anti-type; Said, 307.

64 Photograph of "Kolonisten und Waechter aus der Kolonie Metulah in Galilaea" in Trietsch, Bilder, 127; photographs in Max Grunwald, "Das neue Palaestina."

65 The first Zionist paramilitary organizations were *Bar Giora*, founded in 1907, and *Ha-Shomer*, founded in 1909; Jonathan Frankel, "The 'Yiskor' Book of 1911 – A Note on National Myths in the Second Aliya" in *Religion, Ideology and Nationalism in Europe and America: Essays Presented in Honor of Yehoshua Arieli* (Jerusalem: The Historical Society of Israel and the Zalman Shazar Center for Jewish History, 1986), 356.

66 "The Jewish Hope – Dr Shmarja Levin's Address" [from the Eleventh Zionist Congress] in *Jewish Chronicle*, September 12, 1913, 25; Jonathan Frankel, "The 'Yiskor' Book"; the *Yiskor Book* "served to highlight deep disagreements within the Second Aliya about both the rhetoric and substance of Jewish nationalism and of Jewish-Arab relations," 359ff, 381–4.

67 Trietsch, *Bilder*, 127.
68 Auerbach, 175.
69 Sokolow, quoted in *Jewish Chronicle*, September 12, 1913, 23.
70 Goldmann, 81.
71 Jesaias Press, 22.
72 Goldmann, 81.
73 Motzkin, 122–5.
74 Goldmann, 81.
75 Gerstman, 28, 35.
76 *Zionist Work in Palestine*, 89; Shmarya Levin, in SP VIII., 220ff.; See Ch. 4.
77 Cf. M. Ussischkin, "Palestine and Other Countries," in *Zionist Work in Palestine*, 22.
78 CZA, PC. 15.092; PC. 1869; *Zionist Work in Palestine*, 58.
79 CZA, PC. 4913.
80 CZA, PC. 4911.
81 Goldmann, 84; CZA, PC. 215, PC. G 12.344.
82 David Yellin, "The Renaissance of the Hebrew Language in Palestine" in *Zionist Work in Palestine*, 156; Gerstman, 28; on the controversies over the religious content, see Walter J. Ackerman, 1–13.
83 Goldmann, 43.
84 Sokolow to Herzl, September 1, 1902, quoted in Josef Wenkert, "Herzl and Sokolow," in *Theodor Herzl Year Book III*, 210; Armard Kaminka, 38.
85 Elias Auerbach, "Herzl and Haifa" in *Die Welt*, July 17, 1914, 739–40; Nahum Goldmann, 58.
86 Nahum Goldmann, 57–58; cf. Norman Bentwich, *Jewish Schools in Palestine* [reprinted by the *Jewish Review* (London) and published by the Federation of American Zionists, New York, 1912], 10.
87 Goldmann, 58.
88 See Isaiah Friedman, "The *Hilfsverein der deutschen Juden*, the German Foreign Ministry and the Controversy with the Zionists, 1901–1918" in *Year Book XXIV of the Leo Baeck Institute* (London: Secker & Warburg, 1979), 291–319; Yehuda Eloni, *Zionismus in Deutschland*, 313–56.
89 Isaiah Friedman, 291–2, 302.
90 Paul Nathan, *Palaestina und palaestinenschischer Zionismus* (Berlin: H. S. Hermann, 1914), 59.
91 *Im Kampf um die hebraeische Sprache* (Berlin: Zionistischen Actions-Comite, 1914). 3ff.
92 *Die Welt*, December 5, 1913, 1663; January 9, 1914, 35; March 13, 1914, 253; January 2, 1914, 1–2.
93 *Die Welt*, December 5, 1913, 1658–62.
94 Otto Warburg, "Bericht der Palaestinaressorts," in SP IX., 142; photograph of "Turnstunde in der Maedchenschule des Hilfvereins der deutschen Juden in Jerusalem" in *Juedische Turnzeitung*, 1 (January/February 1911): 8.
95 Fischer, 115.
96 Adolf Friedemann and Hermann Struck, *Palaestina* 93–4; Norman Bentwich, 7; Leopold Kahn, SP III., 203–4.

97 Goldmann, 95–7. It was founded in the late 1870s and managed by the Anglo-Jewish Association since 1898; Davis Trietsch, *Handbuch*, 122; *The Zionist Pocket Reference*, ed. Israel Cohen [adapted from the Third Edition of Hugo Schachtel's "Zionistisches Merkbuch"] (London: W. Speaight & Sons, 1914), 48.
98 Friedmann and Struck, 48–9; Goldmann, 97–8; Gerstman, 11–12.
99 Michael Meyer, *The Origins of the Modern Jew* (Detroit: Wayne State University Press, 1975), 23.
100 Joseph Klausner, introduction to *Boris Schatz: 31 Oil Paintings* (Jerusalem, 1929), 4–5; Fischer, 66–7; Goldmann, 28–35.
101 A. Goodrich-Freer, *Inner Jerusalem* (London: Archibald Constable and Company, 1904), 37.
102 Goldmann, 29.
103 Goldmann, 42.
104 Elias Auerbach, "The Jewish Outlook in Palestine," in *Zionist Work in Palestine*, 174–5.
105 Goldmann, 89–90.
106 Fischer, 97–8; CZA, Printed Materials File, Bezalel collection; Otto Warburg, 143–4.
107 Fischer, 72; "Bericht des Aktionskomitees Allgemeine Uebersicht der zionistischen Bewegung" (1907–9) (Kulturell-politischer Teil) in SP IX., 468; Otto Warburg and Heinrich Loewe, SP VII., 241–2; Heinrich Loewe, *Eine Juedische Nationalbibliothek* (Berlin: Juedischer Verlag, 1905), 5–7ff.
108 Gerstman, 40–1.
109 Printed Material File, CZA, Bezalel collection; portrait of Mathias Bogotirew, Salomon Mordechajew, and M. Schloposchnikow distributed at the Seventh Zionist Congress, PMF VII.; photograph of "Caucasian Mountain Jews as Colonists" in *Zionist Work in Palestine*, 40; CZA, PC. 16.238.
110 Elias Auerbach, "The Jewish Outlook in Palestine" in Zionist Work in Palestine, 175.
111 Joshua Feldman, *The Yeminite Jews* (London: W. Speaight and Sons, 1913), c, 26–7ff.
112 Bezalel collection, CZA.
113 Israel Kolatt, "The Organization of the Jewish Population of Palestine and the Development of its Political Consciousness before World War I" in *Studies on Palestine During the Ottoman Period*, ed. M. Ma'oz (Jerusalem: Magnes Press – The Hebrew University, 1975), 211; see Kemal Karpat, "Jewish Immigration in the Ottoman Empire, 1864–1914," in a forthcoming article: "modern Jewish history has been written almost entirely from the viewpoint of the European Jews, notably the Russian and Polish Jews who played leading roles in the establishment of Israel. The history of the Sephardic, Romaiote, Karaim, and a variety of other fringe area Jews, such as those from the Bukhara and the Mountain Jews of the Caucasus . . . has been ignored. This narrowly focused European ethnocentrism has minimized the role of Middle Eastern Jews in Jewish history in general and in the Zionist movement, and the transformation of

Palestine in particular." I thank Professor Karpat for sharing his manuscript.

114 Feldman, 23–4; Goldmann, 42–3.

115 See "Ein parkbild aus den colonien" and "Fourage in den Colonie" [photographs and stories], in *Die Welt*, July 16, 1897, 7; cf. "The Palestinian Cinematograph" in *Jewish Chronicle*, September 19, 1913, 19.

116 Fischer, 23.

117 See Ch. 2.

118 Cf. "Bundeslied des K.z.V." [Kartell zionistische Verbindung], in *Commers in der Burgoggtei Basel*, X. Zionisten-Congress 1911, CZA, Printed Materials File for the Eleventh Zionist Congress.

119 "Jaffa bei der See-seit" [photograph and story] in *Die Welt*, July 9, 1897, 9.

120 See "Diplom fuer Baumspende," and "Diplom fuer Stiftung eines Arbeiterhauses" in Simon Neumann, *Der Traum von der Nationalfondsbuechse: Ein Maerchen fuer Kinder* (Cologne: Hauptbuero des juedischen Nationalfonds, no date), 11, 13; CZA, PC, 1500, 399, covers of the first and sixth Golden Books of the Jewish National Fund; PMF VIII., CZA, official postcard, "VIII Zionistenkongress im Haag, August 14–20, 1907" by Hermann Struck.

121 Fischer, 117.

122 A notable exception to this is Elias Auerbach's contribution to *Zionist Work in Palestine*, "The Jewish Outlook in Palestine," 172–80.

123 Fredrick Treves, *The Land That Is Desolate: An Account of a Tour in Palestine* (London: Smith, Elder and Co., 1912).

124 I am indebted to Joseph M. Greenblatt of the Hebrew University for this insight.

125 See Fischer, 32, 23; Pasmanik, xvi; Friedemann and Struck, 5–6, 36.

126 Fischer, 113, emphasis mine; see Friedemann and Struck, 36.

127 See Ch. 7.

128 Although this was relatively moderate in support of Zionism, it was included in Zionist reading rooms; A. Goodrich-Freer, *Things Seen in Palestine* (London: Seely, Service & Company, 1913), 207.

129 See Jesaias Press, 24.

130 Goldmann, 3–4.

131 Ussischkin, *Our Program*, 36.

132 Goldmann, 77–8.

133 Fischer, 101, 121; J. H. Kann, 153–5.

134 Gerstman, 54–5.

135 Osaias Thon, Y. Tchlenov, Schmelkes in SP X., 91, 128.

136 Cf. Friedemann and Struck, 20; Fischer, 121.

137 Martin Buber, "Das juedische Kulturprobleme und der Zionismus" in *Der Stimme der Wahrheit*, 209.

138 O. Thon, "The Zionist Programme and Practical Work in Palestine" in Zionist Work in Palestine, 18; Gerstman, 55–6; Fischer, 101–2; SPX., 91ff; *Altneuland* 1, 1 (1904), 1–2.

139 Entry for April 9, 1896, in *Theodor Herzl – Briefe und Tagebuecher, II. Band,* 317.

CHAPTER SEVEN: CULTURE AND CHARITY: THE JEWISH NATIONAL FUND

1 See "Der nationalfonds als Erzieher" in *Die Welt,* August 13, 1911, 729; "Nationalfond-Miszellen," in *Festschrift des Zionistischen Vereines "Jeshrun"–Troppau 1901–1911,* no pagination.
2 See Mascha Hoff, *Johann Kremenezky und der Gruendung des KKL* (Frankfurt a.M.: Perter Lang, 1986) and Walter Lehn with Uri Davis, *The Jewish National Fund* (London: Kegan Paul, 1988); these are among the few scholarly works on the prewar JNF. Lehn's book is expressly anti-Zionist but for the most part a scholarly study; see David Vital, "The History of the Zionists and the History of the Jews", in *Studies in Zionism,* 159ff.
3 The most recent example of pseudo-scholarly self-promotion is Shlomo Shva, *One-Day and 90 Years: The Story of the Jewish National Fund* (Jerusalem: Department of Publications and Audio-Visual Aids, Information Division, Jewish National Fund, 1991). An "Institute for the Research on the History of the JNF" was established to promote "scholarship" about the JNF which shows it in a positive light; the publication of Walter Lehn's JNF history was the impetus for the fund's establishment. Gabriel Alexander provided this insight.
4 Gershom Scholem, *From Berlin to Jerusalem,* 1, 23–4.
5 Nahum Goldmann, *Mein Leben als deutscher Jude* (Munich: Langen Mueller, 1980), 38.
6 Leon Simon, "The Need for Emancipation," in *Zionism and the Western Jew: A Symposium Read Before the London Zionist League on the 24th December, 1908* (London: H. Ginzburg, 1909), 24.
7 Jay L. Kaplove, *Stamp Catalogue of the Jewish National Fund* (Youth and Education Department of the Jewish National Fund and the Educational Society of Israel Philatelist, 1973); see JNF stamp collection, Central Zionist Archives [hereafter cited as CZA] estimated from the figures for 1916 provided in Adolf Boehm, *The Jewish National Fund* (The Hague: Head Office of the Jewish National Fund, 1917), 58.
8 THD, 165.
9 Kaplove, 9.
10 See Ch. 5.
11 Kaplove, 9–14, 73–6, 109–111; Boehm, *Jewish National Fund,* 58.
12 See James A. Leith, "The War of Images Surrounding the Commune" in Leith, ed. *Images of the Commune-Images de la Commune* (Montreal: McGill-Queens University Press, 1978), 101ff.
13 Boehm, *Jewish National Fund,* 51–2.
14 "A Herzl Memorial" (Cologne: Head Office of the Jewish National Fund) [probably around 1910], A2/6/7/1, CZA.
15 Boehm, *Jewish National Fund,* 26ff., 48ff., 52–3; "The Jewish National Fund: Its Objects and Achievements," A2/6/7/1, CZA.
16 Boehm, *Jewish National Fund,* 5ff, 16, 26–8.

17 See, e.g., *Spenden-Buch des Judischen Nationalfonds 1912* A2/6/7/1, CZA, and Simon Neumann, *Der Traum von der Nationalfondsbuechse: Eine Maerchen fuer Kinder* (Cologne: Hauptbuero des Juedischen Nationalfonds, [no date; probably around 1911).
18 Boehm, *Jewish National Fund*, 35; *Der Herzl-Wald* (Die Baum-Spende) (Hague: Hauptbuero des Juedischen Nationalfonds, no date [probably around 1914), 3.
19 There were some editions of the tree certificate without Herzl's portrait; it was on the majority of designs until 1914, CZA, A2/6/7/1.
20 Otto Warburg, in SP IX., 462.
21 Boehm, *Jewish National Fund*, 59.
22 "*Mitzvah*" is literally "commandment" in Hebrew, but generally taken to mean "good deed" or "proper act" according to Jewish tradition; Boehm, *Jewish National Fund*, 59; see *Der Herzl-Wald*, 18–19.
23 Otto Warburg, in SP VII., 205.
24 *Der Herzl-Wald*, 6; "A Herzl Memorial."
25 Boehm, *Jewish National Fund*, 23, 19.
26 Marcus Cohn, 13.
27 "An die Vertrauensmaenner" (1902), [no month or signature], from the Zionist Head Office, A138/4/1, CZA; see SP VI., 248–50, 280–1; Johann Kremenezky, in SP VII., 222ff; "Chanukah," Pamphlet No. 4; "Purim," Flugblatt No. 2; "For the 9th of Ab," Pamphlet No. 3, all A2/6/7/1, CZA. *T'Sha b'Av*, the ninth day of the Hebrew month Av, is the holiday commemorating the destruction of the First and Second Temples in Jerusalem.
28 *Der Herzl-Wald*, 17–18.
29 "Opening Address at the Second Zionist Congress" (Delivered in Basel on August 28, 1898), in *Theodor Herzl Zionist Writings*, II, 16–17.
30 *Der Herzl-Wald*, 18.
31 See Max Nordau, in SP VII., 5ff.; see also Ado Kurrein, *Dr Herzls Grab* (Bruenn: Juedischer Buch-und Kunstverlag, [no date]), 3ff.
32 Boehm, *Jewish National Fund*, 18–19.
33 Boehm, *Jewish National Fund*, 19.
34 See David G. Roskies, *Against the Apocalypse: Responses to Catastrophe in modern Jewish Culture* (Cambridge: Harvard University Press, 1984), 276–80.
35 Simon Neumann, 3–4.
36 Neumann, 15.
37 Neumann, 15–16.
38 "Dear Children", Leaflet Nr 7, A2/6/7/1, CZA.
39 "Gedenkt des Juedischen Nationalfonds;" see also "Something for Reflection", A2/6/7/1, CZA.
40 "Leaflet Nr 8," A2/6/7/1, CZA; see also Franz Landsberger, *A History of Jewish Art* (Cincinatti: Union of American Hebrew Congregations, 1946), 277.
41 "The Jewish National Fund: Its Objects and Achievements," A2/6/7/1, CZA.

42 See Photography collection, 40011, 1499, 399, 1500, 996; see also Heinrich Loewe slide show, special collection, CZA.
43 "Wie kann ich etwas fuer meine armen Brueder tun?," Flugblatt No. 6, A2/6/7/1, CZA.
44 "Wie kann ich etwas fuer meine armen Brueder tun?," Flugblatt No. 6, A2/6/7/1, CZA; "Something for Reflection," "The Jewish National Fund: Its Objects and Achievements," A2/6/7/1, CZA; see also 'Erster Aufruf des 'Juedischen Nationalfonds' in Deutschland," in *Dokumente zur Geschichte des deutschen Zionismus 1882–1933*, 64–5.
45 Simon Neumann, 15.
46 Medals collection, boxes 3, 4, CZA.
47 *Hermann Schapira: Founder of the JNF* (New York: Youth and Education Department, Jewish National Fund, 1962).
48 *Programm und Organisations-Statut der Demokratisch-Zionistischen Fraktion* (Heidelberg, June 16–22, 1902) [CZA], 9–10, 13ff.; cf. Gronemann, in SP VII., 162ff.
49 Max Nordau, *Zionistische Schriften* (Cologne and Leipzig: Juedischer Verlag, 1909), 132.
50 SP VII., 177.
51 "Schnorrer und Verschwoerer" in *Shlemiel* (July 1904): 68.
52 "Der Perfekte Zionist" in *Shlemiel* (July 1904): 69.
53 "Der Perfekte Zionist" in *Shlemiel* (July 1904): 69.
54 See, i.e., "Des Zionismus Ende" in *Shlemiel* (December 1903): 6.
55 Herzl to Max Jungmann, December 7, 1903; February 7, 1904, A194/1, CZA.
56 Johann Kremenezky to Max Jungmann, November 20, 1903, A194/1, CZA.
57 Quoted in *Theodor Herzl: A Memorial*, 190.
58 Quoted from *Max Nordau to his People: A Summons and a Challenge*, 161–2.
59 Boehm, *Jewish National Fund*, 15.
60 Boehm, *Jewish National Fund*, 19.
61 "Der Nationalfonds als Erzieher," 729.
62 Boehm, *Jewish National Fund*, 28.
63 *Die Welt*, August 18, 1911, 875; see also "Der Nationalfonds als Erzieher", 729.
64 *Stenographisches Protokoll der Verhandlungen des X. Zionisten-Kongress in Basel vom 9 bis inklusive 15 August 1911* (Berlin and Leipzig: Juedischer Verlag, 1911), 173.
65 See, e.g., *Festschrift zu Ehren Juedischer Turnverein "Makkabi," Graz 1904–1914 im Verbande der Juedischen Turnerschaft* (Graz: "Leykam," 1914), 4; Israel Abrahams, "A University for Jerusalem" in *Zionist work in Palestine* (London and Leipzig: T. Fischer Unwin), 54 ff.; "Eine Turnfahrt nach Palaestina" in *Juedische Turnzeitung* (February 1910): 27–8; "Palaestinareise im Anschluss an den XI. Zionistenkongress," printed material file, XI. Zionist Congress, CZA.
66 See Max Nordau, *Conventional Lies of Our Civilization* (Chicago: Laird and Lee, 1884).

67 See Arthur Ruppin in SP XI., 257ff.

68 *Jewish Chronicle*, September 12, 1913, 29.

69 See David Vital, *Zionism: The Formative Years*, v–vii; Leon Simon, *Ahad Ha-Am*, 191.

70 See "Der Nationalfonds als Erzieher," 729.

71 *Der Herzl-Wald*, 4, 17–18; "Nationalfond-Miszellen."

72 Adolf Boehm, *Jewish National Fund*, 70; "Nationalfond-Miszellen."

73 David Hartman and Tzvi Marx, "Charity" [*Zedakah*], in *Contemporary Jewish Religious Thought: Original Essays on Critical Concepts, Movements, and Beliefs*, eds. Arthur A. Cohen and Paul Mendes-Flohr (New York: Free Press, 1987), 53–4.

74 See Nash, 1.

CONCLUSION: A SUPPLEMENTAL NATIONALISM

1 Bergman, *Faith and Reason*, 150.

2 Herzl, *Der Judenstaat*, 10; Bergman, 150.

BIBLIOGRAPHY

ARCHIVES, LIBRARIES, MUSEUMS

Buber Archive, Jerusalem
Central Archives for the History of the Jewish People, Jerusalem
Central Zionist Archives, Jerusalem
Ehrenpreis Archive, Jerusalem
Herzl Museum, Jerusalem
Jewish National and University Library, Jerusalem
Memorial Library, University of Wisconsin-Madison
Museum of Swiss Jewry, Basel, Switzerland
Rad Film Archives, Jerusalem
Weizmann Archives, Rehovot, Israel
Weizmann Museum, Rehovot

SELECTED REFERENCE WORKS

Bulletin des Leo Baeck Instituts
Encyclopaedia Judaica
Herzl Year Books
Leo Baeck Year Books
Studies in Contemporary Jewry
Studies in Zionism
Zionism

PERIODICALS

Altneuland
Die Welt
The Jewish Chronicle
Juedische Rundschau
Juedische Turnzeitung
Ost und West
Palaestina
Shlemiel

PRIMARY SOURCES

Aaronshon, Aaron. "The Jewish Agricultural Experiment Station and its Programme." In *Zionist Work in Palestine*, ed. Israel Cohen. pp. 114–20. Leipzig and London: T. Fischer Unwin, 1911.

Abrahams, Israel. "A Jewish University for Jerusalem." In *Zionist Work in Palestine*, ed. Israel Cohen. pp. 54–7. Leipzig and London: T. Fischer Unwin, 1911.

Ahad Ha-Am. "Altneuland." *Ost und West* 3, 4 (April 1903): 237–44.

Selected Essays. Translated by Leon Simon. Philadelphia: Jewish Publication Society of America, 1912.

Nationalism and the Jewish Ethic: Basic Writings of Ahad Ha-Am. Edited by Hans Kohn. New York: Schocken, 1962.

Alexander, Jacob. "Centrifugal and Centripetal Forces." In *Zionism and the Western Jew: A Symposium read before the London Zionist League on the 24th December 1908*. pp. 9–14. London: H. Ginzburg, 1909.

Asch, Schalom. *Im Lande der Vaeter: Bilder und Dichtungen aus Palaestina*. Berlin: Juedischer Verlag. no date.

Auerbach, Elias. "Herzl und Haifa." In *Die Welt* (July 17, 1914): 739–40.

"The Jewish Outlook in Palestine." In *Zionist Work in Palestine*. Edited by Israel Cohen. pp. 172–81. Leipzig and London: T. Fischer Unwin, 1911.

Palaestina als Judenland. Berlin and Leipzig: Juedischer Verlag, 1912.

Pionier der Verwirklichung. Stuttgart: Deutsche Verlags–Anstalt, 1969.

Aus dem Protokoll der Kommission der Demokratisch-zionistischen Fraktion. Berlin: 1902.

Bauer, Leonhard. *Volksleben im Lande der Bibel*. Leipzig: H. G. Wallmann, 1903.

Ben Ami, "Erinnerungen an Theodor Herzl." *Die Welt* (July 3, 1914): 691.

Ben-Gurion, David. *Memoirs*. Edited by Thomas Bransten. Cleveland: World, 1970.

Bentwich, Norman. *Jewish Schools in Palestine*. [Reprinted from the *Jewish Review*] New York: Federation of American Zionists, 1912.

Bernfeld, Simon. "Zwei juedische Kongresse." *Ost und West* (February 2, 1910): 71–6.

Beschluesse und Resolutionen der Zionisten-Kongresse I–VII. Edited by Hugo Schachtel. Vienna: Zionistischer Zentralverein, 1906.

Bialik, C. N. *Bialik on the Hebrew University*. Jerusalem: Palestine Friends of the Hebrew University, 1935.

Die Bibel. In Auswahl fuers Haus mit Zeichnungen vom E. M. Lilien. Martin Luther translation. Edited by Edu. Lehmann and Petersen. Braunschweig and Berlin: Verlag von George Westermann, no date.

Blueher, Hans. *Die Rolle der Erotik in der maennlichen Gesellschaft: Eine Theorie der menschlichen Staatsbildung nach Wesen und Wert*. Stuttgart: Ernst Klett Verlag, 1962.

Bodenheimer, Max Isidor. *Prelude to Israel: The Memoirs of M. I. Bodenheimer*. Edited by Henriette Hannah Bodenheimer and translated by Israel Cohen. New York: Thomas Yoseloff, 1963.

Boehm, Adolf. *The Jewish National Fund*. The Hague: Head Office of the Jewish National Fund, 1917.

Bruenn, W. *Forderungen an den Zionismus*. Berlin: Max Schildberger, no date.

Buber, Martin. *Briefwechsel aus sieben Jahrzeiten*. I: 1897–1918. Edited by Grete Schader. Heidelberg: Verlag Lambert Schneider, 1972.

"Die Entdeckung Palaestinas." *Ost und West* (2 February 1905): 128–30.

"Das juedischer Kulturproblem und der Zionismus." In *Die Stimme der Wahrheit*. p. 205–17. Edited by Lazar Schoen. Wuerzburg: N. Philipp, 1905.

ed. *Juedische Kunstler*. Berlin and Leipzig: Juedischer Verlag, 1903.

"Maennerlied." *Juedischer Turnzeitung*. 7, 8 (1901): 101.

"Theodor Herzl and History." In *Theodor Herzl and We*. Translated by Chaim Arlosoroff. New York: Zionist Labor Party, 1929.

Feiwel, Berthold, and Weizmann, Chaim. *Eine juedische Hochschule*. Berlin: Juedischer Verlag, 1902.

Die Buecher der Bibel. Illustrated by E. M. Lilien. Braunschweig: George Westermann, 1908.

Cohen, Israel. *The German Attack on the Hebrew Schools in Palestine*. London: Offices of the "Jewish Chronicle" and the "Jewish World," 1918.

ed. *The Zionist Pocket Reference*. (Adapted from the Third Edition of Hugo Schachtel's "Zionistisches Merkbuch.") London: W. Speaight and Sons, 1914.

ed. *Zionist Work in Palestine*. London and Leipzig: T. Fischer Unwin, 1911.

Commers in der Burgvogtei Basel X. Zionisten–Congress 1911. Basel: Lithographic Wolf, 1911.

Crane, Walter. *The Claims of Decorative Art*. Boston and New York: Houghton, Mifflin, and Co., 1892.

Eckardt, R., Zickermann, and Fenner, F. *Palaestina Kulturbilder*. Leipzig: Georg Wigand, 1907.

Ehrenpreis, Marcus. "Herzl und der Kultur-Zionismus." In *Zeitgenossen ueber Herzl*. Edited by T. Nussenblatt. pp. 54–60. Bruenn: Juedische Buch und Kunstverlag, 1929.

"Moralische Zionismus." In *Die Welt* (December 17, 1897): 44.

The Soul of the East: Experiences and Reflections. Translated by Alfhild Huebsch. New York: Viking, 1928.

Feiwel, Berthold. "Stroemungen im Zionismus." In *Ost und West* (October 1902): 687–93.

ed. *Juedischer Almanach*. Berlin: Juedischer Verlag, 1902.

ed. *Juedischer Almanach*, II Berlin: Juedischer Verlag, 1904.

Feldman, Joshua. *The Yeminite Jews*. Published on Behalf of the Head Office of the Jewish National Fund. London: W. Speaight and Sons, 1913.

Festcommers zu Ehren des IX. Zionisten-Kongresses zu Hamburg am 28 Dez. 1909. Berlin: Satling and co., 1909.

Festschrift der Juedische Turnverein "Makkabi" Graz 1904–1914 im Verbande der Juedischen Turnerschaft. Graz: "Leykam," 1914.

Festschrift des Vereins Juedischer Studenten zum 10. Stiftungs-fest. Breslau, 7 February 1910.

Festschrift des zionistischen Vereines "Jeshrun," Troppau 1901–1911.

Feuchtwang, Bertold. "Juedische Statistik als Kulturarbeit des Zionismus." In *Die Stimme der Wahrheit.* pp. 218–33. Edited by Lazar Schoen. Wuerzburg: N. Philippi, 1905.

Fischer, Jean. *Das heutige Palaestina.* Antwerp: "Hatikvah," 1907.

Fortlage, Arnold, and Schwarz, Karl. *Das Graphische Werk von Hermann Struck.* Berlin: Paul Cassirer, 1911.

Fraenkel, Josef. *Dr Sigmund Werner: Ein Mitarbeiter Herzls.* Prague: Zionistische Propogandastelle, no date.

Friedemann, Adolf. "Juedische Kunst in Palaestina." in *Ost und West* (May 5, 1911): 445–52.

Das Leben Theodor Herzls. Berlin: Juedischer Verlag, 1914.

and Struck, Hermann. *Palaestina: Reisebilder.* Berlin: Bruno Cassier, 1904.

Friedlander, Israel. "Achad Ha-am." *The Jewish Exponent* (February 16 and 23, 1906).

Gerstman, Josef. *Kultur- und Bildungsfortschritte unter den Juden Palaestinas.* Munich: Max Steinbach Buch und Kunstverlag, 1909.

Gluecksohn, M. "Die Streitfrage." In *Die Welt* (July 10, 1914): 717.

Gold, Alfred. "E. M. Lilien." In *Juedische Kunstler,* ed. Martin Buber. pp. 77–103. Berlin: Juedischer Verlag, 1903.

Goldmann, Nahum. *Erez Israel (Reisebriefe aus Palaestina).* Frankfurt a.M.: Voigt and Gleiber, 1914.

Mein Leben als deutscher Jude. Munich: Langen Mueller, 1980.

Goodrich-Freer, A. *Inner Jerusalem.* London: Archibald Constable and Company, 1904.

Things Seen in Palestine. London: Seely and Service, 1913.

Gronemann, Sammy. *Memoirs of a Yekke.* [Hebrew] Tel Aviv: Lador, 1946.

Grunwald, Max. "Das neue Palaestina." In *Ost und West* (June 6, 1913): 460–4.

Guthe, Hermann. *Palaestina.* Bielefeld and Leipzig: Velhagen and Klating, 1908.

Hauptbuero des Juedischen Nationalfonds. *Der Herzl-Wald.* The Hague, no date.

Hecht, Georg. "Max Nordau und Wir Jungen." *Die Welt* (July 23, 1909): 672.

Die Neue Jude. Leipzig: Gustav Engel Verlag, 1911.

Herrmann, Hugo. "Erziehung im Judentum." In *Vom Judentum: ein Sammelbuch Herausgegeben vom Verein juedischer Hochschuler Bar Kochba in Prag.* Leipzig: Kurt Wolff, 1913.

Herzl, Theodor. *Altneuland.* Leipzig: H. Seeman Nachfolger, 1902.

Theodor Herzl Briefe und Tagebuecher. 3 vols. Edited by Alex Bein, Hermann Greive, Moshe Schaerf, and Julius H. Schoeps. Berlin, Frankfurt a.M, and Vienna: Propylaeen Verlag, 1983–5.

The Complete Diaries of Theodor Herzl. 5 vols. Edited by Raphael Patai and translated by Harry Zohn. New York: Herzl Press and Thomas Yoseloff, 1960.

Herzl Feuilletons, 2 vols. Berlin and Vienna: Verlag Benjamin Harz, 1911.

Der Judenstaat. Versuch einer Modernen Loesung der Judenfrage. Leipzig and Vienna: M. Breitenstein's Verlags-Buchhandlung, 1896.

Theodor Herzl Zionist Writings. 2 vols. Translated by Harry Zohn. New York: Herzl Press, 1973–5.

Theodor Herzls Zionistische Schriften. Berlin-Charlottenburg: Juedischer Verlag, 1908.

Hoelscher, G. *Die Geschichte der Juden Palaestina seit dem Jahre 70 nach Chr.* Leipzig: J. C. Heinrichs'sche Buchhandlung, 1909.

Huntington, Ellsworth. *Palestine and its Transformation*. London: Constable and Co., Boston and New York: Houghton Mifflin Co., 1912.

Jiskor: Ein Buch des Gedenkens an gefallene Waechter und Arbeiter im Lande Israel. Introduction by Martin Buber. Berlin: Juedischer Verlag, 1918.

"'Juedische Renaissance:' Press Stimmen ueber den *Juedischen Almanach.*" Berlin: Juedischer Verlag, 1903.

Juedischer Volkskalender fuer das Jahr 5658 (1897–98). Cologne: Stelter and Company, 1897.

Juedischer Volkskalender fuer das Jahr 5659 (1898–99). Cologne: Stelter and Company, 1898.

Juedischer Volkskalender fuer das Jahr 5700 (1899–1900). Cologne: Stelter and Company, 1899.

Jungmann, Max. *Erinnerungen eines Zionist*. Jerusalem: Rubin Mass, 1959.

Kaminka, Armand. *Meine Reise nach Jerusalem: Skizzen aus Aegypthen und Palaestina*. Frankfurt a.M.: J. Kaufman, 1913.

Kann, J. H. *Erez Israel: Das juedische Land*. Cologne and Leipzig: Juedischer Verlag, 1909.

Klausner, Joseph. Introduction to *Boris Schatz: 31 Oil Paintings*. Jerusalem: 1929.

Kohn, Hans. Introduction to *Vom Judentum: Ein Sammelbuch Herausgegeben vom Verein juedischer Hochschuler Bar Kochba in Prag*. Leipzig: Kurt Wolff, 1913.

Kurrein, Ado. *Dr. Herzls Grab*. Bruenn: Juedischer Kunst und Buchverlag, no date.

Lazare, Bernard. *Job's Dungheap: Essays on Jewish Nationalism and Social Revolution with a Portrait of Bernard Lazare by Charles Péguy*. Edited by Hannah Arendt. New York: Schocken, 1948.

Lessing, Gotthold Ephraim. "Nathan the Wise." Translated by Walter Frank Charles Ade. Woodbury, New York: Barron's, 1972.

Levin, Shmarya. *Forward from Exile*. Translated and edited by Maurice Samuel. Philadelphia: Jewish Publication Society of America, 1967.

"Unsere Kulturaufgaben in Palaestina." In *Ost und West* (September 25, 1912): 1209–11.

Levussove, M. S. *The New Art of an Ancient People: The Work of Ephraim Moses Lilien*. New York: B. W. Huebsch, 1906.

Lipsky, Louis. *A Gallery of Zionist Profiles*. New York: Farrar, Straus, and Cudahy, 1956.

Lilien, E. M. *Jerusalem*. New York: KTAV, 1976.

The Holy Land. Berlin and Vienna: Benjamin Harz, 1922.

Sein Werk. Introduction by Stephan Zweig. Berlin: Schuster and Loeffler, 1903.

Loewe, Heirich. "Aus den Wurzeln unserer Kraft." *Die Welt* (March 22, 1912): 391–4.

Eine Juedische Nationalbibliothek. Berlin: Juedischer Verlag, 1905.

"Der Juedischer Kulturfonds" 'KEDEM.'" *Die Welt* (September 7, 1913).

Liederbuch fuer juedische Vereine. Berlin: Verlag von Hugo Schildberger, 1898.

"Vorwort zum Protokoll des ersten Kongresses." [Central Zionist Archives.]

Miller, E. *Palestine and the Hebrew Revival*. London: "The Zionist," 1915.

Motzkin, Leo. *Die Judenpogrome in Russland*. II Baende. Cologne and Leipzig: Juedischer Verlag, 1909–10.

von Muenchhausen, Boerries. *Juda, Gesaenge*. Illustrated by E. M. Lilien. Berlin: F. A. Lattmann-Goslar, 1900.

Nathan, Paul. *Palaestina und palaestinensischer Zionismus*. Berlin: H. S. Hermann, 1914.

Nawratzki, Curt. *Die juedische Kolonisation Palaestinas*. Munich: E. Reinhardt, 1914.

Neumann, Simon. *Der Traum von der Nationalfondsbuchse: Ein Maerchen fuer Kinder*. Cologne: Hauptbuero des Juedischen Nationalfonds, no date.

Nordau, Max. "Achad Ha'am ueber Altneuland." In *Die Welt* (March 13, 1911): 1–4.

Conventional Lies of Our Civilization. Chicago: Laird and Lee, 1884.

Degeneration. Introduction by George L. Mosse. New York: Howard Fertig, 1968.

Erinnerungen. Leipzig and Vienna: Renaissance-Verlag, 1910.

"Juden vom Gestern" (Eine Erwiderung). In *Ost und West* (April 4, 1903): 233–9.

Vom Kunst und Kunstlern. Liepzig: B. Elischer.

Max Nordaus Zionistische Schriften. Cologne and Leipzig: Juedischer Verlag, 1909.

Paradoxes. Chicago: L. Schick, 1886.

A Question of Honor: A Tragedy of the Present in Four Acts. Translated by Mary J. Safford. Boston: John W. Luce, 1907.

The Right to Love. Translated by Mary J. Safford. New York and Chicago: John W. Luce, 1907.

"Socialism in Europe." *The Cosmopolitan* 36 (March 1904): 517–24.

and Gustav Gottheil. *Zionism and Anti-Semitism*. New York: Scott-Thaw, 1903.

Nossig, Alfred. "Ausstellung juedischer Kuenstler." In *Ost und West* 12 (December 1912): 743–53.

Das juedische Kolonisationsprogramm. Berlin: Juedischer Verlag, 1904.

ed. *Juedische Statistik*. Berlin: Juedischer Verlag, 1903.

Oppenheimer, Franz. *Cooperative Colonisation in Palestine*. The Hague: Head Office of the Jewish National Fund and the Settlement Company "Erez Israel," 1914.

Palaestina Ansichten von denkwuerdigen Staetten in des heiligen Landes und Doerfen juedischen Bauern. Berlin: Hugo Schildberger, 1896.

Palaestina-Informationsbureau. *Kleiner Reisefuehrer durch Palaestina fuer juedische Touristen*. Vienna, no date.

Pinkus, Lazar Feliz. *Palaestina und Syrien: Untersuchung zur Wirtschaftspolitik.* Geneva: Verlag der Zionistischen Monatshefte, 1903.

Press, Jesaias. *Die juedischen Kolonien Palaestinas.* Leipzig: J. C. Heinris'sache Buchhandlung, 1912.

Rathenau, Walter. *Walter Rathenau Gesammelte Schriften,* 5 vols. Berlin: S. Fischer Verlag, 1918.

Rosenberger, Erwin. *Herzl as I Remember Him.* Translated by Louis Jay Hermann. New York: Herzl Press, 1959.

Rosenfeld, Morris. *Lieder des Ghetto.* Translated by Berthold Feiwel and illustrated by E. M. Lilien. Berlin: B. Harz, 1907.

Rosenhek, Ludwig, ed. *Festschrift zu Feier des 100. Semesters der akademischen Verbindung Kadimah.* Vienna, 1933.

Ruppin, Arthur. *Die Juden der Gegenwart. Eine sozialwissenschaftliche Studie.* Berlin: Verlag von S. Calvary and Co., 1904.

Memoirs, Diaries, Letters. Edited by Alex Bein and translated by Karen Gershon. New York: Herzl Press, 1971.

"The Return of the Jews to Agriculture." In *Zionist Work in Palestine,* ed. Israel Cohen. pp. 137–42. Leipzig and London: T. Fischer Unwin, 1911.

Ruskin, John. *The Political Economy of Art.* London: Smith, Elder, and Co., 1857.

Sahuwi, Nathanja. "Vor Hermann Struck's Herzl-Portrait." *Ost und West* (September 9, 1903): 709–14.

Schalit, Isidor. "1890 bis 1904." In *Festschrift zu Feier des 100. Semesters der akademischen Verbindung Kadimah,* ed. Ludwig Rosenhek. Vienna, 1933.

Schatz, Boris. "The Bezalel Institute." In *Zionist Work in Palestine,* ed. Israel Cohen. pp. 58–64. Leipzig and London: T. Fischer Unwin, 1911.

Scholem, Gershom. *From Berlin to Jerusalem: Memories of My Youth.* Translated by Harry Zohn. New York: Schocken Books, 1980.

Walter Benjamin: The Story of a Friendship. Translated by Harry Zohn. New York: Schocken Books, 1981.

Schoen, Lazar, ed., *Die Stimme der Wahrheit: Jahrbuch fuer wissenschaftlichen Zionismus.* Wuerzburg: N. Philippi, 1905.

Simon, Leon. "The Need for Emancipation." In *Zionism and the Western Jew: A Symposium read before the London Zionist League on the 24th December, 1908.* London: H. Ginzburg, 1909.

ed. *Selected Essays of Ahad Ha-Am.* Philadelphia: Jewish Publication Society of America, 1912.

Spenden-Buch des Juedischen Nationalfonds, no date.

Stenographisches Protokoll der Verhandlungen des II. Zionisten-Kongresses gehalten zu Basel vom 28. bis. 31. August 1898. Vienna: "Erez Israel," 1898.

Stenographisches Protokoll der Verhandlungen des III. Zionisten-Kongresses gehalten zu Basel vom 15. bis. 18. August 1899. Vienna: "Erez Israel," 1899.

Stenographisches Protokoll der Verhandlungen des IV. Zionisten-Kongresses in London, 1900. Vienna: "Erez Israel," 1900.

Stenographisches Protokoll der Verhandlungen des V. Zionisten-Kongresses in Basel vom 26. 27. 28. 29. und 30. Dezember 1901. Vienna: "Erez Israel," 1901.

Stenographisches Protokoll der Verhandlungen des VI. Zionisten-Kongresses in Basel vom 23. 24. 25. 26. 27. 27. und 28. August 1903. Vienna: "Erez Israel," 1903.

Stenographisches Protokoll der Verhandlungen des VII. Zionisten-Kongresses und des ausserordentlichen Kongresses in Basel vom 27. 28. 29. 31. Juli, 1. und 2. August 1905. Berlin: Juedischer Verlag, 1905.

Stenographisches Protokoll der Verhandlungen des VIII. Zionisten-Kongresses im Haag vom 14. bis inklusive 21. August 1907. Cologne: Juedischer Verlag, 1907.

Stenographisches Protokoll der Verhandlungen des IX. Zionisten-Kongresses im Hamburg vom 26. bis inklusive 30. Dezember 1909. Cologne: Juedischer Verlag, 1910.

Stenographisches Protokoll der Verhandlungen des X. Zionisten-Kongresses in Basel vom 9. bis inklusive 15. August 1911. Berlin: Juedischer Verlag, 1911.

Stenographisches Protokoll der Verhandlungen des XI. Zionisten-Kongresses in Wien vom 2. bis 9. September 1913. Berlin and Leipzig: Juedischer Verlag, 1913.

Struck, Hermann. "As an Artist Saw Him." In *Theodor Herzl: A Memorial*, ed. Meyer Weisgal. p. 36. New York: New Palestine, 1929.

Radierung von Hermann Struck: Mit einem Essay von Max Osborne. Berlin: Berliner Verlag, 1904.

Thon, Jacob. "Jewish Schools in Palestine." In *Zionist Work in Palestine*, ed. Israel Cohen. pp. 86–98. Leipzig and London: T. Fischer Unwin, 1911.

Thon, Osaias. "Achad Haam." In *Die Welt* (March 13, 1914): 254.

"The Zionist Programme and Practical Work in Palestine." In *Zionist Work in Palestine*, ed. Israel Cohen. pp. 13–20. Leipzig and London: T. Fischer Unwin, 1911.

Trietsch, Davis. *Bilder aus Palaestina*. Berlin: Orient Verlag, no date.

Palaestina Handbuch. Berlin-Schmargendorf: Orient-Verlag, 1910.

Ussischkin, M. *Our Program: An Essay*. Translated by D. S. Blonheim. New York: Federation of American Zionists, 1905.

Weinberg, Jehuda Louis. *Aus der Fruehzeit des Zionismus. Heinrich Loewe*. Jerusalem: Rubin Mass, 1946.

Weizmann, Chaim. *The Letters and Papers of Chaim Weizmann*. Edited by Meyer Weisgal et al. English ed., vols. I–III, ser. A. London: Oxford University Press and Yad Chaim Weizmann, 1968–72; vols. IV–VII, ser. A. Jerusalem: Israel Universities Press , 1973–5.

Trial and Error. New York: Schocken Books, 1949.

Yellin, David. "The Renaissance of the Hebrew Language in Palestine." In *Zionist Work in Palestine*. pp. 143–56. Edited by Israel Cohen. Leipzig and London: T. Fischer Unwin, 1911.

Zangwill, Israel. Introduction to *The Holy Land*, [drawings] by E. M. Lilien. Berlin and Vienna: Benjamin Harz, 1922.

Speeches, Articles, and Letters of Israel Zangwill. London: Soncino Press, 1937.

Zionisten-Congress in Basel (29. 30. und 31. August 1897). Officielles Protocoll. Vienna: Verein "Erez Israel", 1898.

Zionistisches A–B–C–Buch. Berlin-Charlottenburg: Zionistisches Zentralbureau, 1908.

Zionistisches Actions Comite. *Im Kampf um die Hebraeische Sprache*. Berlin: Zionistisches Actions Comite, 1914.

Zweig, Stefan. *The World of Yesterday*. Translated by Harry Zohn. Lincoln and London: University of Nebraska Press, 1964.

SECONDARY SOURCES

Ackerman, Walter I. "Religion in the Schools of Eretz-Israel, 1904–1914." In *Studies in Zionism*, 6 1 (1985): 1–13.

Agulhon, Maurice. *Marianne Into Battle: Republican Imagery and Symbolism in France, 1780–1880*. Translated by Janet Lloyd. Cambridge: Cambridge University Press, 1981.

Almog, Shmuel. "Alfred Nossig: A Reappraisal." *Studies in Zionism*, 7 (Spring 1983): 1–29.

Zionism and History: The Rise of New Jewish Consciousness. Jerusalem: Magnes Press and St Marin's Press, 1987.

ed. *Zionism and the Arabs*. Jerusalem: The Historical Society of Israel and the Zalman Shazar Center, 1983.

Alsberg, Paul A. "Documents on the Brussels Conference of 1906." *Michael*. Edited by Shlomo Simonsohn and Jacob Toury, II, pp. 145–77. Tel Aviv: The Diaspora Research Institute, 1973.

Altmann, Alexander. *Essays in Jewish Intellectual History*. Hanover, New Hampshire, and London: University Press of New England, 1981.

Moses Mendelssohn: A Biographical Study. Philadelphia: Jewish Publication Society of America, 1975.

Arendt, Hannah. *The Jew as Pariah*. Edited by Ron H. Feldman. New York: Grove, 1978.

The Origins of Totalitarianism. Cleveland: World, 1966.

Asch, Adolph. *Geschichte des K.C. (Kartellverband juedischer Studenten) im Licht der deutschen kulturellen und politischen Entwickelung*. London: published by the author, 1964.

Aschheim, Steven. *Brothers and Strangers: The East European Jew in Germany and German-Jewish Consciousness, 1800–1923*. Madison: University of Wisconsin Press, 1982.

Avineri, Shlomo. *The Making of Modern Zionism*. New York: Basic, 1982.

Avishai, Bernard. *The Tragedy of Zionism: Revolution and Democracy in the Land of Israel*. New York: Farrar, Straus, Giroux, 1985.

Avni, Haim, and Shimoni, Gideon, eds. *Zionism and Its Jewish Opponents*. [Hebrew] Jerusalem: Hssifriya Hazionit, 1990.

Bach, H. I. *The German Jew: A Synthesis of Judaism and Western Civilization*. New York: Oxford University Press, 1985.

Barthes, Roland. *Image-Music-Text*. Translated by Stephen Heath. New York: Hill and Wang, 1977.

Baldwin, P. M. "Liberalism, Nationalism, and Degeneration: The Case of Max Nordau." In *Central European History* 13 (June 1980): 90–120.

Bein, Alex. "Arthur Ruppin: The Man and His Work." In *Leo Baeck Institute Year Book 17* (1972): 117–71.

"The Origin of the Term and Concept 'Zionism.'" In *Herzl Year Book*, II. Edited by Raphael Patai. pp. 1–27. New York: Herzl Press, 1959.

Theodore Herzl. New York and Philadelphia: Jewish Publication Society of America, 1962.

Beller, Steven. *Herzl.* London: P. Halban, 1991.

Vienna and the Jews, 1867–1938: A Cultural History. Cambridge: Cambridge University Press, 1989.

Ben-Horin, Meir. *Max Nordau: Philosopher of Human Solidarity.* London: London Jewish Society, 1956.

Benjamin, Walter. *Illuminations.* Edited by Hannah Arendt and translated by Harry Zohn. New York: Schocken, 1969.

Berger, John. *About Looking.* New York: Pantheon, 1980.

Bergman, Samuel Hugo. *Faith and Reason: An Introduction to Modern Jewish Thought.* Edited and translated by Alfred Jospe. New York: Schocken, 1972.

Berkowicz, Michael. "Herzl and Hebrew." In *Theodor Herzl: A Memorial.* Edited by Meyer Weisgal. p. 74. New York: New Palestine, 1929.

Berlin, Isaiah. *Chaim Weizmann.* New York: Farrar, Straus, and Cudahy, 1958.

Bernstein, Deborah. *The Struggle for Equality: Urban Women Workers in Pre-State Israel.* New York: Praeger, 1987.

Bernstein, Herman. *Celebrities of Our Time.* London: Hutchinson, 1924.

Bezalel 1906–1929. Edited by Nurit Shilo-Cohen. Jerusalem: Israel Museum, 1983.

Biale, David. *Gershom Scholem: Kabbalah and Counter-History.* Cambridge: Harvard University Press, 1982.

Power and Powerlessness in Jewish History. New York: Schocken, 1987.

Boehm, Adolf. *Die Zionistische Bewegung bis zum Ende des Weltkrieges,* I. 2nd edn, rev. Berlin: Juedischer Verlag, 1935.

Bredin, Jean-Denis. *The Affair: The Case of Alfred Dreyfus.* Translated by Jeffrey Mehlman. New York: George Braziller, 1986.

Brieger, Lothar. *E. M. Lilien: Eine kuenstlerische Entwickelung um die Jahrhundertewende.* Berlin and Vienna: Verlag Benjamin Harz, 1922.

Brod, Harry, ed. *A Mensch Among Men: Explorations in Jewish Masculinity.* Freedom, California: Crossing Press, 1988.

Bychowski, Z. "Die Intuition Herzls." In *Zeitgenossen ueber Herzl.* Edited by T. Nussenblatt. pp. 46–9. Bruenn: Juedischer Buch und Kunstverlag, 1929.

Cohen, Arthur A., ed. *The Jew: Essays from Martin Buber's Journal "Der Jude" 1916–1928.* University, Alabama: The University of Alabama Press, 1980.

The Natural and the Supernatural Jew: An Historical and Theological Introduction. London: Valentine, Mitchell, 1967.

and Mendes-Flohr, Paul, eds. *Contemporary Jewish Religious Thought: Original Essays on Critical Concepts, Movements, and Beliefs.* New York: Free Press, 1987.

Cohen, Mitchell. *Zion and State: Nation, Class, and the Shaping of Modern Israel.* New York: Basil Blackwell, 1987.

Cohen, Stuart A. *English Zionists and British Jews: The Communal Politics of Anglo-Jewry, 1895–1920.* Princeton: Princeton University Press, 1982.

Cohn, Emil Berhnard. *David Wolffsohn, Herzl's Successor.* New York: Zionist Organization of America, 1944.

Cohn, Markus. "Erinnerungen eines Baslers an den ersten Zionistenkongress." *Sonderdruck aus der Festschrift des Schweizerischen Israelitischen Gemeindebundens*. Basel: Brin, 1954.

Craig, Gordon. *Germany 1866–1945*. New York: Oxford University Press, 1980.

Cuddihy, John Murray. *The Ordeal of Civility: Freud, Marx, Levi-Straus, and the Jewish Struggle with Modernity*. New York: Basic Books, 1981.

Davies, W. D. *The Territorial Dimension of Judaism*. Berkeley: University of California Press, 1982.

De Haas, Jacob. *Theodor Herzl: A Biographical Study*. New York: The Leonard Co., 1927.

Deutscher, Isaac. *The Non-Jewish Jew and Other Essays*. Edited by Tamara Deutscher. Boston: Alyson, 1968.

Dubnov, Simon. *The History of the Jews*. 4th rev. edn. 5 vols. Translated from the Russian and edited by Moshe Spiegel. South Brunswick, N.J.: Thomas Yoseloff, 1971 (IV); 1973 (V).

History of the Jews in Russia and Poland. 3 vols. Philadelphia: Jewish Publication Society of America, 1916–20.

Edelman, Murray. *Politics as Symbolic Action: Mass Arousal and Quiescence*. Chicago: Markham, 1972.

Elias, Norbert. *The Civilizing Process: The Development of Manners*. Translated by Edmund Jephcott. New York: Urizen Books, 1978.

Elon, Amos. *Herzl*. New York: Holt, Rinehart and Winston, 1975.

The Israelis: Founders and Sons. New York: Penguin, 1981.

Eloni, Yehuda. *Zionismus in Deutschland: Von den Anfaengen bis 1914*. Gerlingen: Bleicher Verlag, 1987.

Elston, Esther N. *Richard Beer-Hoffman: His Life and Work*. University Park, Pennsylvania: Pennsylvania State University Press, 1983.

E. M. Lilien: Zeichnungen fuer Buecher: Ausstellung vom 15. Oktober bis 20 November 1981. Munich: M. Hasenclever, 1981.

Emerson, Rupert. *From Empire to Nation: The Rise to Self-Assertion of Asian and African Peoples*. Boston: Beacon, 1969.

Even-Zohar, Itmar. "The Emergence of a Native Hebrew Culture in Palestine: 1882–1948." In *Studies in Zionism*, 4 (October 1981): 167–84.

Fischmann, Ada. *Die Arbeitende Frau in Erez Israel*. Tel Aviv: Moazasth Hapoaloth, 1930.

Flapan, Simha. *The Birth of Israel: Myths and Realities*. New York: Pantheon, 1986.

Foster, Milton P. "The Reception of Max Nordau's *Degeneration* in England and America." Ph.D. dissertation, University of Michigan, 1954.

Foucault, Michel. *The Archaeology of Knowledge and the Discourse on Language*. Translated by A. M. Sheridan Smith. New York: Pantheon, 1972.

Fraenkel, Josef. "Chaim Weizmann and Haham Moses Gaster." In *Herzl Year Book, VI pp. 183–237. New York: Herzl Press, 1963–4.*

Dubnow, Herzl, and Ahad Ha-Am: Political and Cultural Zionism. London: Ararat, 1963.

"The Jewish Chronicle and the Launching of Political Zionism." *Herzl Year Book*, II pp. 217–27. New York: Herzl Press, 1959.

Theodor Herzl: A Biography. London: Ararat, 1946.

Frankel, Jonathan. *Prophecy and Politics: Socialism, Nationalism, and the Russian Jews, 1862–1917*. Cambridge: Cambridge University Press, 1981.

"The 'Yiskor' Book of 1911: A Note on National Myths in the Second Aliya." In *Religion, Ideology, and Nationalism in Europe and America: Essays Presented in Honor of Yehoshua Arieli*. pp. 356–84. Jerusalem: The Historical Society of Israel and the Zalman Center for Jewish History, 1986.

Friedman, Isaiah. "The *Hilfsverein der deutschen Juden*, the German Foreign Ministry and the Controversy with the Zionists." In *Leo Baeck Institute Year Book 24* (1979): 291–319.

Friedman, Maurice. *Martin Buber's Life and Work: The Early Years, 1878–1923*. New York: Dutton, 1981.

Furet, François. *In the Workshop of History*. Translated by Jonathan Mandelbaum. Chicago and London: University of Chicago Press, 1984.

Gaisbauer, Adolf. *Davidstern und Doppeladler: Zionismus und juedischer Nationalismus in Oesterreich 1882–1918*. Vienna, and Graz: Boehlau, 1988.

Gay, Peter. *Freud, Jews, and Other Germans: Masters and Victims in Modernist Culture*. New York: Oxford University Press, 1978.

Gelber, Mark H. "The *jungjuedische Bewegung*." In *Leo Baeck Institute Year Book 31*. (1986): 105–19.

Gilman, Sander. *Jewish Self-Hatred. Anti-Semitism and the Hidden Language of the Jews*. Baltimore: Johns Hopkins University Press, 1986.

Goldmann, Nachum. *The Genius of Herzl and Zionism Today*. Jerusalem: Organization Department of the Zionist Executive, 1955.

Goldstein, Joseph. *Between Political and Practical Zionism: The Beginnings of Zionism*
in Russia. [Hebrew] Jerusalem: Magnes Press of the Hebrew University, 1991.

"The Zionist Movement in Russia, 1897–1904." [Hebrew] Ph.D. dissertation. The Hebrew University of Jerusalem, 1982.

Goodman, Paul, ed. *Chaim Weizmann: A Tribute on His Seventieth Birthday*. London: Victor Gollancz, 1945.

Goren, Arthur A., ed. *Dissenter in Zion: From the Writings of Judah L. Magnes*. Cambridge: Harvard University Press, 1982.

Greenberg, Louis. *The Jews in Russia: Their Struggle for Emancipation*. New Haven: Yale University Press, 1965.

Grunwald, Kurt. "Jewish Schools under Foreign Flags in Ottoman Palestine." In *Studies in Palestine during the Ottoman Period*, edited by Moshe Maoz. pp. 164–74. Jerusalem: Magnes Press, 1975.

Halpern, Ben. *A Clash of Heroes: Brandeis, Weizmann, and American Zionism*. New York: Oxford University Press, 1987.

The Idea of the Jewish State. 2nd rev. edn. Cambridge: Harvard University Press, 1969.

Harbaki, Yehosafat. *The Bar Kochba Syndrome: Risk and Realism in International Politics*. Chappaqua, New York: Russell, 1983.

Hayes, Carlton J. H. *Essays on Nationalism*. New York: Macmillan, 1933.

Hertzberg, Arthur. *The French Enlightenment and the Jews: The Origins of Modern Anti-Semitism*. New York: Schocken, 1968.

ed. *The Zionist Idea: A Historical Analysis and Reader*. New York: Atheneum, 1977.

Heyd, Milly. "Lilien and Beardsley: 'to the pure all things are pure.'" In *Journal of Jewish Art* 7 (1982): 58–69.

Heymann, Michael, ed. *The Uganda Controversy*. I Jerusalem: Israel Universities Press, 1970; II Jerusalem: Ha-Sifriyah ha-Zionit, 1977.

Hobsbawm, Eric, and Terrence Ranger, eds. *The Invention of Tradition*. Cambridge: Cambridge University Press, 1988.

Hoff, Mascha. *Johann Kremenezky und der Gruendung des KKL*. Frankfurt a.M.: Peter Lang, 1986.

Hunt, Lynn. *Politics, Culture, and Class in the French Revolution*. Berkeley: University of California Press, 1984.

Hyman, Paula. *From Dreyfus to Vichy: The Remaking of French Jewry, 1906–1939*. New York: Columbia University Press, 1979.

"The History of European Jewry: Recents Trends in the Literature." In *Journal of Modern History* 54, 2 (June 1982): 303–19.

Jacobsohn, Herman. "Max Nordau – The Jeremiah of the Century." In *Open Court* 37 (April 1923): 224–8.

Janik, Allan, and Toulmin, Stephen. *Wittgenstein's Vienna*. New York: Simon and Schuster, 1973.

Jannaway, Frank G. *Palestine and the World*. London: Sampson, Low, Marston, and Co., 1925.

Jones, Ernest. *The Life and Work of Sigmund Freud*. New York: Basic, 1966.

Kampf, Avram. *Jewish Experience in the Art of the Twentieth Century*. Hadley, Massachusetts: Bergin and Garvey, 1984.

Kaplan, Marion. *The Making of the Jewish Middle Class: Women, Family, and Identity in Imperial Germany*. New York and Oxford: Oxford University Press, 1991.

Kaplove, Jay L. *Stamp Catalogue of the Jewish National Fund*. Jerusalem: Youth and Education Department of the Jewish National Fund and the Educational Society of Israel Philatelist, 1973.

Karpat, Kemal. "Jewish Immigration in the Ottoman Empire, 1864–1914." [manuscript.]

Studies in Ottoman Population 1864–1914. Madison: University of Wisconsin Press, 1984.

Katz, Jacob. *From Prejudice to Destruction: Anti-Semitism 1700–1933*. Cambridge: Harvard University Press, 1980.

Out of the Ghetto: The Social Background of Jewish Emancipation, 1770–1870. New York: Schocken, 1978.

Kedourie, Elie, and Sylvia Haim, eds. *Palestine and Israel in the 19th and 20th Centuries*. London: Frank Cass, 1982.

Klausner, Israel. *Opposition to Herzl*. [Hebrew] Jerusalem: Achiever, 1960.

Klausner, Joseph. *The Story of the Hebrew University in Jerusalem*. American Friends of the Hebrew University, no date.

Kleeblatt, Norman L., ed. *The Dreyfus Affair: Art, Truth and Justice.* Berkeley: University of California Press, 1987 (for the Jewish Museum, New York).
Klein, Dennis B. *Jewish Origins of the Psychoanalytic Movement.* Chicago and London: University of Chicago Press, 1985.
Kling, Simcha. *Joseph Klausner.* New York and London: Thomas Yoseloff: 1970.
"Leo Motzkin." In *Herzl Year Book,* II. Edited by Raphael Patai. New York: Perzl Press, 1959.
Nahum Sokolow: Servant of His People. New York: Herzl Press, 1960.
Kohn, Hans, ed. *Martin Buber: Sein Werk und seine Zeit.* Cologne: Joseph Melzer Verlag, 1961.
ed. *Nationalism and the Jewish Ethic: Basic Writings of Ahad Ha-Am.* New York: Schocken, 1962.
Kolatt, Israel. "The Organization of the Jewish Population of Palestine and the Development of Its Political Consciousness Before World War I." In *Studies in Palestine during the Ottoman Period,* edited by Moshe Maoz, pp. 211–45. Jerusalem: Magnes Press, 1975.
"Theories on Israel [sic] Nationalism." In *In the Dispersion,* 7 (1967): 13–50.
"Zionism and Political Messianism." In *Totalitarian Democracy and After: An International Colloquium in Memorial of Jacob L. Talmon.* Jerusalem: Magnes Press, 1984.
Kornberg, Jacques, ed. *At the Crossroads: Essays on Ahad Ha-am.* Albany: State University of New York Press, 1983.
"Theodor Herzl: A Reevaluation." *Journal of Modern History* 52 (June 1980): 226–52.
Lamberti, Marjorie. *Jewish Activism in Imperial Germany: The Struggle for Civil Equality.* New Haven and London: Yale University Press, 1978,
Landsberger, Franz. *A History of Jewish Art.* Cincinnati: Union of American Hebrew Congregations, 1946.
Laqueur, Walter. *A History of Zionism.* New York: Holt, Rinehart and Winston, 1972.
Lederhendler, Eli. *The Road to Modern Jewish Politics.* New York: Oxford University Press, 1989.
Lehn, Walter, in association with Uri Davis. *The Jewish National Fund.* London: Kegan Paul, 1988.
Leith, James. "The War of Images Surrounding the Commune." In *Images of the Commune-Images de la Commune,* ed. James Leith. Montreal: Queens University Press, 1978.
Levi-Strauss, Claude. *Structural Anthropology.* Translated by Claire Jacobson and Brooke Grundfer Schoepf. Harmondsworth, Middlesex: Penguin, 1968.
Lewis, Beth Irwin, and Paret, Peter. "Art, Society, and Politics in Wilhelmine Germany." In *Journal of Modern History* 4, 1 (December 1985): 696–710.
Lichtheim, Richard. *Die Geschichte des deutschen Zionismus.* Jerusalem: Rubin Mass, 1954.
Lidtke, Vernon L. *The Alternative Culture: Socialist Labor in Imperial Germany.* New York: Oxford University Press, 1985.
Loewenberg, Peter. "A Hidden Zionist Theme in Freud's 'My Son, the Myops'

Dream." In *Journal of the History of Ideas* 31 (January–March 1970): 129–32.

"Theodor Herzl: A Psychoanalytic Study in Charismatic Political Leadership." In *The Psychoanalytic Interpretation of History*, edited by Benjamin B. Wolman, pp. 150–91. New York: Basic Books, 1971.

"Sigmund Freud as a Jew: A Study in Ambivalence and Courage." In *Journal of the History of the Behavioral Sciences* 7, 4 (October 1971): 363–9.

"Walter Rathenau and German Society." Ph.D. dissertation, University of California, Berkeley, 1966.

Luz, Ehud. *Parallels Meet: Religion and Nationalism in the Early Zionist Movement*. Translated by Lenn J. Schramm. Philadelphia: Jewish Publication Society of America, 1988 .

Mandel, Neville J. *The Arabs and Zionism before World War I*. Berkeley: University of California Press, 1976.

Ma'oz, M., ed. *Studies on Palestine During the Ottoman Period*. Jerusalem: Magnes Press, 1975.

Marmorstein, Emile. *Heaven at Bay: The Jewish Kulturkampf in the Holy Land*. London: Oxford University Press, 1969.

Marrus, Michael. *The Politics of Assimilation: A Study of the French Jewish Community at the Time of the Dreyfus Affair*. London: Oxford University Press, 1971.

Massing, Paul W. *Rehearsal for Destruction: A Study of Political Anti-Semitism in Imperial Germany*. New York: Harper Brothers, 1949.

McCagg, William. *A History of Habsburg Jews, 1670–1918*. Bloomington: Indiana University Press, 1989.

McGrath, William J. *Freud's Discovery of Psychoanalysis: The Politics of Hysteria*. Ithaca: Cornell University Press, 1986.

Mendelsohn, Ezra. *Class Struggle in the Pale*. Cambridge: Cambridge University Press, 1970.

The Jews of East Central Europe Between the World Wars. Bloomington: Indiana University Press, 1983.

Zionism in Poland: The Formative Years 1915–1926. New Haven: Yale University Press, 1981.

Mendes-Flohr, Paul R., and Jehuda Reinharz, eds. *The Jew in the Modern World: A Documentary History*. New York: Oxford University Press, 1980.

Meyer, Michael. *The Origins of the Modern Jew: Jewish Identity and European Culture in Germany 1749–1824*. Detroit: Wayne State University Press, 1984.

Response to Modernity: A History of the Reform Movement in Judaism. New York: Oxford University Press, 1988.

Mosse, George L. *The Crisis of German Ideology: Intellectual Origins of the Third Reich*. New York: Grosset and Dunlap, 1964.

The Culture of Western Europe. Chicago: Rand McNally, 1974.

Fallen Soldiers: Reshaping the Memory of the World Wars. New York: Oxford University Press, 1989.

German Jews Beyond Judaism. Bloomington: Indiana University Press, 1985.

Germans and Jews: The Right, the Left, and the Search for a "Third Force" in Pre-Nazi Germany. New York: Howard Fertig, 1970.

Nationalism and Sexuality: Respectability and Abnormal Sexuality in Modern Europe. New York: Howard Fertig, 1985.

The Nationalization of the Masses: Political Symbolism and Mass Movements in Germany from the Napoleonic Wars through the Third Reich. New York: Meridian, 1977.

Toward the Final Solution: A History of European Racism. New York: Harper and Row, 1978.

Narkess, M. "The Arts Portray Herzl." In *Theodor Herzl: A Memorial*, ed. Meyer Weisgal. pp. 119–20. New York: New Palestine, 1929.

Nash, Stanley. *In Search of Hebraism: Shai Hurwitz and His Polemics in the Hebrew Press*. Leiden, Netherlands: E. J. Brill, 1980.

Netanyahu, Benjamin. *Max Nordau to His People: A Summons and a Challenge*. New York: Scopus, 1941.

Nordau, Anna and Maxa. *Max Nordau: A Biography*. New York: Nordau Committee, 1943.

Nussenblatt, Tulo, ed. *Theodor Herzl Jahrbuch*. Vienna: Dr Heinrich Glanz, 1937.

Zeitgenossen ueber Herzl. Bruenn: Juedischer Buch und Kunstverlag, 1929.

Ofrat-Friedlander, Gideon. "The Periods of Bezalel," pp. 31–79, "Bezalel Culture," "Bezalel Sales and Promotion," and " The Bezalel Museum," pp. 283–359. In *Bezalel 1906–1929*, ed. Nurit Shilo-Cohen. Jerusalem: The Israel Museum, 1983.

Orlan, Haiyim. "The Participants in the First Zionist Congress." In *Herzl Year Book*, VI. pp. 133–52. Edited by Raphael Patai. New York: Herzl Press, 1964–5.

Pawel, Ernst. *The Labyrinth of Exile: A Life of Theodor Herzl*. Farrar, Straus, and Giroux, 1989.

The Nightmare of Reason: A Life of Franz Kafka. New York: Farrar, Straus and Giroux, 1984.

Penslar, Derek J. *Zionism and Technocracy: The Engineering of Jewish Settlement in Palestine, 1870–1918*. Bloomington: Indiana University Press, 1991.

Pollak, Adolf. *Die Welt Index – Zionistische Chronologie* (von Juni 1897 bis Juli 1914). Tel Aviv, no date.

Poppel, Stephen. *Zionism in Germany 1897–1933*. Philadelphia: Jewish Publication Society of America, 1977.

Porath, Y. *The Emergence of the Palestinian-Arab National Movement 1918–1929*. London: Frank Cass, 1974.

Rabinowicz, Oskar K. *Fifty Years of Zionism*. London: Robert Anscombe, 1950.

Reinharz, Jehuda. "Achad Haam und der deutsche Zionismus." *Bulletin des Leo Baeck Instituts* 61 (1982): 3–27.

"Ahad Ha-Am, Martin Buber, and German Zionism." In *At the Crossroads: Essays on Ahad Ha-Am*, edited by Jacques Kornberg, pp. 142–55. Albany: State University of New York Press, 1983.

Chaim Weizmann: The Making of a Zionist Leader. New York: Oxford University Press, 1985.

ed. *Dokumente zur Geschichte des deutschen Zionismus, 1882–1933*. Tuebingen: J. C. B. Mohr, 1981.

Fatherland or Promised Land? The Dilemma of the German Jew, 1893–1914. Ann Arbor: University of Michigan Press, 1975.

"Ideology and Structure in German Zionism, 1882–1933." *Jewish Social Studies* 42, 2 (Spring 1980): 119–46.

Rosenberg, Harold. *Rediscovering the Present*. Chicago: University of Chicago Press, 1973.

Rozenblit, Marsha L. *The Jews of Vienna: Assimilation and Identity, 1870–1914*. Albany: State University of New York Press, 1983.

Sachar, Howard M. *A History of Israel*. New York: Knopf, 1976.

The Course of Modern Jewish History. Cleveland: World, 1958.

Said, Edward. *The Question of Palestine*. New York: Vintage Books, 1980.

Orientalism. New York: Vintage, 1977.

Salmon, Yosef. *Religion and Zionism: First Encounters*. [Hebrew] Jerusalem: Hassifriya Haziyonit, 1990.

Sanders, Ronald. *The High Walls of Jerusalem*. New York: Holt, Rinehart and Winston, 1983.

Schaerf, Moshe. "Herzl's Social Thinking." *Herzl Year Book*, III. Edited by Raphael Patai. pp. 199–206. New York: Herzl Press, 1960.

Scholem, Gershom. *Judaica I*. Frankfurt a.M.: Suhrdamp Verlag, 1981.

The Messianic Idea in Judaism and Other Essays on Jewish Spirituality. New York: Schocken, 1971.

Major Trends in Jewish Mysticism. New York: Schocken, 1961.

On Jews and Judaism in Crisis. Edited by Werner Dannhauser. New York: Schocken, 1978.

Schorsch, Ismar. "Art as Social History: Oppenheim and the German Jewish Vision of Emancipation." In *Moritz Oppenheim: The First Jewish Painter*. pp. 31–58. Jerusalem: Israel Museum, 1983.

Schorske, Carl E. *Fin-de-Siècle Vienna: Politics and Culture*. New York: Vintage, 1981.

Schwarz, Karl. *Jewish Artists of the 19th and 20th Centuries*. Freeport, New York: Books for Libraries Press, 1970.

ed. *Hermann Struck Memorial Exhibition*. Tel Aviv: Tel Aviv Museum, 1944.

Segre, Dan V. *A Crisis of Identity: Israel and Zionism*. Oxford: Oxford University Press, 1980.

Shapira, Anita. *Visions in Conflict*. [Hebrew] Jerusalem: Am Oved, 1988.

Shva, Shlomo. *One Day and 90 Years: The Story of the Jewish National Fund*. Jerusalem: Department of Publications and Audio-Visual Aids, Information Division, 1991.

Silberschlag, Eisig. *From Renaissance to Renaissance: Hebrew Literature from 1492 to 1970*. I. New York: KTAV, 1973.

Sokolow, Nahum. *History of Zionism 1600–1918*, II. London: Longmans, Green, 1919.

Sorkin, David. *The Transformation of German Jewry, 1780–1840*. New York and Oxford: Oxford University Press, 1987.

Stewart, Desmond. *Theodor Herzl*. Garden City, New York: Doubleday, 1974.

Straus, Leo. "Zionism in Max Nordau." In *The Jew*. Edited by Arthur Cohen and translated by Joachim Neurgroschel. pp. 121–9. University, Alabama: University of Alabama Press, 1980.

Tagg, John. *The Burden of Representation: Essays on Photographies and Histories*. Amherst: University of Massachusetts Press, 1988.

Tal, Uriel. *Christians and Jews in Germany: Religion, Politics, and Ideology in the Second Reich*. Translated by Jonathan Jacobs. Ithaca, New York and London: Cornell University Press, 1975.

Tartakover, David, ed. *Herzl in Profile: Herzl's Image in the Applied Arts*. Tel Aviv: Tel Aviv Museum, 1978–79.

Teveth, Shabtai. *Ben Gurion: The Burning Ground 1886–1948*. Boston: Houghton Mifflin, 1987.

Thon, Osaias. "The First Big Visions." In *Theodor Herzl: A Memorial*. Edited by Meyer Weisgal. pp. 54–6. New York: New Palestine, 1929.

Toury, Jacob. "Herzl's Newspapers: The Creation of *Die Welt*." In *Studies in Zionism* 1, 2 (Autumn 1980): 159–72.

Ussischkin, M. *Ussischkin Tells the Story of 35 Years of Keren Kayemeth: An Address Delivered at the 35th Anniversary Celebration of the Keren Kayemeth in Tel Aviv on January 5, 1937*. New York: Jewish National Fund of America, 1937.

Vital, David. "The History of the Zionists and the History of the Jews." In *Studies in Zionism* 6 (Autumn 1982): 159–70.

The Future of the Jews. Cambridge: Harvard University Press, 1990.

The Origins of Zionism. Oxford: Oxford University Press, 1975.

Zionism: The Crucial Phase. Oxford: Oxford University Press, 1987.

Zionism: The Formative Years. Oxford: Oxford University Press, 1982.

Waxman, Meyer. *A History of Hebrew Literature*. IV, pt. 2. New York: Thomas Yoseloff, 1960.

Weisbrod, Robert. *African Zion: The Attempt to Establish a Jewish Colony in the East Africa Protectorate 1903–1905*. Philadelphia: Jewish Publication Society of America, 1965.

Weisgal, Meyer, ed. *Theodor Herzl: A Memorial*. New York: New Palestine, 1929.

and Carmichael, Joel, eds. *Chaim Weizmann: A Biography by Several Hands*. London: Weidenfeld and Nicolson, 1962.

Weltsch, Robert. "Theodor Herzl and We." In *Theodor Herzl and We*. Translated by Chaim Arlosoroff. New York: Zionist Labor Party, 1929.

Wenkert, Josef. "Herzl and Sokolow." In *Herzl Year Book*, II. Edited by Raphael Patai. pp. 184–216. New York: Herzl Press, 1959.

Werner, Alfred. "Boris Schatz: Father of an Israeli Art." *Herzl Year Book*, VII. Edited by Raphael Patai. pp. 395–410. New York: Herzl Press, 1971.

"The Story of Jewish Art." In *Jewish Affairs*, 14 (December 15, 1946): 3–48.

"The Tragedy of E. M. Lilien." In *Herzl Year Book*, II. Edited by Raphael Patai. pp. 92–112. New York: Herzl Press, 1959.

Wistrich, Robert S. *Revolutionary Jews from Marx to Trotsky*. London: Harrap, 1976.

Youth and Education Department, Jewish National Fund. *Hermann Schapira: Founder of the JNF*. New York: 1962.

Zaloma, Yigal. "Boris Schatz," pp. 125–49, "Trends in Zionism and the Question of Art before the Establishment of Bezalel," pp. 23–30, and "Hirsenberg, Lilien, and Pann: Painters at Bezalel." pp. 197–211. In *Bezalel 1906–1929*. Edited by Nurit Shilo-Cohen. Jerusalem: The Israel Museum, 1983.

Zionism. [Israel Pocket Library] Jerusalem: Keter Books, 1973.

Zipperstein, Steven J. *The Jews of Odessa: A Cultural History, 1794–1881*. Stanford: Stanford University Press, 1985.

Zohn, Harry. *Karl Kraus*. New York: Twayne, 1971.

INDEX